THE
HEALING
PATH

Thorsons
An imprint of HarperCollins*Publishers*
77–85 Fulham Palace Road
Hammersmith, London, England W6 8JB

Published in the United States by
Thorsons 2001

Conceived, created, and designed by
Duncan Baird Publishers Ltd.
Sixth Floor, Castle House,
75–76 Wells Street
London, England W1T 3QH

Copyright © Duncan Baird Publishers 2001
Text copyright © Jacqueline Young 2001
Commissioned artwork copyright © Duncan
Baird Publishers 2001
For copyright of photographs see
page 176, which is to be regarded as
an extension of this copyright

Designer Ian Midson
Photographic direction Rachel Cross
Picture research Cee Weston-Baker
Commissioned photography Sian Irvine,
Matthew Ward
Illustrator Hanna Firmin
Editorial assistants Hanne Bewernick,
Jessica Hughes

Medical consultants
China Elisabeth Hsu
India Dominik Wujastyk
Tibet Marianne Winder
Japan Gretchen de Soriano

Library of Congress Cataloging-in-Publication
data is available

10 9 8 7 6 5 4 3 2 1

ISBN: 0-00-761263-X

Typeset in Garamond and Rotis Sans Serif
Color reproduction by Colourscan, Singapore
Printed by Imago, Singapore

Publisher's note
Before following any advice or practice
contained in this book, it is recommended
that you consult your doctor as to its suitability,
especially if you suffer from any health problems or special conditions. The publisher, the
author, and the photographers cannot accept
responsibility for any injuries or damage
incurred as a result of following the exercises
in this book, or by using any of the therapeutic
methods that are mentioned herein.

THE
HEALING PATH

THE PRACTICAL GUIDE TO THE HOLISTIC
TRADITIONS OF CHINA, INDIA, TIBET, AND JAPAN

Jacqueline Young

Thorsons
Directions for Life

CONTENTS

INTRODUCTION

In 1981, I went to Japan for a three-week holiday and I ended up staying for five years. That time marked the beginning of my intensive study and practice of oriental medicine, and my passion for sharing its benefits with others which has continued to this day. Despite being born and raised in England, I had been fascinated by the Orient since early childhood and, in 1963, I lived for six months in Hong Kong, where my father was working. There he was introduced to acupuncture and to yoga, which became a lifelong interest for the whole family.

Yet in the 1960s and 1970s, most oriental therapies were practically unknown and rarely practised in the West. In 1975, while an undergraduate, I had a back injury and was recommended for spinal surgery. Horrified at this prospect I searched for an alternative and consulted an osteopath. When his treatment failed to bring relief he recommended me to a colleague – one of the first people in the U.K. to practise acupuncture.

I was intrigued by his pulse-taking and needle treatment and by his incredibly accurate diagnosis: it was made on the basis of tongue, pulse and palpatory techniques with only minimal questioning. Yet it accurately described not only my current back problem but every aspect of my health, both past and present. Over the next few treatments I took every opportunity to ask him about Chinese medicine and when the acupuncture cured my back problem I resolved to study it myself.

However, acupuncture training in the U.K. was then in its infancy and so I decided to complete my academic and professional training in clinical psychology first. Working in the National Health Service and in the field of primary care as a clinical psychologist gave me experience of both the strengths and weaknesses of the Western medical system. Yet I yearned to find a more holistic system that encompassed mind, body and spirit and that focused more on preventive approaches and health promotion than on disease management.

I found what I was looking for in the medical traditions of Japan, China, India and Tibet. In Japan I trained in acupuncture, herbal medicine (*kanpo*), *shiatsu* and *anma* massage, and various forms of movement therapy, martial arts and meditation. I also undertook advanced acupuncture training and *qi gong* training in China. I later went to India and have now been visiting regularly for over fifteen years, taking the opportunity to study with Tibetan and Ayurvedic physicians. I have spent much time at the Tibetan medical institutes in Dharamsala and Delhi in northern India, as well as with Tibetan physicians in the Tibetan settlements of southern India and in Europe.

A particular highlight of my study was a private audience with His Holiness the Dalai Lama in Dharamsala, during which we discussed the practice and future of Tibetan medicine. One of his particular comments on that day is included in the text of this book (see page 52). Since returning to the West I have continued my study and practice of these traditions and joyfully witnessed their growing popularity and transmission here through many great teachers.

In learning about these traditions and witnessing the physicians at work, I have been deeply impressed by the accuracy of their diagnosis, the efficacy of their techniques, the range of self-care and preventive approaches employed and the compassion shown to patients. I have also been struck by both the similarities within the traditions as well as their unique individual differences. All share the concept of the five primordial elements, and of both internal and external pathogenic factors, and Indian and Tibetan medicine share the concept of three humours. Yet Tibetan medicine has the most extensive and subtle system of pulse-taking, including the "wondrous pulses" (see page 67); Ayurvedic medicine has devised a unique system of

purification treatments, the *panchakarma* (see pages 38–39); Japanese medicine is the only tradition that uses *ampuku* – diagnosis and treatment through the abdomen alone (see page 139); and Chinese medicine has a uniquely comprehensive system of tongue diagnosis (see pages 106–107) – to give but a few examples.

Each of these traditions represents a complete system of medicine, rather than just a collection of individual therapies, and has been practised over thousands of years. Each has an underlying philosophy; thorough concepts of the body, incorporating anatomy of both the physical and subtle bodies; comprehensive diagnostic systems, including pulse, tongue, abdominal, urine and astrological diagnosis; a wide range of treatments; and an extensive knowledge of medicinal substances (materia medica). Each takes account of the patient's environment, diet, behaviour and mental state, and even of the seasons, celestial cycles and spirit influence. At the root of all these traditions is the idea that health is a reflection of leading a life of balance and that the true goal in life goes beyond mere physical health to the achievement of balanced function of body, mind and spirit and ultimately spiritual liberation itself.

Jacqueline Young

This book is dedicated to my most precious and beloved son, Shanphan Norbu (Michael Alan Young), who embodies the best of both East and West and who has been raised according to the health principles described in these pages. May he, and all readers of this book, be joyfully guided and inspired by the ancient healing wisdom of the East to live a long, happy, healthy and productive life for the benefit of all sentient beings.

INDIA

KNOWLEDGE FOR LIVING

Ayurveda, the principal medical tradition of India, is said to have developed from the sacred texts – the Vedas – and is known to have been practised for more than 2,000 years. It views the body as a miniature cosmic universe regulated by the balance of three primordial humours – wind (*vata*), choler (*pitta*) and phlegm (*kapha*). A holistic system that covers both prevention and cure, Ayurveda advocates a lifestyle of moderation and encompasses recommendations for diet, seasonal behaviour, exercise and moral living. Diagnosis is based on observation, palpation and questioning, and the physician uses perception, reasoning and what is referred to as "the tradition of the wise" to correctly diagnose and to select the most appropriate therapy. Treatments are mainly herbal, but also include purification techniques, known as *panchakarma*, which are used for detoxifying the body and regulating the humours. Spiritual remedies take into account the person's karma and astrological influences.

Women float oil lamps onto the water at Udaipur, Rajasthan, as part of the ritual celebrations during India's great autumn festival of lights, Diwali. It is held each year to honour Lakshmi, the consort of Vishnu and a goddess of good fortune who is associated with fertility.

SACRED ROOTS AND EARLY TEXTS

Ayurveda literally means "the knowledge" or "science" (*veda*) of "life" or "longevity" (*ayus*). It is said to have derived from sacred Hindu texts, the Vedas, but modern-day scholars argue that only fragmentary references to health and healing actually exist in them and that it is more likely that the Ayurvedic tradition evolved gradually, absorbing Buddhist and other influences in the process.

Early healing approaches were based on magic and ritual, and disease was seen mainly in the context of demonic possession, to be cured by prayer and the recitation of mantras, or as external injury, to be healed with herbal remedies and simple surgery.

The earliest formalized Ayurvedic texts, written in Sanskrit, date back some 2,000 years. The medical compendiums by Charaka and Sushruta cover a vast array of topics from pathology, diagnosis, therapy and surgery to philosophy and advice for daily living. Copies of these texts have survived to the present day and are still used as the basis of medical training. Other significant medical texts cover, among other topics, specialized treatments for women and children and there are numerous texts about materia medica, as well as useful volumes offering concise summaries of herbal prescriptions. Ayurvedic medicine developed pioneering forms of surgery that were later adopted in Europe. It also influenced, and was influenced by, the Greco-Arabic tradition of Unani medicine (see pages 14–15).

THE HISTORY OF AYURVEDA

According to Hindu mythology, the contents of the ancient spiritual texts, the four Vedas, was revealed by the creator god Brahma (see box, page 13) to ancient seers, known as *rishis*. They passed the knowledge down to others in the form of Sanskrit verses known as *suktas* and the Vedas are thought to have first been written down between 1500 and 1200BCE. The oldest text is the *Rig Veda*, which contains 1,028 hymns praising the gods. The second and third Vedas, the *Yajur Veda* and *Sama Veda*, contain the principal tenets of Indian philosophy and religion. The *Atharva Veda*, which was written last, deals principally with magic and ritual.

Brahma, the god of creation, is often represented with four heads, facing in the directions of the compass, and with the four Vedas in his hands.

Contained within the Vedas, especially the *Atharva Veda*, there are references to health and healing and to therapeutic remedies. Early healing practices appear to have been based on hygiene, herbal remedies, religious rituals and prayers, including mantras. A primary cause of disease was thought to be demonic possession, and penances, prayers and incantations were used in treatment. However, there is no formalized or complete system of medicine contained within the Vedic texts and claims that Ayurveda descended directly from the Vedas may be unfounded. Rather, it appears that the system of medicine developed over time, absorbing influences from Buddhism and other traditions along the way. Remarkable similarities exist between early Buddhist medical texts and later Ayurvedic

texts to support this idea, and it would appear that some Ayurvedic texts underwent some religious reworking some time after they were originally written. It is also known that early Buddhist monks and followers were encouraged to administer healing as a way of exercising compassion for humanity and that they developed new forms of medical practice.

The earliest Ayurveda textbooks were originally written in Sanskrit on palm leaves or birch bark, some of which still survive today. Two great medical texts, the *Charaka Samhita*, or *Charaka's Compendium*, and the *Sushruta Samhita*, or *Sushruta's Compendium*, compiled by Charaka and Sushruta respectively, are the oldest surviving texts and form the backbone of the Ayurvedic medical system. A third ancient text, the *Bhela Samhita*, or *Bhela's Compendium*, was written around the same time, but has survived only in fragments and has not yet been fully explored.

The earliest layers of the *Charaka Samhita* have been dated to the second or third centuries BCE. According to legend, the work contains the medical teachings that the sage Atreya received from the god Indra and then passed on to his student, Agnivesa. Charaka himself is thought to have been a physician who lived around the first or second century CE and compiled and edited the teachings for a wider readership. Another author, Drdhabala, made further revisions in the fourth or fifth century.

Krishna, the eighth incarnation of Vishnu (see box, right), presents a lotus to his favourite, Radha. The lotus flower is commonly used in Indian art as a symbol of purity, transcendent consciousness and fertility.

The *Charaka Samhita* deals with a vast range of topics, including the classification of disease, types of therapy, how to abandon bad habits and cultivate good ones in their place, and the harmful consequences of suppressing "natural urges". It has 120 chapters with eight main sections: *Sutra*, covering pharmacology, diet, some diseases, treatments and philosophical topics; *Nidana*, which describes the causes of the eight main diseases; *Vimana*, covering taste, nourishment, pathology and medical study; *Sharira*, on philosophy, anatomy and embryology; *Indriya*, on diagnosis and prognosis; *Chikitsa*, on therapy; *Kalpa*, on pharmacy; and *Siddhi*, on additional general therapy.

The *Sushruta Samhita*, the work of more than one author, claims to contain teachings received directly from the god Dhanvantari (see box, right), who was given them by Indra after having received them from Brahma. Scholars nowadays believe that this text was first compiled in the last centuries BCE and then revised up to about 500CE. The original is thought to have covered surgical methods and equipment, the necessity for hygiene, techniques for suturing and so on. Gradually this was expanded to include the six comprehensive sections that it has today: *Sutra*, covering the origins of medicine, medical training, diet, treatments and surgery; *Nidana*, on symptoms, pathology, prognosis and surgery; *Sharira*, on philosophy, embryology and anatomy; *Chikitsa*, on therapy; *Kalpa*, on poisons; and *Uttara*, on ophthalmology, children's diseases, demonic attack and dentistry.

Another important text is the *Ashtangahrdaya*, or *Heart of Medicine*, by Vagbhata. Written around 600CE, it consists of a compilation of earlier texts, forming, for the first time, a coherent work that drew together the different strands of Ayurveda. It became the foremost Sanskrit medical text. For centuries it formed the basis of medical teaching, was often memorized by physicians and was translated many times, resulting in Tibetan, Chinese and Arabic versions.

These early texts outline the eight branches of Ayurveda: surgery, medicine, gynecology, pediatrics, toxicology, otorhinolaryngology (ear, nose and throat), rejuvenation and virilification (male virility and female fertility) therapy. They also describe the Ayurvedic concepts of the body (see pages 16–23), including the three humours. Historically, there may be a link here with the Greek concept of the humours. First proposed by Hippocrates around 400BCE, and later elaborated by Galen in 150CE, four humours of blood, phlegm, black and yellow bile and four corresponding emotional types – the sanguine, phlegmatic, melancholic and choleric – were described.

These concepts dominated European medical thinking up to the early sixteenth century when the first anatomical studies were carried out. In Ayurveda, the concept of the humours is still current; yet acceptance of this is at the root of the dispute between those who support pure *shuddha* Ayurveda – believing that the underlying fundamental principles of Ayurveda are superior to other forms of medicine – and those who believe that it has to be brought into the modern world by dropping certain precepts and integrating with the principles and practice of Western medicine.

During British rule in India there was a gradual decline in support for Ayurveda, but it enjoyed a revival after independence and has now gained the support of the Indian government. As a result, many new Ayurvedic colleges, clinics and pharmacies were established during the latter part of the twentieth century and Ayurvedic practitioners are once again numerous and widespread in India. There is also a burgeoning industry in Ayurvedic pills, potions and ointments, both in India and abroad. Ayurveda is becoming increasingly popular as a complementary therapy in the West. Ayurvedic beauty treatments are also becoming more well known and gaining acceptance outside of the Asian communities in Western countries.

Dhanvantari, the god of Ayurveda, holds a vase filled with the "nectar of immortality", which has the power to cure all diseases.

THE HEAVENLY PHYSICIAN

The Hindu pantheon has countless deities but the most well known are the three gods who constitute the holy trinity or *trimurti*: Brahma, the creator, Vishnu the preserver and Shiva, the creator and destroyer. Vishnu, who is the preserver of righteousness (Dharma) and the protector for suffering humanity, has many different incarnations of which the most well known is Krishna.

In another incarnation he takes on the form of Dhanvantari who, in a famous story, is said to have arisen from the primordial Ocean of Milk, which was being churned by gods and demons in order to retrieve good things that had sunk to its depths. He rose to the surface carrying a vase containing the "nectar of immortality" and brought with him knowledge of the science of medicine and healing. For this reason Dhanvantari has come to be known as the god of Ayurveda and is worshipped for his healing powers (see page 44). His statues appear in most Ayurvedic hospitals and clinics and he is often shown with four arms, like Vishnu, holding the vase of nectar, a conch shell, a disc, and leeches for blood-letting, an Ayurvedic therapy.

UNANI AND SIDDHA MEDICINE

A number of other medical traditions exist in India alongside Ayurveda and these have significantly influenced one another. Particularly worthy of mention are the Unani *tibb* tradition of Islam and the Siddha tradition of the Tamils.

Unani *tibb* was brought to India by the invading Muslim armies in the eleventh and twelfth centuries. It was based on the Greek humoral tradition – *unani* means "of the

A surgeon or jarrah *swabs the leg of a patient following the cleansing and repair of a wound. When it was required, the anesthetic of choice was derived from opium.*

Greeks", or Ionian, while the Arabic word *tibb* means "medicine" – and the works of the Persian Ibn Sina (980–1037), known as Avicenna in the West. His medical canon, the *Quanun*, formed the basis of Unani theory and practice.

The tradition spread in the large cities of India, such as Delhi, Agra and Hyderabad, due to the patronage of Muslim rulers who established hospitals. As a result, many Persian *hakims* (doctors) travelled to India, where some settled and established great lineages of *hakim* families. Indian physicians also went to Persia to learn Unani *tibb*. From the ninth century, Sanskrit texts were translated into Persian and

Arabic, and from the thirteenth century, Unani texts were written in India and translated into local languages, such as Urdu, leading to a rich exchange of ideas.

The traditions of Ayurveda and Unani *tibb* have many things in common, but also important differences. Both recognize the concept of humours, but the Unani system has the four humours of Greek medicine whereas Ayurveda has just three. The materia medica of both was extended as practitioners shared information on the usage or substitution of different herbs. The Unani tradition had neglected surgery and began to adopt some of the Ayurvedic techniques, while Ayurveda adopted the more refined Unani practice of pulse diagnosis, and began to give it more prominence within its own diagnostic approach.

In the twentieth century, Unani flourished alongside Ayurveda as India's independence led to the establishment of new Unani training institutions as well as Ayurvedic ones. However, in general, Unani has remained urban, hospital-based and is utilized predominantly by Muslims, while Ayurveda tends to be practised on a more individual basis, or in small clinics, is widespread in both rural and urban areas and is favoured by Hindus.

Siddha medicine (*cittar* in Tamil), still popular today in southern India, shares humoral theory with Ayurveda but lays greater emphasis on tantric rituals, the alchemical use of metallic compounds in its medicines and the attainment of longevity through intense yoga practices. It is said to have been developed by ancient Tamil sages (*siddhas*), who were believed to possess superhuman powers. Agastyar, Tirumular and Bhogar, living around the fifth and sixth centuries, are the most famous of these. Pulse diagnosis is prominent in this system and urine diagnosis and moxibustion (*muccukkalayam*) are also used. One prominent medicine is *muppu*, a secret combination of salts believed to enhance other Siddha medicines and spiritual transformation. A unique technique for rejuvenation, *kaya kalpa*, involves taking *muppu* and mercurial medicines, combined with breathing and other exercises.

A 1795 engraving of Cowasjee's successful rhinoplasty (nose reconstruction). This surgical technique was pioneered in India before gaining popularity in Europe.

PIONEERING SURGERY

Surgery was first conducted in India in the first millennium BCE. Vedic texts of that time record the use of a reed as a catheter to relieve urine retention, and the later *Sushruta Samhita* (see page 12) outlines detailed surgical procedures. It is believed that later physicians rarely practised surgery because of a taboo against contact with "impure" bodily fluids, such as blood. Instead, its practitioners seem to have been a caste of barber-surgeons. One famous case is the rhinoplasty performed on a bullock-cart driver named Cowasjee who lost his nose during a war in 1792. The operation involved grafting skin onto the site from the forehead. British surgeons witnessed the surgery and brought the technique to Europe.

CHAPTER 2

CONCEPTS OF THE BODY AND DISEASE

In Ayurveda the healthy body is conceptualized as a microcosmic universe with its vital components in a delicate state of equilibrium. At its base are the five great primordial elements – the *panchamahabhutas* – of ether (*akasha*), air (*vayu*), fire (*agni*), water (*jala*) and earth (*prithvi*), which combine to form the three humours, or *doshas*, known as wind (*vata*), choler (*pitta*) and phlegm (*kapha*). The humours each have their own qualities and can combine in a variety of ways, and it is their relative balance which determines individual constitution (*prakriti*) and predisposition to disease. The constitution is also affected by the strength of a person's "digestive fire" (*agni*) and bowel function (*kostha*).

The physical body is made up of seven tissues (*dhatus*), their waste products (*malas*) and a network of "pipes", ducts and channels for circulating fluids and essences around the body. When all these components work together in a balanced way the person is healthy. However, negative mental attitudes or external factors can upset this equilibrium and the result is disease, which may also be affected by the law of karma.

Psychological make-up is influenced by the relative balance of the humours and by the equilibrium of three interdependent universal constituents known as the three *gunas*, which are purity (*sattva*), activity (*rajas*) and stagnation (*tamas*). These play a part in determining different mental qualities.

THE PHILOSOPHY OF CREATION

The basic principles of Ayurveda are based on one of the oldest systems of Indian philosophy, the Sankhya (the word indicates the idea of enumerating or reckoning). According to the Sankhya, the ultimate source of all existence is a state of absolute reality, *purusha*, which existed before creation and the manifestation of the universe. This absolute reality, sometimes translated as "spirit", is characterized as *sat-chit-ananda* – a state of total unity of being, awareness and bliss. From this unity arises the desire for creation, and thus what is unified in the one starts to evolve and transform itself to give birth to the many.

Vishnu, the preserver, seated on the cosmic serpent Ananta-Shesha, holding a conch shell (the elements), mace (time), disc (the sun) and lotus (creative power).

The first component to emerge from the unity of *sat-chit-ananda* is *prakriti*, or nature. *Prakriti* is characterized as female, the eternal Mother Nature that gives birth to all form in the physical world. *Prakriti* is made up of three interdependent constituents, known as the three *gunas*. They are *sattva*, (purity), *rajas* (activity) and *tamas* (solidity). These three are antagonistic yet complementary and exist in a state of equilibrium within *prakriti* to create balance and harmony in the universe.

From *prakriti* comes cosmic intelligence, or intellect (*mahat*), and individualized identity (*ahamkara*). This is sometimes translated as "ego" but it has a much wider meaning, referring to the individual identity of every atom and cell. Within *ahamkara* the three *gunas* manifest as consciousness (*sattva*), activity (*rajas*) and inertia (*tamas*). *Sattva* represents the subjective world of perception, *tamas* the objective world of material reality and the operation of the five elements, and *rajas* the force that binds these two together.

Sattva evolves into eleven *indriyas* (sense and motor organs): the mind, the five organs of cognition (ears, skin, eyes, tongue and nose) and the five motor organs or organs of action (*manas*). These are speech, hands, feet, genitals and anus, which relate to communication, creativity, locomotion, reproduction and elimination respectively. *Rajas* represents life-force and movement and has a role in balancing *sattva* and *tamas*. *Tamas* evolves into the five sense organs, namely sound, touch, sight, taste and smell, known as the *tanmatras*.

From the subtle aspects of these five senses evolve the five elements, the *panchamahabhutas*. Sound is linked with the element of space or ether (*akasha*), touch with the element of air (*vayu*), sight to the element of fire (*agni*), taste to the element of water (*jala*) and smell to the element of earth (*prithvi*). These elements are the basis of everything in the physical world and are in a constant, dynamic state of change.

The principles that constitute the cosmic universe are mirrored in the make-up of the individual. Here, *purusha* represents the soul and *prakriti* the individual constitution. The three *gunas* represent the qualities of the mind and the five elements (*bhutas*) combine to make up the three *doshas* that regulate health (see pages 18–19).

THE BODY IN AYURVEDA

There has never been one unified concept of the body in Ayurveda. Over time, various theories have emerged and disappeared, with some concepts, particularly that of the three humours (*doshas*), becoming predominant. There is no real theory of anatomy within Ayurveda either, although many of the ancient texts contain detailed lists of bones, muscles, tendons, and so on. The body is principally conceived as a collection of vital fluids and essences that course through the body in a network of channels and

A girl dousing herself with water, which in India is considered to be a highly potent spiritual symbol. Rivers are identified with Shiva's power and represent purification and rebirth.

important centres. In line with this, many of the interactions between the gods, and between gods and humans, are described in terms of a symbolic exchange of fluids too.

The *Sarngadhara Samhita*, or *Sarngadhara's Compendium*, describes the body as composed of the three humours (*doshas*); the seven tissues (*dhatus*), their subsidiaries and impurities; the seven membranes, or skins; the seven receptacles, such as the bladder which retains urine, and other internal organs; the 210 ligaments, 300 bones, 500 muscles, 16 tendons and 10 orifices (women have 20 extra muscles and 13 extra orifices); the 107 *marma* points (see box, page 35); 700 ducts; and 24 "pipes" or channels (see page 21).

The three *doshas*, known as *vata*, *pitta* and *kapha*, are each made up of two of the elements. *Vata*, or wind, is produced from a combination of air and ether and has the quality of movement (*rajas*). It is light, subtle, cold, dry and erratic. *Pitta*, also known as choler or bile, is composed primarily of the fire element, but is combined with the water element and has the quality of purity (*sattvas*). It is hot, oily, liquid and sharp. *Kapha*, or phlegm, is a combination of water and earth elements, with water predominating, and has the qualities of darkness, solidity and inertia (*tamas*). It is heavy, cold, oily, slimy and soft. Each humour is also associated with particular tastes or savours. *Vata* has astringent savours, *pitta* has pungent and bitter savours, which turn sour after digestion, and *kapha* has a sweet savour, which turns salty after digestion (see pages 32–33 and 36–37).

The elements and humours are each associated with particular body parts and functions. The ether element relates to speech and sound. The air element influences respiratory function, joint mobility and touch. The fire element

MAHABHUTAS: THE FIVE GREAT ELEMENTS

According to the Sankhya philosophy (see page 17) all matter in the universe is composed from five primordial elements, each of which is associated with particular qualities, properties and actions. In the body, each is identified with specific organs, faculties and functions. The elements also combine to form the three humours (*tridoshas*).

ELEMENT	QUALITY	SENSE ORGAN	SENSE FACULTY	MOTOR ORGAN	MOTOR FUNCTION
SPACE (*AKASHA*)	Sound	Ears	Auditory	Vocal chords	Speech
AIR (*VAYU*)	Touch	Skin	Tactile	Hands	Handling and touch
FIRE (*AGNI*)	Sight	Eyes	Visual	Feet	Movement
WATER (*JALA*)	Taste	Tongue	Gustatory	Genitals	Procreation
EARTH (*PRITHVI*)	Smell	Nose	Olfactory	Anus	Excretion

regulates temperature, heat, skin hue and vision. The water element influences all that is liquid in the body, and also taste, sweat and urine. The earth element governs the solid organs, bones, teeth, nails, flesh and sense of smell.

There are five types of each *dosha*, each located in a specific part of the body and related to certain mental and physical functions. The five types of *vata* are described as five "breaths". *Prana*, the "fore-breath", enters via the mouth and is located in the head and chest. It regulates mental function, respiration and helps food to enter the stomach. *Udana*, the "up-breath", is located in the chest and neck and governs vocal functions. *Samana*, the "mid-breath", is located in the stomach and small intestine and aids digestion and the separation of waste products. *Vyana*, the "intra-breath", is located throughout the body and governs movement, the circulation of blood and sweating. *Apana*, the "down breath", is located in the intestines and bladder and aids excretion of faeces and urine. It also influences menses in women and semen production in men. *Vata* is often regarded as the most powerful of the humours as it can also move choler and phlegm in the body.

The five types of *pitta* are *alochaka pitta*, located in the eyes and governing vision; *sadhaka pitta*, in the heart centre of consciousness and related to memory and consciousness; *bhrajaka pitta*, located in the skin and controlling skin hue, lustre and temperature; *pachaka pitta*, located in the stomach and small intestine and related to digestion and absorption of nutrients; and *ranjaka pitta*, located in the liver and spleen and governing blood and lymph.

The five types of *kapha* are *tarpaka kapha*, located in the head, which relates to brain and sense organ function; *bodhaka kapha*, in the tongue and throat, which governs taste; *avalambaka kapha*, in the heart centre, which relates to cardiac function; *kledaka kapha*, located in the stomach, which plays a part in the liquefaction of foodstuffs; and *shleshmaka kapha*, located in the joints, which plays a part in lubrication and locomotion.

The seven tissues (*dhatus*) that nourish and support the body are chyle, blood, flesh, fat, bone, marrow and semen. Each one of these produces another, so that blood is derived from chyle, flesh from blood and so on. They also produce the impurities of mucus, "ear dirt", impurities of the orifices, and of nails and eyes, oiliness of the face and spots respectively. The subsidiary *dhatus* are women's breastmilk and menstrual blood, fat, sweat, teeth, head hair and energy (*ojas*).

THE HEALTHY BODY

Ayurveda defines health as a state of equilibrium between each of the three *doshas* and the normal function of the seven *dhatus* and their waste products (*malas*) – namely, urine (*mutra*), feces (*purisha*) and sweat (*sveda*). When the *doshas* work together correctly, the body is strong and healthy, mental faculties are good and the emotions are in balance. Health conceived in this way is said to enable the individual to freely pursue Dharma (righteous living), *artha* (prosperity), *kama* (pleasure) and, ultimately, *moksha* (spiritual liberation).

In their normal state, the three *doshas* balance one another by virtue of the fact that they have both shared and antagonistic qualities. For example, both *vata* and *kapha* have cold qualities, although the former is dry-cold and the latter wet-cold. In addition, both *pitta* and *kapha* have oily qualities, but the former is only slightly oily whereas the latter is very oily and slimy. Also, within *pitta*, if the fire element is too strong the water element will diminish, causing dryness. Alternatively, if the water element is strengthened, the excess fire will be quenched.

LOCATIONS OF THE THREE HUMOURS

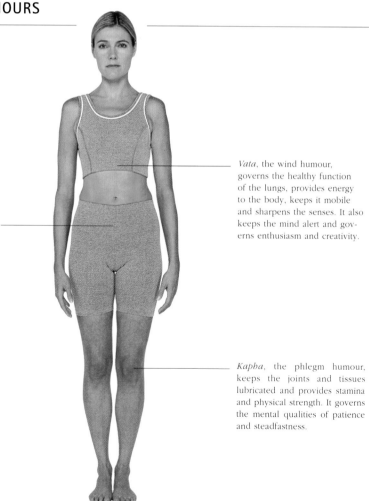

Pitta, the choler or bile humour, governs healthy digestive function and appetite, regulates body temperature and helps maintain good eyesight. It aids memory, intellectual function and confidence.

Vata, the wind humour, governs the healthy function of the lungs, provides energy to the body, keeps it mobile and sharpens the senses. It also keeps the mind alert and governs enthusiasm and creativity.

Kapha, the phlegm humour, keeps the joints and tissues lubricated and provides stamina and physical strength. It governs the mental qualities of patience and steadfastness.

Each of the *doshas* has specific functions within the body and in mental processing. *Vata*'s normal function is to provide the body with energy, efficient respiration, mobility, "natural urges" (such as sneezing) and sharp sensory ability; it provides the mind with alertness, enthusiasm and creativity. The normal role of *pitta* is to enable good digestion, regulate body temperature, vision and suppleness, and aid good memory, intellectual function and confidence. *Kapha*'s functions involve lubricating the joints and tissues, and providing unctuousness, stamina and physical strength combined with mental steadiness and patience.

The *doshas* combine to form the basic constitution (*prakriti*) of a person. Ayurveda identifies seven constitutional types: in the first three, just one of the *doshas* predominates; in the second three, any two *doshas* combine together with equal strength; while in the last type all three *doshas* have equal strength. The latter is rare and most people have a predominance of one or two *doshas* determining their individual make-up.

Vata individuals are generally short, lightly built, with an angular face and thin, dry skin. They tend to sweat little, talk rapidly and are creative and enthusiastic but erratic. *Pitta* types are usually of average height and build with a well-proportioned face and soft skin. They often sweat profusely, are physically strong and confident but may be prone to anger. *Kapha* types are usually tall, sturdy, with a large, round face and oily, pale skin. They dislike cold, love sleeping, sweat moderately and are caring and patient, although their mental functions may be slow.

Individual constitution and health also depend on the strength of the person's *kostha* ("bowel predisposition") and *agni* ("digestive fire"), both of which are affected by the *doshas*. If *vata* is too strong, *agni* becomes erratic and inefficient and constipation or irregular bowel movements may be experienced; if *pitta* is in excess, the *agni* fire becomes intense and all-consuming and the stools are loose and soft; *kapha* excess causes weak and dull *agni* fire and causes mucus to be present in the stools.

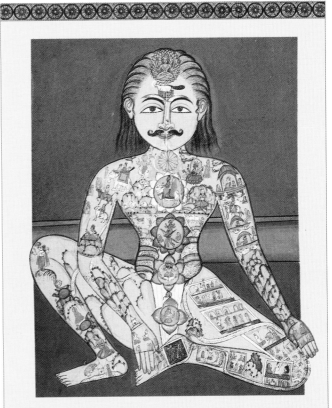

This figure shows the chakras *of the subtle body. The yogi has attained enlightenment and so the entire universe is represented on his body.*

THE SUBTLE BODY

In Ayurveda little reference is made to the subtle energetic body that is described in such detail in the yoga and *tantra* traditions, but there appears to be some overlap in the descriptions of the *marma* points (see box, page 35). In the yoga tradition the *nadis* are the subtle nerve channels of the astral, or energetic, body through which *prana*, the life-force, flows. There are said to be more than 72,000 *nadis*, of which the main three are the *sushumna*, which runs parallel with the spine, and the *ida* and *pingala*, which run on either side of the spine and intersect it at several major points. These points of intersection correspond with the seven energy centres known as the *chakras*. For there to be good physical and emotional health it is essential that *prana* flows freely through these channels. This can be achieved through the practice of yoga (see pages 40–43).

UNDERSTANDING DISEASE

*Fresh lemons, chilli, garlic and ginger in a market in New Delhi. Indian medicine
has long advocated the importance of eating local, seasonal produce.*

The root cause of all disease, according to Ayurveda, is "perversity of mind" – that is, the mental attitudes that prevent us from taking good care of ourselves even though we know how to protect and promote our own health. Instead of living in harmony with nature and the seasons and the natural cycles of life, we push the boundaries for our own selfish reasons, regardless of the ultimate cost to health, and allow ourselves to be consumed with negative emotions such as grief, fear, anger, envy and pride. Ayurveda calls this *prajnaparadha*, which means "a crime against wisdom". Diseases which spring directly from *prajnaparadha* are described as "internally caused" and relate directly to imbalance of the *doshas* (humours). Other

"external" factors such as accidents, epidemics, adverse planetary influences and possession by spirits can also precipitate disease. In these cases, the symptoms occur first and these then cause imbalance of the *doshas*.

Ayurveda has many ways of classifying disease, but there are seven main categories: genetic (*adibalapravritta*), congenital (*janmabalapravritta*), constitutional or metabolic (*doshabalapravritta*), traumatic (*sanghatabalapravritta*), seasonal (*kalabalapravritta*), divine (*daivabalapravritta*) and natural (*swabhavbalapravritta*).

Constitutional diseases are due directly to imbalance of the *doshas*. This balance can be affected by many factors such as age, constitution, season, suppression of "natural urges", lifestyle (such as indulging in bad habits or keeping bad company), misuse of the senses, poor diet and impaired digestion (see page 21). Specific factors that are similar in nature to a *dosha* will increase its propensity, while factors dissimilar in nature will decrease it. So, for example, *vata* is increased by exposure to cold, fasting, lack of sleep and worry, but decreased by keeping warm, moderate eating, warm foods, adequate sleep and mental calm. Similarly, *pitta* is increased by overexposure to heat, overeating spicy foods, strenuous physical exertion, anger and hatred, and decreased by their opposites. The *kapha* humour is increased by exposure to cold, too much sweet food, sleeping after eating, inactivity, doubts and greed, and decreased by their opposites. If the nature of the disorder is of the same nature as your basic constitution it will be harder to treat, while if it is dissimilar it will be easier to remedy.

Diseases are also classified by whether they are curable. There are those that can be cured (*sadhya*), those that can only be eased (*yapya*) and those that are incurable (*asadhya*). Those that are curable may be either easy to cure or difficult, depending on conditions. If the patient is young, the disease is relatively recent and limited in its effects and the planets are in auspicious alignment, then the cure is likely to be easy. If the opposite is true and the treatment requires surgery, it will be harder to cure. If the person still has some physical vitality, then changes of lifestyle and diet will mitigate the symptoms. However, if the person is weak and consumed with mental negativity, and the disease is intractable, then the patient cannot be cured. Physicians are advised not to take such patients on.

Diseases may also be classified in terms of their symptoms, severity, causes, location, timing, prognosis and treatment. The disease may be primary (due to one particular cause) or secondary (arising as a complication of an existing set of symptoms).

The first stage of disease is "accumulation", as the *dosha* imbalance increases. It then becomes aggravated and the symptoms increase. In the final stage of disease, the aggravated *dosha* spreads and new symptoms are created. If untreated at this stage, the disease may become incurable.

The Ayurvedic texts describe eight "great" diseases (*mahagadas*), all serious in nature. These are severe fevers, bleeding and haemorrhage, tumours, diabetes and other severe urinary disorders, serious skin conditions, tuberculosis and other related diseases, convulsions and epilepsy, and, finally, insanity. Mental illness can be triggered by an imbalance of *rajas* and *tamas* (see page 17), disequilibrium of the three humours, the experience of intense emotions, such as shock or grief, alcohol abuse or demonic influence.

A key factor to be considered in all diseases is the concept of karma. This law of cause and effect states that the roots of an illness may lie in actions performed in a past life, the fruits of which are resulting in the present. Accordingly, the individual has ultimate responsibility for the experience of disease and its consequences. Such illnesses cannot be treated with medicines and lifestyle changes alone, but also require spiritual remedies (see pages 44–45).

AILMENTS ASSOCIATED WITH THE DOSHAS

Vata	Pitta	Kapha
Joint pain	Digestive problems	Weight gain
Muscular pain	Hot flushes	Food cravings
Menstrual irregularity and scanty flow	Burning sensation in soles and palms	Water retention and bloating
Dry, hacking cough	Cystitis and painful urination	Lethargy and fatigue
Dry skin	Excess sweating	Indigestion, cramps
Headache	Sore eyes, migraine	Breast tenderness
Anxiety and Nervousness	Anger and irritability	Disinterest and mental dullness

CHAPTER 3

DIAGNOSTIC PROCEDURES

Diagnosis in Ayurveda is aimed principally at establishing the relative balance of the *doshas* in relation to the patient's health. The physician examines the patient by means of observation, touching (palpation) and questioning. In the Eightfold Examination (see pages 26–27), the physician observes the tongue, eyes, skin, and general appearance, listens to the tone of the voice, examines a sample of, or asks about, urine and stools, and takes the pulse on the wrist. In each of these procedures, signs of the relative imbalance of a particular *dosha*, or *doshas*, are noted and gradually combined to form an overall picture of the pattern of imbalance. Questions are used to supplement and confirm the diagnosis and to decide on appropriate treatment.

The diagnosis of the actual disease is made by determining the underlying cause, the initial signs, the symptoms, their consequences and the stage that the disease has reached. Ten different aspects are considered in relation to the nature of the disease and the likely outcome of treatment (see page 27). These relate to the person's individual constitution, build, body proportions, mental and physical capacity, general level of vitality, adaptability, digestive strength, age and the level of pathology of the disease.

Spiritual diagnoses, the analysis of dreams or the use of astrological natal charts – may also be used to determine the role of karma or any spirit influence in the disease. Different planets are sometimes associated with particular types of ailments and their transits with so-called "karmic cycles".

CONSULTING A PRACTITIONER

An Ayurvedic consultation begins with the physician observing the patient, their gait, general appearance, complexion, and so on, as they enter the room. The patient is put at ease and the physician may ask certain questions. These will cover family medical history – to ascertain congenital influences on the constitution of the patient – and personal medical history. Questions also focus on lifestyle to determine the influence of habits, diet, stress and specific behaviours, such as smoking and drinking, on the patient's health. The physician will carry out the Eightfold Examination (see pages 26–27), which includes taking the patient's pulse. Some Ayurvedic physicians rely almost solely on pulse diagnosis and take it silently before making any comments or asking any questions. These three forms of diagnosis – observation (*darshana*), questioning (*prashna*) and palpation (*sparshana*) – enable the physician to determine the *dosha*-type of the person and their strengths as well as their weaknesses.

The physician will carefully determine the exact nature of symptoms and disease in order to select the correct form of treatment. This is done by investigating the likely causes of the disease (*nidana*) – be they external (due to diet, behaviour and so on) or internal (due to physical imbalance) – and its signs and symptoms, both advance warning signs (*purvarupa*) and actual ones (*rupa*). The manifestation of the disease – that is, where in the body it originated

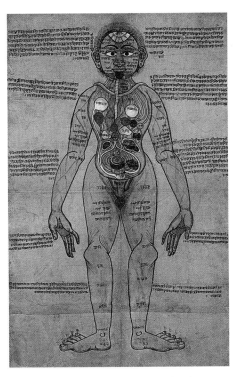

A rare, illustrated Indian medical text, originating from Nepal but annotated in Sanskrit and featuring interesting anatomical detail.

(*udbhava sthana*), where it appeared (*adhisthana*) and how it was transported around the body (*sanchara marga*) – will also be considered and exploratory therapy (*upashaya*) may be carried out to confirm diagnosis. If the treatment alleviates symptoms, then the diagnosis is correct, whereas if it does not then the diagnosis and the treatment must be modified.

In arriving at a correct diagnosis the physician employs the skills of perception, inference and authoritative reasoning. Perception (*pratyaksha*) refers to information received through the senses which is processed and understood not only by the mind but also by the heart. Inference (*anumana*) refers to the physician's ability to infer information about a disease on the basis of signs and symptoms – in the same way as fruit can be inferred from a seed – and to produce a prognosis through assessment of the patient's strength, adaptability and so on. Authoritative reasoning includes making correct diagnostic conclusions based on expert testimony, medical texts and historical knowledge – using this skill, the physician is said to act as an "authoritative person" (*apta*) and is able to build up a picture of the patient's past, present and likely future health.

Astrology may also be used, for the position of the planets at birth is said to exert an influence on the *prakriti* (constitution) of the individual (see pages 16–17) and to offer an explanation of the karmic causes of disease.

EXAMINATION AND DIAGNOSIS

The Eightfold Examination (*ashtavidha pariksha*) involves examination of pulse (*nadi*), tongue (*jihva*), voice (*sabda*), skin (*sparsa*), vision (*drk*), general appearance (*akrti*), urine (*mutra*) and stools (*mala*).

The pulse is taken on the radial artery and is used to determine specific pulse qualities in relation to the balance of the *doshas*. A healthy pulse is firm, strong and regular. A *vata* pulse is fast and slippery, described as moving "like a leech" or "like a snake"; a *pitta* pulse is jumpy, akin to the movement of a sparrowhawk or frog; and a *kapha* pulse is slow and steady, resembling a swan or pigeon. If two *doshas* are imbalanced the pulse may be alternately slow or fast; when all the *doshas* are imbalanced the pulse becomes erratic and unpredictable. A rapid, throbbing pulse indicates

Pulse diagnosis is an important part of the Eightfold Examination but in Ayurveda the pulse positions do not correspond to individual organs as they do in Chinese and Tibetan medicine.

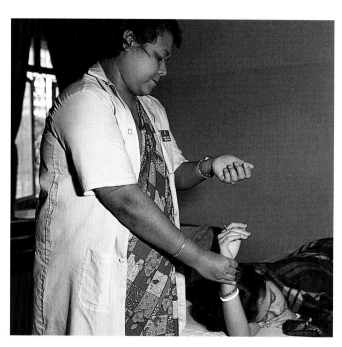

that a fever has entered the body, while a weak, slow pulse indicates a lack of digestive fire and cold or chronic conditions. If the pulse stops and starts the disease has reached the fatal stage.

In tongue diagnosis, the general appearance, colour and coating of the tongue are examined. *Vata* signs are a dry, rough tongue with cracks and little coating or moisture; *pitta* signs are a red tongue with a burning sensation and sometimes an oily, yellow coating; *kapha* signs are a full, swollen, tongue that is moist with a greasy white coating. The voice also reflects the *dosha* balance: a coarse voice indicates *vata* disturbance, a cracked voice indicates *pitta* imbalance, and a heavy, thick voice suggests *kapha*.

Skin diagnosis involves observation of colour and texture and palpation of certain points to detect disturbance or tenderness (see box, page 35). *Vata* imbalance results in dry, rough, sensitive skin that is cool to the touch; *pitta* imbalance causes the skin to redden and feel hot; *kapha* imbalance results in clammy, moist and cold skin.

The key diagnostic clue in eye examination is the colour of the whites of the eyes and the overall sensation around the eyes. *Vata* signs are dry, sensitive eyes with a dull hue to the whites; *pitta* signs are a burning sensation in the eyes, with yellowed eye whites; *kapha* signs are heaviness of the eyelids and watery eyes.

Diagnosis of general appearance takes into account posture and movement. *Vata* types are often thin and wiry and fast-moving; *pitta* types are often strong and upright but restless; *kapha* types are often heavily built and slow in their movements.

Urine diagnosis involves questioning the patient about the frequency of, and sensation during, urination and examining a urine sample for its colour and odour. Normal,

TEN ASPECTS OF DIAGNOSIS IN AYURVEDA

ALONGSIDE THE EIGHTFOLD EXAMINATION, THE PHYSICIAN TAKES ACCOUNT OF THE FOLLOWING TEN FACTORS:

SANSKRIT TERM	ENGLISH TERM	ASPECTS OF DIAGNOSIS
Prakriti	Individual constitution	Evaluates genetic factors and balance of the five *mahabhutas* (elements) (see pages 18–19) and the three *doshas* (see pages 22–23) in the body.
Sattva	Mental/emotional constitution	Evaluates the relative dominance of the three *gunas* (mental properties) (see page 17), which determine individual psychological constitution (*manasa prakrti*)
Vikriti	Pathological state	Analysis of the signs and symptoms of the disease, their effect on the body and the stage of disease (see page 23)
Sara	Tissue state	Evaluates the relative vitality of each of the seven *dhatus* (tissues) (see page 19)
Ahara Shakti	Digestive vigour	Evaluates the strength of the digestive 'fire' (*agni*), which governs digestive capacity, metabolism and assimilation of nutrients.
Satmya	Affinity	Evaluates what is normal for the person according to genetic factors, upbringing and habitual factors – for example, according to the environment and climate in which they live and the normal diet for that place.
Samhanana	Physical make-up	The physician views the build, postural balance, condition of the skin and hair, and so on, to determine the general state of health of the patient.
Pramana	Body proportion	The physician looks for good proportions in the patient's body using the guide of finger-breadth measurement. Relative proportion is taken as a sign of general good health.
Vayas	Age	Considers the stage of life of the patient and diseases specifically associated with that time of life; for example, childhood or old age.
Vyayama shakti	Physical vigour	Evaluates the patient's capacity for physical movement and exercise.

healthy urine is usually light yellow in colour and has a fresh odour. *Vata*-type urine is clear and odourless; *pitta*-type urine is brown or deep yellow with a burnt odour; *kapha*-type urine is turbid and whitish in colour with a stale smell. In ancient times it was believed that dropping a little oil onto the surface of a urine sample and watching the results could predict the outcome of a disease. If the oil spread over the surface the disease was curable, but if it did not the disease would be either harder to cure or incurable.

A normal healthy stool is considered to be firm and light brown in colour. *Vata* disturbance causes the stool to be hard and dry and grey in colour; *pitta* disturbance causes loose stools that are yellow, dark brown or green in colour; *kapha* disturbance results in slimy, pale stools with mucus.

CHAPTER 4

HEALING IN
INDIAN MEDICINE

Ayurvedic healing is both curative and preventive and treats the whole person, not just the symptoms or specific disease. By restoring equilibrium through rebalancing the *doshas* in the body, it also aims to strengthen the constitution, restore the *agni* (digestive fire), improve health generally and promote longevity. Good health enables the individual to pursue the three goals of life outlined in the Vedas – Dharma (virtuous living), *artha* (prosperity) and *kama* (pleasure). These three lead to the fourth, and ultimate, goal of *moksha* (spiritual liberation).

Ayurvedic treatments range from herbal medicine, manual therapies, diet and lifestyle recommendations to exercise therapy (yoga), meditation, spiritual remedies and spiritual advice. There are both external and internal therapies – which can be used individually or in combination with one another – and also spiritual therapies (see pages 44–45), which deal with the mental and emotional aspects of disease.

Prevention methods include personal hygiene, treatments for enhancing fertility and virility, rejuvenation techniques and yoga. According to the ancient medical texts, the patient, physician and his or her attendant must each embody certain characteristics, and treatment must be selected appropriately and given in the correct form and at the right time. Religious rituals, pilgrimages and prayer are used to invoke divine protection and healing.

THE FOUR PILLARS OF TREATMENT

According to Charaka (see page 11) there are four "pillars", or foundations, underlying Ayurvedic treatment: the physician, the assistant, the patient and the medicine. All play a part in the therapeutic process and the Ayurvedic medical texts stipulate certain requirements for each.

The physician must be accomplished in terms of medical knowledge, training and clinical experience, and should exhibit physical cleanliness and purity of mind. Charaka said that he or she must be "able to deliver comfort and be companions of life itself". Physicians' attendants should display the same qualities.

The patient has a duty to follow any instructions accurately and obediently. He or she must describe their symptoms accurately and have the courage and motivation to be healed. The medical writer Sarngadhara warns that a sick person should only be regarded as suitable for treatment "if he has a proper constitution and appearance, if he is alert, if he is devoted to the physician, and has his senses under control". Vagbhata counsels that a patient should be rejected if he "is ferocious, grief-stricken, timid, ungrateful or thinks of himself as a physician".

The ingredients used in medicine should be grown, harvested and prepared correctly (see pages 36–37) in order to be effective. Medicine must be prescribed in accordance

A painting from 1825 of a perfumer preparing a pharmaceutical treatment. A knowledge of drugs and prescriptions was an area in which Unani and Ayurveda medicine shared expertise.

with the diagnosis and in the appropriate form – such as a pill, a powder or a paste.

In Ayurveda there are said to be three types of medicine: those based on reasoning, those based on the sacred and those based on good character. Medicine based on reasoning encompasses Ayurveda's four main forms of treatment: medicinal, which involves herbs (*aushadha*); cleansing and purificatory techniques (*panchakarma*); dietary therapy; and lifestyle modification (*pathya*).

Medicines based on the sacred include the recitation of mantras, ritual prayers and the dedication of offerings to the gods (*puja*), fasts, penances and pilgrimages, while those based on good character involve staying away from bad influences, avoiding stimulants such as alcohol, cultivating moral qualities and developing mental strength and decisiveness through concentration and meditation.

Actual therapies are divided into three types: those that involve internal medicine, such as herbs; those that employ external techniques such as massage and manipulation; and surgery (see page 15). The appropriate therapies are selected according not only to the diagnosis, but also to the individual constitution of the patient (including their age, vitality, *agni* and desire to heal), the stage and severity of disease and so on.

LIFESTYLE AND BEHAVIOUR

The ghats *at Varanasi along India's holy River Ganges are frequently visited by pilgrims keen to purify themselves in the waters that symbolize Shiva's power. Varanasi and its river are a* mokshadvara, *or a "door to liberation", where people seek an auspicious rebirth.*

Writing in *Heart of Medicine* in about 600CE, Vagbhata declared, "In all his actions, a wise man has the world as his teacher." In Ayurvedic practice it is recommended that to ensure health and happiness one follows an appropriate daily routine, carries out suitable behaviour and lives according to the seasons.

The most beneficial daily routine (*dinacharya*) involves rising early, bathing and cleaning the body. Medical texts recommend cleaning the teeth and gums, scraping the tongue, cleaning the nails, rinsing the nasal cavities and gargling, putting on clean clothes and adorning the body with garlands, gems and pleasant scents. This can be followed by exercises, the recitation of mantras or prayers and, perhaps, a period of meditation. Beginning the day in this way wakes and strengthens the physical body, sharpens the mind and attunes the self with the divine.

Exercise should be suited to the person's *dosha* type and the season. *Vata* types should undertake gentle exercise, *pitta* types can take on moderate exercise while *kapha* types can exercise the most vigorously. Regular exercise is essential to keep the body supple and the muscles firm, to enable physical labour to be undertaken, as well as to maintain the balance of the *doshas* and the strength of the digestive fire (*agni*). Food (*anna*) is best taken in moderate amounts, chewed well and selected to accord with body type and season (see pages 32–33). Sleep must be sufficient to allow for adequate rest and healing of the tissues. Sleep-needs also vary by season and body type: more is required in the darker, winter months and less in the lighter, summer months; and more sleep is needed by *vata* types, since they are generally active, and less by *kapha* types, because they are more lethargic.

Appropriate behaviour (*sadachara*) involves avoiding detrimental behaviours and cultivating good habits, while not suppressing one's "natural urges". These include defecation, urination, yawning, sneezing, burping, hunger, thirst and sleep. Suppression is believed to trigger particular diseases – medical texts contain long lists of examples. Stifling a sneeze is thought to lead to a stiff neck, headaches and even facial palsy, while ignoring the desire to urinate can cause pain in the urinary organs and urinary infections. In order to cultivate virtue, one should suppress non-virtuous thoughts and deeds such as feelings of anger, greed, fear, envy, pride and attachment or the desire to harm another. Good habits include refraining from over-stimulation of the senses, respecting parents, teachers and gods, showing courage and telling the truth.

Living according to the seasons (*ritucharya*) means adjusting one's daily habits and eating and exercising according to the environmental and climatic demands of the different times of year. Ayurveda divides the year into six seasons: early winter (*hemanta rtu*), running from November to January according to the Western calendar; late winter (*shishira rtu*), from January to March; spring (*vasanta rtu*), from March to May; summer (*grishma rtu*), from May to July); the rainy season (*varsha rtu*), from July to September; and autumn/fall (*sharad rtu*), from September to December. *Dosha* balance is strongly affected by the seasons. *Vata* is strongest in early winter and the rainy season, *pitta* is strongest in summer and *kapha* is strongest in late winter. During the dry seasons (late winter, spring and summer) plenty of fluids should be drunk to hydrate the body, while during the three wetter seasons the body should be oiled and warm foods should be eaten.

Some of the carvings adorning the walls of the temple complex at Khajuraho are erotic and refer to tantric practices.

REJUVENATION

Whole sections of the ancient medical texts are devoted to the subject of rejuvenation (*rasayana*). There are many herbs that are used specifically for rejuvenatory purposes. Some of these are thought to boost the body's natural functions, such as memory or the immune system, while others are believed to delay the aging process and promote longevity. Rejuvenation elixirs are popular over-the-counter remedies, with specific formulas available for boosting mental function and general vitality and for increasing fertility and virility (*vajikarana*) or for use as aphrodisiacs. The principal aim of these fertility formulas was originally to ensure procreation and the continuation of lineages, although sexual pleasure and union are also regarded as an essential aspect of good health.

It is also believed that rejuvenation can be facilitated through wearing gems, and through yoga and good conduct – that is prayer, religious ritual and virtuous action. Rejuvenation therapy reputedly made it possible to live to 100 years of age with the senses intact, the body firm and the intellect sharp.

FOOD AS MEDICINE

Ayurveda has always stressed the vital role of diet and eating habits in determining health. Foods are classified according to six "savours" (or "tastes"), their energetic "potencies" and their post-digestive effects (the long-term effects of different food substances on the body). The six "savours" – said to originate from paired combinations of the five elements (see pages 18–19) – are sweet (earth and water), sour (fire and earth), salty (water and fire), bitter (air and ether), pungent (fire and air) and astringent (air and earth). These refer not only to the taste of the food on the tongue but also to its effects on the tissues of the body.

The two types of energetic "potencies" of foods are warming and cooling. Warming foods are digested more easily. They are beneficial for *vata* and *kapha* types but aggravating for *pitta* types. Cooling foods are slower to digest and will therefore ease *pitta* conditions but are unhelpful for *vata* and *kapha* conditions (see boxes, right). In general, sour, salty and pungent foods and drinks are warming in nature, while sweet, bitter and astringent foods are cooling.

According to this classification the effects of individual foods and beverages on the *doshas* – that is whether they aggravate and increase the *dosha* or pacify and decrease it – can be determined. The most appropriate healing diet for a given individual can then be decided.

Eating habits also exert a strong influence on health. The *Charaka Samhita* (see pages 10–11) advises that food should be eaten in a tranquil and clean environment and that there should be little speech while eating so as not to interfere with digestion. Food should be eaten in moderation and chewed slowly. Local, seasonal produce is considered best and foods should be carefully combined according to their tastes and energetic qualities in order to create the most balanced and healthy diet. Eating should stop before the point of complete satiation is reached.

Food is considered to be a sacred gift and meals are an opportunity to commune with, and expresss gratitude to, the divine.

THE HEALTH BENEFITS OF BASIL

In India the basil (*tulsi*) plant is considered sacred. It is commonly placed at the entrance to the home and is worshipped as an embodiment of Lakshmi, the goddess of prosperity, good luck and longevity.

Basil is believed to have numerous health benefits and is included in many home remedies. Chewing a few leaves of basil every day sweetens the breath. Juiced basil leaves, or basil-leaf infusions, drunk daily, are regarded as a heart and nerve tonic. A hot tea made from basil leaves, a clove and half a teaspoonful of ginger juice eases sore throats and coughs.

VATA FOODS

Vata is aggravated by pungent, bitter and astringent foods and pacified by sweet, sour and salty ones. *Vata* types should eat warming, cooked foods and avoid frozen, raw and fried ones. Most sweet and dried fruits are beneficial. Dairy produce can be consumed in moderation.

Left to right: banana, onion (when cooked and eaten in moderation), asparagus, radishes (cooked), garlic and mango are all considered to be good foods for vata *types.*

PITTA FOODS

Pitta is aggravated by pungent, sour and salty foods and pacified by sweet, bitter and astringent ones. *Pitta* types should eat cooling, uncooked foods and avoid all hot, spicy, fried and sour foods. Sweet fruits, sweet and bitter vegetables and cool dairy or fruit drinks are beneficial.

Left to right: rice (basmati, white or wild types), okra, (top) ghee (clarified butter), (bottom) figs, oats and mint are all good foods for pitta *types.*

KAPHA FOODS

Kapha is aggravated by sweet, sour and salty foods and pacified by pungent, bitter and astringent foods. *Kapha* types should eat light, dry and spicy foods and avoid salt, sugar and dairy produce. Astringent fruits and vegetables, such as cranberries and aubergine (eggplant), can be eaten.

Left to right: couscous, lentils, millet, aduki beans and chickpeas (garbanzos) are grains and legumes suitable for kapha *types.*

MASSAGE AND EXTERNAL THERAPIES

The external therapies (*bahir pari-marjana*) of Ayurveda include various types of general and specialized massage, physiotherapeutic stretches and manipulations, and miscellaneous techniques such as herbal gargles for throat problems. Massage is particularly widely used both as a therapy in its own right and in conjunction with internal, herbal medicine (see pages 36–37); it is also an important preparatory technique used before the deep-cleansing *panchakarma* purification therapies (see pages 38–39).

Ayurvedic massage always uses oils – most of which are of plant origin, although *ghee* (clarified butter), milk and bone marrow are sometimes used. The massage is performed directly on the skin, rather than through clothing as with some other forms of Eastern massage, such as *shiatsu* (see pages 146–147). It is generally performed with the hands (although sometimes with the feet, see below) and utilizes a range of techniques including kneading, squeezing, rubbing and tapping. Hand-held wooden rollers are sometimes used. Massage may be given to the whole body (*abhyanga*) or to particular parts of the body such as the hands, neck and shoulders or the head. Indian head massage (see page 39) has become increasingly popular in the West in recent years and is now offered as a therapy on its own. It is used to relieve stress, promote relaxation and to treat anxiety, insomnia, headaches and migraines.

The primary use of massage is medical, although it provides the secondary benefits of relaxation and a sense of well-being. It promotes circulation, increases flexibility, relieves pain and stiffness, aids the elimination of waste

Therapeutic hand massage is a popular and widely practised element of Ayurvedic medicine.

products and can be used to treat specific ailments. The massage may be given by one or more people, and in one specialized form, known as *chavutti pizhichil*, the masseur(s) are held by ropes attached to the ceiling in order to "walk" over the patient's body, massaging with the feet, while assistants pour oil over the skin to keep it lubricated. This method allows for careful control of the amount of pressure given to different parts of the body.

In another form of massage (*navarakizhi*), several people vigorously rub the patient's skin with linen bags containing a special type of cooked rice soaked in warmed cow's milk. This is said to be especially effective in relieving muscular stiffness and pain.

The oils used for massage are selected according to the diagnosis of the person's *dosha*. *Vata* types are given "calming oils", such as almond, olive, castor and wheatgerm. *Pitta* types are given "cooling oils", such as coconut, pumpkin and sandalwood. *Kapha* types are given "warming oils", such as sesame and mustard. The oils can be used singly or combined and aromatic or therapeutic herbs may sometimes be added.

During specialized massage treatments the patient often lies on a special type of wooden board, a *droni*. The wood is smooth and comfortable and has rimmed edges to prevent any surplus oil or milk from spilling onto the floor. The oil is heated to a comfortable temperature and then trickled onto the body in a steady stream from a metal or wooden container that has a small hole at the base out of which the flow of oil may be controlled by a wick.

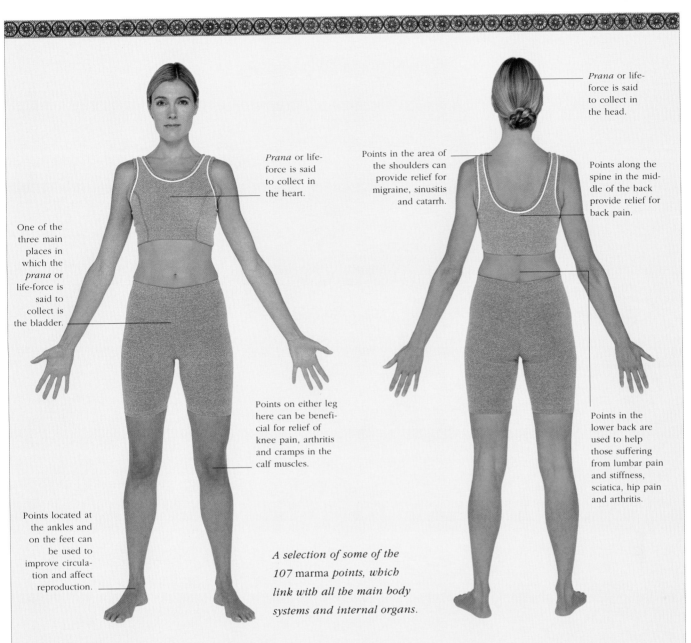

Prana or life-force is said to collect in the heart.

One of the three main places in which the *prana* or life-force is said to collect is the bladder.

Points on either leg here can be beneficial for relief of knee pain, arthritis and cramps in the calf muscles.

Points located at the ankles and on the feet can be used to improve circulation and affect reproduction.

Prana or life-force is said to collect in the head.

Points in the area of the shoulders can provide relief for migraine, sinusitis and catarrh.

Points along the spine in the middle of the back provide relief for back pain.

Points in the lower back are used to help those suffering from lumbar pain and stiffness, sciatica, hip pain and arthritis.

A selection of some of the 107 marma *points, which link with all the main body systems and internal organs.*

THE ENERGIZING MARMA POINTS

Marma therapy is a late twentieth-century development inspired by classical Ayurveda, although it was not originally part of it. *Marma* are energetic points located all over the body. As with the acupoints and massage points of other Eastern cultures, these are thought to connect with both the physiological systems, such as the nerves, blood vessels and endocrine glands, and the subtle energy system of the body.

Just as acupoints are connected by the meridian pathways, the *marma* points are thought to be linked together by the *nadi* system and to connect directly to the vital energy centres, the *chakras* (see box, page 21). *Prana*, or life-force, is said to flow through the *marma* points and to collect in the head, the heart and the bladder.

The use of massage techniques on the points can adjust the flow of *prana* and regulate the balance of the *doshas*. *Marma* therapy provides pain relief and eases fatigue and digestive disturbances; it is highly potent and should only be undertaken with an experienced practitioner.

AYURVEDIC MEDICINES

Sarngadhara wrote in his compendium on Ayurvedic medicine, dating to around 1300CE, "All the different heavenly herbs are like glittering deities. Knowing this, the wise man leaves doubt behind and cultivates an understanding of their different powers." According to Indian mythology, it was great sages living in the Himalayas in ancient times who first identified medicinal herbs. These men are said to have roamed the mountains treating each plant with great reverence, examining and naming them and identifying their properties and healing powers.

Two women preparing Ayurvedic medicine prescriptions in Poona, India, from behind a counter screen.

Many of the ancient Vedic texts mention the therapeutic properties of plants and the compendiums by Charaka and Sushruta list them extensively. The various materia medica that exist classify plants, and other substances, according to their tastes, potencies and "ripening" effects (*vipaka*). This means their sweet, sour, salt, bitter, pungent and astringent qualities; their warming and cooling properties; and their post-digestive effects (see pages 32–33). In addition to these, medicinal plants have been classified according to their unique "potential" (*prabhava*), that is, their specific healing effect on the body, based on observation over centuries of their actions on each of the *doshas* and on different types of body tissues and their digestibility, or effect on the *agni*.

Although Ayurvedic medicines are made principally from plant ingredients, such as the leaves, flowers and fruits of plants, trees and creepers, they may also contain minerals, gems and animal products. Spices, such as cardamom, cinnamon, nutmeg, cloves, ginger, turmeric, cumin and fenugreek are often included, while typical mineral or gem ingredients are iron, calcium, copper, silver and gold. Commonly used animal products are dairy ingredients, such as milk and *ghee*, wax, animal fats and honey. Animal urine, especially from cows and elephants, is also highly prized and used in many compound medicines. If some people find the presence of urine shocking, it is worth noting that many Western beauty products and certain medicines, such as some forms of hormone replacement therapy, also contain or are derived from animal urine. It is used because it is high in nutrients and may contain significant levels of certain hormones. In addition, there is a long tradition of urine therapy in India, where one's own urine is valued for its cleansing and medicinal properties rather than being viewed as merely a distasteful waste product of the body (a notable proponent of urine therapy was Mahatma Gandhi).

Both fresh and dried ingredients are used in Ayurvedic medicines and medical texts contain detailed descriptions of the correct methods and timing for harvesting herbs. It is thought that the attitude and the qualities of the person harvesting the plants can affect the quality, and thereby the healing potential, of the herbs being collected – Sarngadhara instructed that, "Herbs should be gathered on a good day by someone in a good state of mind who is clean, facing the sun, silent, and who has paid homage in his heart to the god, Shiva." Emetic and purgative herbs are

AYURVEDIC REMEDIES

A wide variety of spices feature in Ayurvedic home remedies. A teaspoon of turmeric powder in a cup of warm milk three times daily is an effective treatment for colds and flu. A small glass of ginger juice (0.2fl oz/5ml) taken daily relieves diarrhea, headaches and colds, while a slice of ginger root with a pinch of salt chewed minutes before a meal prevents indigestion. Ginger paste applied to joints can help relieve strains. Clove oil is used to relieve toothache and cardamom powder is used in remedies against colds, flu and vomiting. Cinnamon is used in cold remedies, to improve circulation and in antidote remedies for treating poisoning.

Clockwise, from top left: cinnamon twigs (tvac)*, cloves (*lavanga)*, ginger (*mahaushadha)*, turmeric powder (known variously as* gauri, haridra *or* rajani) *and cardamom pods (*ela *or* sukshmaila)*.

harvested in the late spring, while others are picked in the autumn/fall when they are full of sap and considered to be at their most potent.

Ayurvedic medicines are based on either single ingredients or compounds of up to several dozen different components, selected to work synergistically. A compound medicine is named after the first medical ingredient in it. The fact that naming systems may differ depending on the text, and the substitution of one plant for another for practical or geographical reasons, has meant that there has been some confusion about the exact composition of certain formulas. The historical use of more than one system of measurement has added to the confusion. However, with the standardization of modern Ayurvedic medical training in India and the establishment of huge databases, compounds have become more uniform.

Medicines come in the form of pills (*gutika*), powders (*churna*), pastes (*kalka*), juices (*svarasa*), decoctions (*kvatha*) and medicated oils (*tailas*). Medicinal teas, liquors and elixirs (see box, page 31) are also used. They are made by various methods, including grinding, juicing, diluting, soaking, boiling, fermenting and heating the different herbs. Patients may be prescribed a combination of internal and external remedies: pills may be taken in conjunction with the massage of an oil into the skin. There is now a thriving industry in over-the-counter Ayurvedic remedies from skin creams to medicinal pills for specific remedies.

Certain plants have a uniquely prominent position in Ayurveda – one of these is garlic. Legend has it that the sage Sushruta discovered garlic and declared it to be a universal remedy with the power to subdue all diseases. It is often taken in the form of juice or made into a paste. Western medicine now also widely acknowledges garlic's therapeutic potential in, for example, the prevention of heart disease. Other particularly Indian herbs such as *neem*, derived from the leaves of the neem tree and used in many dental and beauty products, have now become well known and widely used in the West.

PANCHAKARMA PURIFICATION

The five *panchakarma* are purification techniques used in Ayurveda for cleansing and detoxifying the body and for rectifying imbalances of the *doshas* (see pages 18–19). The five consist of therapeutic vomiting, using emetics (*vamana*); purgatives (*virechana*); enemas (*vasti*); nasal cleaning (*nasya*); and blood purification (*raktamokshana*). The five *panchakarma* are used in both the treatment and the prevention of disease.

Before undergoing any of these purification techniques it is essential to ensure that the body is ready. This is done by means of two preparatory techniques (known as *purva karma*): oil therapy (*snehana*) and sweating therapy (*svedana*). These serve to soften and cleanse the skin, beginning the process of releasing the impurities from within.

Oil therapy uses vegetable oils or *ghee*, either singly, together, or in combination with herbal remedies. The oils may be taken orally with food, poured slowly onto or massaged into the body, or introduced in enemas. Ideally this procedure is repeated over several days. The aim is to lubricate the digestive system and soften the stools, allowing old waste matter to pass out of the intestines and detoxification to commence.

Next, sweating therapy is carried out. This can be done in two ways. The first method uses external heat and can be applied by encasing the whole body, except the head, in a specially designed "sauna" box, or by the application of

During oil therapy the oil most appropriate to the person's dosha *type is used. For example, "calming" oils, such as almond or wheatgerm, are used for* vata *types.*

steaming hot packs or herbal poultices onto the body. In the second method the heat is generated within the body by external means, such as vigorous physical exercise or wrapping the body in extra clothes and blankets. The more the person sweats, the more impurities pass out of the body.

Once the preparation has been carried out, the main treatment, which is known as the *pradhana karma*, can begin. The treatment is tailored individually, selected according to the practitioner's diagnosis of the individual patient's *dosha* imbalance (see pages 26–27) and his or her existing symptoms.

To induce therapeutic vomiting (*vamana*), rock-salt, honey and certain emetic herbs are ingested. This technique is good for *kapha* conditions (see pages 22–23) and helps to relieve nasal congestion, mucus and other problems of stagnation in the upper body. It is often used to treat rhinitis, bronchitis, throat problems, and chest and heart problems.

Purgative treatment (*virechana*) involves drinking combinations of herbal laxatives or, depending on the condition, mild or strong purgative herbs. It is often used to treat *pitta* conditions (see pages 22–23), but it can also be used for other types of *dosha* imbalance. It is recommended for conditions such as piles, intestinal worms, fevers and skin diseases, but is not considered suitable for the very young, the very old or the chronically sick. Purgatives can be used on their own or given after emetic therapy.

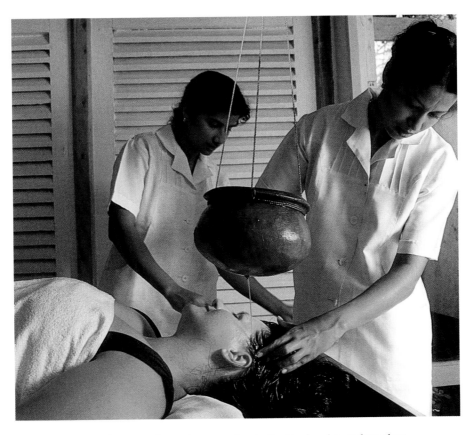

A steady stream of warm oil may be poured onto the forehead to induce deep relaxation. The oil is stroked into the hair and massaged into the scalp.

Enemas (*vasti*) are best for *vata* conditions (see pages 22–23) and help to relieve toxins accumulated in the large intestine. Oily enemas (*anuvasana vasti*) relieve skin dryness and digestive imbalance, but are inadvisable for people who are obese or have skin diseases. Decoction enemas (*asthapana vasti*) use herbs to treat nervous problems and fatigue; they are not suitable for people with respiratory problems or pregnant women. Vaginal douches are also sometimes used for female genito-urinary disorders.

Nasal cleaning (*nasya*) is used for problems such as sinusitis, headache and nasal congestion. Medicinal oils or powders are inhaled into the nose, causing irritants or blockages to be discharged. The nose may be massaged with oil before the drops or paste is put into each nostril, or the medicine can be inhaled with steam at regular intervals over several days. This therapy is not suitable for the very young, the elderly or those suffering from fevers.

Blood-letting (*raktamokshana*) is carried out using surgical instruments or leeches and is used for blood (*rakta*) disorders and *pitta* diseases such as skin problems, boils and abscesses. Pastes made from herbs, such as turmeric and mustard, are sometimes smeared on the skin first to cleanse it and to bring the blood to the surface. It is not used for pregnant women or those with anemia or edema.

Once the main *panchakarma* treatment has been completed, it is followed by a period of careful monitoring and after-care (*paschatah karma*), which involves rest, rehabilitation and special attention to diet.

These purification techniques may sound unattractive to Westerners, but most patients who undergo them are amazed at the beneficial effects. However, these treatments must be administered correctly under the close supervision of a qualified practitioner. In India they are usually carried out in a hospital or clinic.

YOGA

Yoga has been practised for thousands of years in India and constitutes a complete health system in its own right. The Sanskrit word *yoga* means "union" and the practice of yoga is designed to balance physical and mental aspects of the self and pave the way for spiritual development. Indian sages and ascetics were probably yoga's first practitioners. Carvings from 2500BCE show figures in yogic postures and yoga is mentioned in the sacred texts, the Vedas, parts of which are thought to date from 1200BCE or earlier. Yoga also forms part of the advice given by the gods to the warrior Arjuna in his epic battle against the forces of evil described in the *Bhagavad Gita* (c.200BCE–200CE).

It was scholars of Vedic texts who introduced yoga to the West in the nineteenth century. Later, Westerners studied with leading Indian yoga practitioners and different forms of yoga training became established and gained steadily in popularity.

In the fourth century CE, the great sage Patanjali laid down in the *Yoga Sutras* the eight-part framework for yoga practice: *yamas* (moral codes), *niyamas* (daily observances), *asanas* (exercise postures), *pranayama* (breathing exercises), *pratyahara* (withdrawal of the senses), *dharana*

*The lotus pose (*padmasana*) is the classic, stable position for meditation and* pranayama *breathing exercises. The spine is straight and the legs are bent with the feet placed on each thigh. The index fingers and thumbs are joined.*

(concentration), *dhyana* (meditation) and *samadhi* (superconsciousness and spiritual union).

The five *yamas* are non-violence, truth (of word, thought and deed), moderation, non-stealing and non-possessiveness. The practice of these is aimed at overcoming the lower aspects of human nature and desires. In their place the five, positive *niyamas* are encouraged. They are the fostering of purity, contentment and austerity, daily study of sacred texts and constant awareness of the divine in all things.

Hatha yoga consists of the *kriya* cleansing techniques, the *asanas* and the *pranayama* breathing exercises. The *asanas*, or physical poses, are designed to gently stretch the spine, improve flexibility, suppleness and muscle tone, stimulate the nerves and enhance the function of the internal organs. The *pranayama* techniques are designed to improve oxygen flow to the body and to enable the individual to gain control of *prana*, the vital energy or life-force in the body. This facilitates mental control and is a preparatory step for the later stage of meditation. The five *kriyas* are methods for purifying and detoxifying the body, also as a preparation for higher spiritual practices.

Pratyahara (withdrawal of the senses) and *dharana* (concentration) practices help to calm and focus the mind so that *dhyana* (meditation) can be practised. The ultimate goal is to reach the bliss of *samadhi* (superconsciousness and spiritual union with the divine).

There are four main paths of yoga: *karma yoga*, the yoga of action; *bhakti yoga*, the yoga of devotion; *jnana yoga*, the yoga of knowledge and wisdom; and *raja yoga*, the yoga of physical and mental control. All the paths have the same goal of *samadhi*, but they differ in nature and should be selected according to the individual. *Karma yoga* suits people with an active nature who find it hard to sit in meditation. This path teaches the importance of selfless service and the dedication of all actions to the divine without attachment to results or expectations of reward. *Bhakti yoga* suits people with a spiritual nature; it involves the expression of devotion to a chosen form of the divine – chanting, singing and writing the divine name, together with ritual devotions and invocational prayer, are used to generate feelings of unconditional love as an expression of divine love. *Jnana yoga* suits people with a philosophical and intellectual nature: mental power and the study of sacred texts produce insight and self-realization. This path is said to be the hardest, requiring tremendous will and self-discipline, as well as some mastery of the two previous paths, in order to go beyond the ego. *Raja yoga* incorporates the *asanas* and the *pranayama* of *hatha*

ALTERNATE NOSTRIL BREATHING (ANULOMA VILOMA)

This exercise balances prana *in the body. Using your right hand, place the thumb by your right nostril and the ring finger by your left. Close the right nostril with your thumb and inhale through the left one to the count of eight. Next close the left nostril with your ring finger, release the thumb and exhale through the right for eight. Then inhale from the right to the count of eight, close it and exhale on the left. Continue this for several minutes. Once you are used to the technique you can use the proper ratio of 2:8:4 – that is, inhale to the count of two; close both nostrils and hold for eight; exhale for four and then repeat on the other side.*

yoga and emphasizes learning control over body and mind in order to attain spiritual awareness. Sometimes called "the royal path", it is comprehensive in nature, containing physical, mental and spiritual practices, and is suitable for anyone. The five important principles for the practice of *raja yoga* are: relaxation of body and mind; regular practice of yoga *asanas*; correct breathing learnt through *pranayama* exercises; proper diet (see pages 32–33); and meditation.

Yoga *asanas* should be practised slowly and with awareness. There are many different *asanas* and most are named after the animal or shape they represent, such as the cobra pose (see below) in which the body is raised like a king cobra with its great hood. It is important to learn the correct procedure for adopting the pose in order to prevent strain or injury and to obtain the appropriate health benefits from it. Each pose has specific as well as general benefits that relate to the part of the body or the energetic pathways (*nadis*) being stimulated. The *nadis* are thought to be nerve channels that course through the body and connect with the energetic centres, the *chakras* (see box, page 21). Research in the latter part of the twentieth century by Dr Hiroshi Motoyama in Japan has suggested that there is a strong correspondence between the Indian *nadi* system and the Chinese acupuncture meridian system (see pages 98–99).

THE COBRA POSE (BHUJANGASANA)

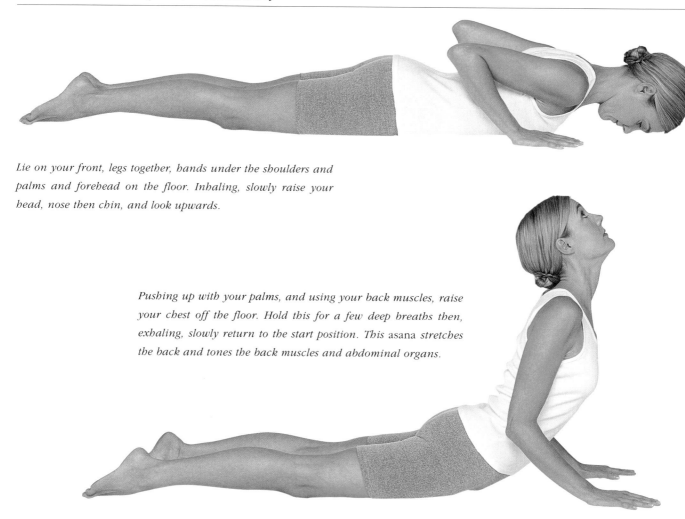

Lie on your front, legs together, hands under the shoulders and palms and forehead on the floor. Inhaling, slowly raise your head, nose then chin, and look upwards.

Pushing up with your palms, and using your back muscles, raise your chest off the floor. Hold this for a few deep breaths then, exhaling, slowly return to the start position. This asana *stretches the back and tones the back muscles and abdominal organs.*

Asana practice coordinates with breathing. In general, inhalation takes place as the body is stretched and exhalation when it is contracted. If the final position is held in a relaxed way, while breathing deeply, it is usually possible to extend the stretch with each deep breath.

Yoga is constantly evolving into different approaches with particular emphases. *Kundalini* yoga, for example, contains exercises designed to raise the dormant *kundalini* (spiritual energy or power, said to reside at the base of the spine like a coiled serpent) up through the spine. This is said to activate, and eventually awaken, the *chakras* and lead to superconsciousness. *Tantra* yoga also works with the *chakras* and uses sexual union, real or visualized, as a means of stimulating the *kundalini*. Modern *ashtanga* yoga has linked various *asanas* together as a dynamic and vigorous form of exercise. Finally, biomedical yoga emphasizes the medical benefits of different poses for common ailments, such as backache and respiratory and digestive problems.

Yoga can benefit and be performed by anyone, regardless of age or physical condition. Most of the postures have simple forms to suit the inexperienced, the weak, the elderly, the young or pregnant women, as well as more advanced forms. There are no special requirements although loose clothing and a clean, calm, warm and comfortable environment are best.

FORWARD BEND POSE (PASCHIMOTHANASANA)

This asana *benefits the spine, tones the internal organs, especially the urinary system, and regulates the nervous system. Sit with your legs together and stretched out in front with the toes pointing to the ceiling. While inhaling, raise your arms upwards and stretch your back.*

Exhaling, slowly bend forwards keeping the back as straight as possible. Relax. Do not force or bounce. Hold on to the feet or ankles for a few deep breaths then, inhaling, slowly sit up.

PRAYER AND WORSHIP

*The sacred bull Nandi guards the Shiva shrine at Pattadakal Temple, Karnataka.
Nandi symbolizes strength and sexual potency and represents triumph over
uncontrolled aggression and lust. The floral garlands serve as a mark of respect,
for Nandi is worshipped as Shiva's great battle mount.*

Prayer and worship play an important part in effecting cures in Ayurvedic medicine. Given that disease is viewed in Ayurveda as a product of individual karma (see pages 22–23), it is considered essential to try to purify and transcend negative karma by means of regular prayer, good deeds and ritual observances and by invoking help from deities. The performance of *puja* – prayer and worship rituals – takes place at home, in temples and in the form of elaborate ceremonies held on religious festival days throughout India.

Various deities from the Hindu pantheon are worshipped for the healing powers they possess. Vishnu, the preserver, is often worshipped in the *avatar* form of Dhanvantari (see page 13), also known as the god of Ayurveda, or as Krishna, with his consort Radha. Shiva, the

god of creation and destruction, is worshipped together with his powerful consort, the goddess Durga, and their sons, Kartikeya and Ganesha. The lord Ganesha, who has a human body with an elephant's head, is believed to be able to remove obstacles, including disease.

At home, most families maintain an altar dedicated to their favourite deity or deities. The altar houses an image, or images, "dressed" in ornate clothes and jewels and given offerings of food, water, scented flowers and so on. The shrine may also have a *linga* to represent the deity Shiva. *Lingas* are smooth, phallic or egg-shaped stones, either naturally occurring or carved, which are often set in a rounded *yoni* to represent the vulva and female energy. Together these two symbols represent the joining of male and female energies, the union of heaven and earth and the power of creation. A *linga* is washed daily in water and then "anointed" with milk or *ghee* while mantras are recited (see box, right).

Each deity has special mantras that are used to invoke his or her divine power. The recitation of mantras, known as *japa*, is normally carried out at dawn and dusk every day, or when the person rises and goes to bed. In certain devout homes and in temples, *japa* might also occur at noon and midnight. Certain numbers of repetitions, such as three, seven or 108, are held to be particularly auspicious; to help with accurate counting either the fingers or prayer beads, known as *mala*, may be used.

Finger-counting is done on the right hand by touching the thumb to the top crease of the little finger, then the middle crease and then the lower crease and repeating this for each finger in turn (twelve counts) and then nine times over to make a count of 108. Counting with a *mala* is done by holding the string of beads, or seeds, in the right hand and rolling one between the thumb and middle finger for each recitation. The *mala* has 108 beads and one larger one, the *meru* bead, that symbolizes Mount Meru, the sacred, mythical mountain believed to be at the centre of the universe. When performing *japa mala*, the *meru* bead is the starting point from which the mantra is counted. When the 108 recitations are completed and the *meru* bead is felt again, one can stop or begin again in the opposite direction.

Mantras can also be written down on paper – a practice called *likhita japa*. This involves concentrating with full awareness on the mantra each time it is written and focusing both one's thought and physical activity (the actual writing) on the deity. Often the writing is arranged in beautiful patterns. Another way of praying is by concentrating on *yantra* – symbolic diagrams. By studying and meditating on these diagrams, the energies of the deities they represent can be drawn into the body.

Many people also go on pilgrimages to sacred sites associated with particular deities in order to absorb their invigorating and healing divine power, known as *shakti*.

The sacred syllable Om *has three phonetic elements (*a-u-m*) and a soundless fourth. It is the most well known mantra and is said to be the primordial sound of the universe.*

THE HOLY SOUND OF THE MANTRA

Mantras are syllables, words or sentences in Sanskrit that have a particular sound vibration conducive to meditation and spiritual development. There are three main types: *saguna* mantras, which invoke particular Hindu deities such as Shiva, Krishna or Rama; *nirguna* mantras, which are abstract and identify with absolute consciousness, such as *Om* or *So-ham* (meaning "I am that"); and *bija* mantras (or "seed mantras"), which are derived from the fifty fundamental sounds of Sanskrit. Mantras are either given by a *guru* to a disciple as part of an initiation during spiritual training or are chosen by the individual according to their preference. For example, a person who feels particularly devoted to Shiva might choose to recite *Hare om nama shivaya*. Mantras can be recited silently or vocalized, and it is said that their repetition fills the body and mind with spiritual vibrations and elevates consciousness. Certain mantras are also believed to facilitate healing. To have the best effects the mantra must be pronounced correctly so that its power, or *shakti*, can be released. Mantras are said to have been handed down from ancient sages and to contain divine energy.

TIBET

HEALING THE BODY TO LIBERATE THE SPIRIT

The Tibetan medical system is exacting and comprehensive. It has developed over more than 2,000 years,
absorbing influences from Greece, India, Persia and
China as well as from Tibetan Buddhism and the Bon
religion. Tibetan medicine is now taught and practised
in several countries and interest in its holistic approach
is growing.

Based on the Buddhist concept that all human life
involves suffering and that this can only be trans-
cended as one develops true understanding, wisdom
and compassion, the aim of Tibetan medicine is to
liberate the individual not only from physical disease
but also from mental ignorance. Disease is viewed as a
process of imbalance brought about by negative
thoughts, harmful actions, improper behaviour, inappropriate diet and sometimes the influence of malevolent spirits. These factors disturb the delicate equilibrium of humours and elements in the body (see pages
57–59), disrupting its normal processes and eventually
resulting in sickness.

*Medical charts adorn the library at the school of medicine in Lhasa's
Mentsekhang Hospital. Tibet's medical literature is one of the greatest
legacies of its civilization, and some works date from the seventh century
CE. The* Four Great Medical Tantras *remain the basis of medical practice.*

CHAPTER 5

AN UNBROKEN HERITAGE

The history of Tibetan medicine is rich in accounts of legendary figures, but many real-life developments can also be traced through written records about known historical people. It is thought that the ideas of the country's earliest inhabitants concerning religion and health were based on nature – no doubt influenced by the powerful beauty of the mountain environment and its dramatic climate. Early Tibetan religion incorporated a myriad of good and evil spirits linked to the forces of nature and a wealth of rituals intended to honour and appease them. These rites formed the basis of pre-Buddhist cults, which were later formalized as the Bon tradition. Early medical practices are thought to have been based on simple herbal remedies and religious incantations.

Later developments can be credited to several great kings, such as Songtsen Gampo, who devoted themselves to developing Tibetan culture. A script was created and translations of India's Sanskrit medical *tantra*s were made in the seventh century CE, when Buddhism was introduced to Tibet. The medical teachings of these *tantra*s date back to the time of the Shakyamuni Buddha (sixth to fifth centuries BCE). Through contact with physicians from India, China and further afield, new ideas were added to these teachings and to the extant oral traditions and the distinct system known today began to evolve, with the first formal Tibetan medical texts, the *rGyud-bzhi* (pronounced "gyu-zhi") or *Four Medical Tantras*, emerging in definitive form in the twelfth century CE.

BUDDHISM AND BON

According to legend, Tibet's first king, Nyatri Tsenpo, descended from the heavens by means of a spirit ladder which he would ascend once his earthly tasks were completed. Six successors came to Earth in the same way, but black magic was cast upon the eighth king and he was bound to Earth, his ladder broken. Unable to return to the heavens, he died and left his body behind. The death rites that characterized the Bon tradition of Tibet were developed from this legend.

Bon is thought to be the Tibetan form of the shamanism and animism that existed in northern and Central Asia in the pre-Buddhist era. It incorporates a rich pantheon of gods and involves elaborate recitations and trance states, as well as divination and rudimentary astrology. After the introduction of Buddhism to Tibet, Bon practices became formalized by noble families in an attempt to undermine the power of the royal house which favoured Buddhism. Aspects of Bon were later incorporated into Tibetan Buddhism. Bon is still practised in Tibet today and is also taught abroad.

Tibetan medicine is believed to originate from the Shakyamuni (or Gautama) Buddha. Formerly an Indian prince named Siddhartha (563–483BCE), the Shakyamuni Buddha attained enlightenment after many years of

A thangka or cloth icon image of the Medicine Buddha, Bhaishajyaguru, in his celestial realm. He holds a bowl of life-giving nectar and a myrobalan fruit, said to cure all diseases.

spiritual practice and began to teach humanity the path to liberation. At the core of his teachings are the twin doctrines of the Four Noble Truths and the Eightfold Path. The Four Noble Truths recognize that human life involves suffering but that there are identifiable causes and that suffering can be ended if one can live according to the principles of the Eightfold Path: that is, by right views, right intention, right speech, right action, right livelihood, right effort, right mindfulness and right concentration. Adherence to these principles will lead to the attainment of a pure state of enlightened consciousness and bliss (*nirvana*).

The Buddha sought to provide a practical method for seeking salvation rather than focusing on rituals or metaphysical speculation. To transmit specific teachings, he is said to have taken on different manifestations – one such was the Medicine Buddha, also known as Sangye Menla or Bhaishajyaguru.

Buddhism was introduced into Tibet from India some 1,000 years after the Buddha's death, during the reign of Songtsen Gampo (*c.*627–649). It quickly became the dominant religion, influencing every aspect of life, including medicine. Under Songtsen a written Tibetan language was developed, texts from India and China began to be translated and Tibet's first medical texts were written.

THE TRANSMISSION OF KNOWLEDGE

Because of Tibet's relative isolation from much of the world, its indigenous medical tradition has enjoyed an unbroken lineage over the centuries. The lack of formal and written teachings during the very early period meant that practical knowledge was passed on orally within families from father to son and great medical dynasties were created in the process, some of which still exist today. Even after the introduction of Tibetan script, the oral tradition remained widespread among practitioners because texts were utilized largely by scholars only.

Although the origins of the medical system can be traced back to the teachings of the Buddha himself, the lineage of Tibetan physicians dates back to the fifth century CE when King Nyatri Tsenpo invited two great Indian physicians, Vijay and Gajay, to Tibet. Their healing was so successful that they stayed for ten years, and in recognition of his services Gajay was given a Tibetan princess as a wife. Their son, Dungi Thorchog, later became a renowned physician in his own right and it is to him that Tibetan doctors are said to trace back their roots.

The same lineage was shared by Yuthok Yonten Gonpo the Elder, a famous and accomplished physician who lived during the eighth century CE. Yuthok visited India several times to study the country's medical traditions and is said to have lived to be 125 years old. He authored several medical works, including one on surgery, and oversaw many important translations. Yuthok is known as "the father of Tibetan

The fourteenth Dalai Lama, Tenzin Gyatso, both spiritual and secular head of his people, has encouraged international research into Tibetan medicine and promotes its study and practice worldwide.

medicine" because of his important work in consolidating Tibetan medical practices as a viable system.

Yuthok Yonten Gonpo was among the participants at a great medical conference held in 794CE that was attended by representatives from India, China, Persia, Nepal, Sinkiang, Kashmir and Afghanistan. It was so successful that another was staged soon after. Held during the reign of Trisong Detsen (755–797CE), both these conferences led to a cross-fertilization of ideas and resulted in a number of lengthy visits to Tibet by foreign physicians and by Tibetan doctors to neighbouring countries. This led ultimately to the development of Tibet's own unique system of medicine, based on a synthesis of specifically Tibetan elements, the traditions from surrounding countries and cultures, and the influence of Buddhism.

From the ninth century onwards Tibet entered a period of anarchy with the collapse of the Tibetan dynasty and feudal infighting. It was not until the seventeenth century that the country was reunited and a golden period commenced under the rule of Ngawang Losang Gyatso, the fifth Dalai Lama (1617–1682), the spiritual leader and head of state. He had a great interest in medicine and became an ardent scholar of medical texts and had many translated and rewritten. His work was continued by his spiritual son, usually called his regent, Sangye Gyatso (1653–1705). In 1696 the first great medical college, Chakpori, was established in

Lhasa, the capital of Tibet, close to the Dalai Lama's principal residence, the Potala Palace.

Later, a college of medicine and astrology was established at Mentsekhang and other teaching institutes were set up elsewhere in Tibet. Medical education was arduous – it involved seven years of study, which included the memorization and recitation of large sections of medical texts, and several years of practical training. Traditionally, each monastery and village chose a suitable candidate to study at one of the great colleges. This ensured that medical care was provided in all the monastic and secular communities and it also encouraged local study of both medicine and astrology. Tibetan medicine flourished and spread to neighbouring Mongolia, where it was formally adopted.

Forming the basic cornerstone of Tibetan medical teaching, both then and now, are the works known as the *Four Tantras* or *Four Medical Tantras* (see box, right). Of these, the *First*, or *Root*, *Tantra* provides an introductory outline to the medical system and types of disease. The *Second*, or *Explanatory*, *Tantra* outlines underlying concepts and the Tibetan medical view of physiology and pathology. The *Third*, or *Instructional*, *Tantra* describes each type of disorder in detail and the *Final*, or *Last*, *Tantra* outlines methods of diagnosis and therapy.

With the invasion of Tibet in 1959 by the Communist Chinese, the traditional Tibetan way of life was severely disrupted. Many monasteries and colleges were damaged or destroyed and a large number of physicians fled to India. Although this period began a decline in Tibetan medicine within Tibet itself, it has been re-established abroad. In 1961 the fourteenth Dalai Lama set up a new school of medicine – the Tibetan Medical and Astrological Institute – in Dharamsala in northern India, the seat of Tibet's government-in-exile. The institute trains new Tibetan doctors and has clinics in various parts of India, providing a vital medical service to both Tibetan and Indian people. Renowned Tibetan physicians also travel abroad to practise, teach and engage in research.

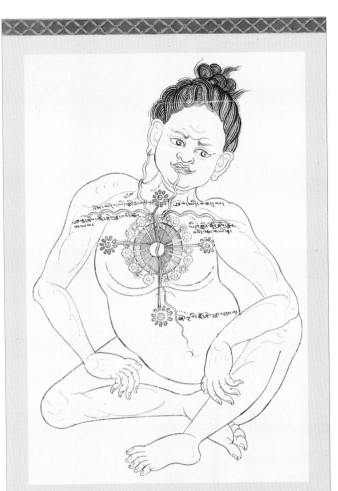

A medical thangka *from a commentary on the ancient* Four Tantras, *prepared by Sangye Gyatso to codify Tibetan medical science. The consciousness of the five senses is shown moving through the heart centre.*

THE FOUR GREAT MEDICAL TANTRAS

The most important text in Tibetan medicine is the *Four Tantras* (*rGyud-bzhi*). The exact origin and history of this four-part treatise is unknown. Some passages show similarities to certain Sanskrit medical texts, notably Vagbhata's *Ashtangahrdaya* (see page 12) but others suggest original Tibetan authorship. Yuthok Yonten Gonpo the Younger made a comprehensive compilation of this work in the twelfth century.

The *Four Tantras* comprise 156 chapters and 5,900 verses. These four volumes are still studied in detail by medical students today, with large portions of the text having to be memorized.

QUALITIES OF THE PRACTITIONER

Following Tibet's first great medical conference (see page 50), King Trisong Detsen decreed that all physicians should adhere to a code of behaviour encapsulated in four vows. Like Western medicine's Hippocratic Oath, these vows are still made by graduating physicians today and they encapsulate the essence of the Tibetan medical approach.

According to the Four Vows, the doctor should have an attitude of selflessness and altruism, should be diligent and avoid procrastination and should be of good character and abstain from alcohol. He or she should also put the patient at ease and embody compassion and love. Essentially, the physician is expected to behave in an exemplary way at all times.

As well as the Four Vows, King Trisong Detsen passed the Thirteen Laws, whereby patients should, in return, demonstrate their respect for their physician. These laws include stipulations that the doctor should be transported by horse (even if the patient is only next door) and that he or she should always be given the best seat.

The training doctors undergo and the vows that they are required to take demonstrate the strong link in Tibet between Buddhism and medicine. The profession of medicine is considered to be altruistic work that can generate merit for the benefit of all sentient beings. Although monk-physicians are now rarer, the physician will normally be a practising Buddhist and is reminded to rely on the Three Jewels, which are the Buddha, the Dharma (the Buddha's teachings) and the Sangha (the Buddhist community).

A Tibetan doctor examining a child's ear as part of an initial diagnosis. One of the vows the physician makes concerns the need to put the patient at ease – and with younger patients this is, of course, particularly important.

In addition to these instructions, doctors are expected to see the Buddha's form in all patients and to invoke it during treatment. Buddhist prayers are recited during both the collection of herbs and the preparation of medicines, and the patient is asked to do the same when taking the medicines that have been prescribed.

In the seventh month of every Tibetan year medical students traditionally set out on a two- or three-week trip to the mountains to harvest medicinal herbs. Physicians have to be able to identify and correctly name numerous types of herbs, know their therapeutic qualities, and be able to prepare them by combining them appropriately into different forms of remedies.

In the words of the famous female Tibetan doctor Lobsang Dolma Khangkar, a student entering a Tibetan medical school "must have perseverence for the task ahead. He should not tire easily from chores like going up the mountains to choose and collect medicinal herbs. The student must be energetic and think of facing any hardship, in connection with medical training, with enthusiasm."

Although today it is predominantly Buddhist thought and doctrine that informs and allegedly empowers Tibetan medicine, it is important to note the opinion of His Holiness the fourteenth Dalai Lama, who claims that faith is not necessary for Tibetan medicine to be efficacious. He argues that research has demonstrated that Tibetan medicines and treatments can stand alone, but that, in his view, their effectiveness can be further enhanced by Buddhist practice.

HEAVENLY REALMS AND BUDDHIST IDEALS

According to ancient Tibetan belief, the world is divided into three, layered parts: Heaven, Air and Earth (sometimes called Heaven, Earth and Underworld). The highest realm (Heaven) is that of the gods and spirits that protect and guide human beings; the middle realm (Air/Earth) is inhabited by human beings; the lower realm (Earth/Underworld) is populated by snakes, water-beings, vampires and mountain gods. The universe is conceptualized as a world with Mount Sumeru as its centre, surrounded by a great ocean and four continents (*gling*) situated at the four corners of the compass. Each continent is populated by a pantheon of benevolent gods and goddesses, as well as malevolent spirits; each one also has two sub-continents and is influenced by both the sun and the moon.

The Buddha recognized the existence of gods but not of one God or immortal soul. He promoted the "Arhat" ideal, whereby an individual can overcome suffering and attain the desireless, perfected state of *nirvana*. Over time, differences of opinion among followers of the Buddha led to the establishment of a variety of Buddhist sects. In Tibet, the Mahayana, or Great Vehicle, became the dominant form of Buddhism. It promoted the ideal of the *bodhisattva* – an enlightened being who delays achieving *nirvana* out of compassion for those suffering. *Bodhisattvas* come to the aid of humankind in response to being venerated and shown devotion.

A later sect, the Vajrayana or Diamond Vehicle, promotes the idea of developing both the "lower perfections" of alchemy and the "higher perfections" or *siddhis* (supernatural powers). It teaches that Tantric practices can enable individual enlightenment in this lifetime. Some of the rituals in Tibetan medicine are drawn from Vajrayana Buddhism.

MANDALAS: CIRCLES OF LIFE

Many of the Tibetan Buddhist deities and concepts have been represented visually to form meditation aids known as mandalas. Symbolically representing the Buddhist cosmos, mandalas are circular diagrams showing various Buddhas and *bodhisattvas* and the qualities they embody.

Mandalas used in Tibetan medicine feature the Medicine Buddha with a bowl of wish-fulfilling nectar and a myrobalan fruit. There are several levels of meaning within these mandalas. The external level is the practice of medicine by the physician and devotion to the Medicine Buddha. The internal level is the physician identifying with the Medicine Buddha and his energies. The most subtle, or secret, level is actually realizing the Medicine Buddha's nature as one's own – that is, attaining enlightened consciousness.

Typical features of a mandala are depictions of a divine presence at its centre, in this case Vasudhara, consort of the god of riches, as well as the use of interrelating circles and squares surrounded by protector-deities and saints.

CHAPTER 6

CONCEPTS OF THE BODY AND DISEASE

Tibetan medicine is based on the concept that health depends on a delicate balance of mental and physiological processes and of the vital life forces – the "humours" and "elements" – in the body. Illnesses are understood in terms of deviation from the optimum state of balance – and of humoral imbalance – rather than being identified as specific diseases in their own right.

The workings of the body are described in both a literal and a figurative way in the Tibetan tradition. The body is compared to a palace inhabited by courtiers (vital organs) with different roles and functions. It is thought that in a healthy body all the vital organs, body constituents and body functions work together in a harmonious way without any undue stress, while bodily fluids and subtle energy flow smoothly through both visible and invisible body channels.

In understanding the process of disease, emphasis is placed not only on the internal conditions, but also on the external environmental, seasonal and meteorological factors, and the role of diet, daily habits and general lifestyle. Close attention is paid to the different stages of disease in order to describe how it becomes rooted in the body.

A prominent feature of Tibetan medicine is its explicit acknowledgment of the role and importance of spirits and demons in disease. According to Bon belief a myriad of spirit beings may provoke bodily imbalance, while the Buddhist belief in rebirth suggests that actions in a past life may cause illness in this life.

THE HEALTHY BODY

The fundamental principle underlying a healthy mind and body is said to be a balance between what are known as the Three Humours or *nyes-pa* (pronounced "nyepa"). These are wind or air (*rlung*, pronounced "loong"), bile (*mKhris-pa*, pronounced "tripa") and phlegm (*bad-kan*, pronounced "peken"). The literal translation of *nyes-pa* is "fault" or "defect", indicating the link between the humours and the Three Poisons that are thought to be the root of disease (see pages 58–59). Wind is linked to the poison of desire, bile to that of aversion and phlegm to that of delusion. When the humours are in balance the body is strong and healthy and the mind calm and clear, but when imbalance occurs disease and mental afflictions result.

The concept of the humours was developed from the Ayurvedic system of the three *doshas* (see pages 18–19). The term humours has a broad meaning, encompassing not only the body fluids and constituents of the physical body but also the energies and essences of the subtle body (see pages 84–85). The humours are made up of the elements that are said to be the basis of the cosmos – that is, earth

LOCATIONS OF THE THREE HUMOURS

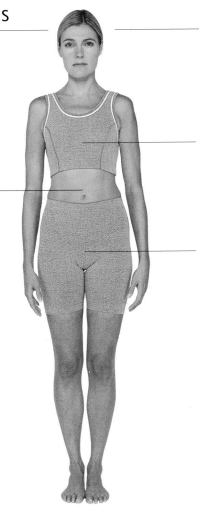

The bile humour predominates in the centre of the body and influences hunger and thirst, digestive function, eyesight and the quality and tone of the skin.

The phlegm humour predominates in the upper body and sinks downwards. It influences sleep, mobility of the joints, digestion and excretion.

The wind humour predominates in the abdomen and lower body and moves upwards to the head. It influences reproduction, digestion, respiration, mental function and consciousness.

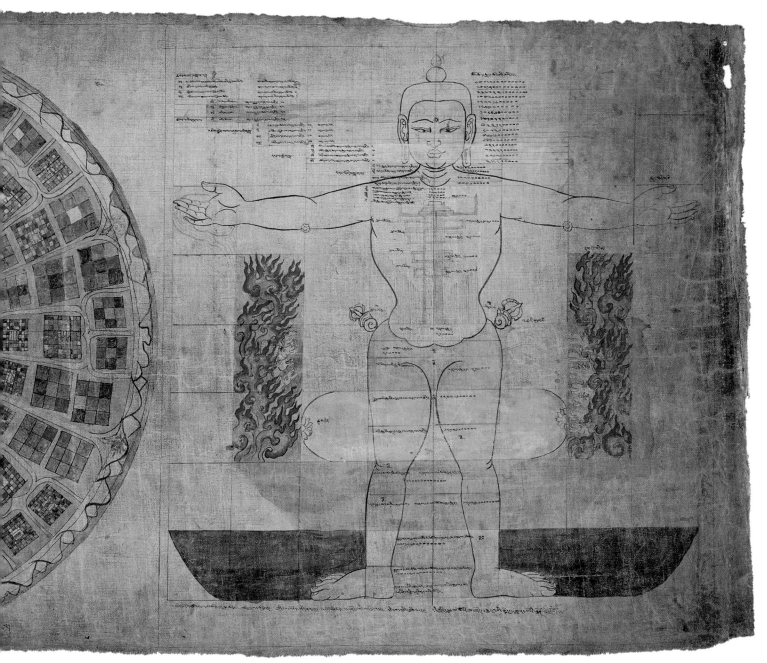

In Tibetan medicine, the physical health of an individual is inextricably linked to his or her spiritual well-being; medical knowledge is considered to be inseparable from religious and cosmological beliefs. This Tibetan thangka *linking the body and the cosmos is taken from the* Kalacackra Tantra, *which contains information about the body's network of channels for the circulation of essential fluids.*

(*sa*), water (*chu*), fire (*me*), air (*rlung*) and space (*nam-mkha*). In the body, wind is the manifestation of air, bile is the manifestation of fire and phlegm is the manifestation of earth and water. The element of "space"' is one which transcends the physical and links with the subtle energy channels of the body.

Each humour has its main location in a particular part of the body and has certain qualities and functions with which it is associated. Wind is said to predominate in the abdomen and the lower body and has the qualities of motion, lightness and dryness. It is linked to the bodily functions of movement, respiration, thought, digestion and reproduction, and it affects vitality, mental clarity and gynaecological health. Wind has five types: "life-sustaining wind" is based in the heart centre and relates to breathing; "ascending wind" is based in the chest and relates to speech; "pervasive wind" is based in the head but travels all round the body and relates to muscular function; "fire-accompanying wind" is based in the abdomen and digestive organs and aids digestion; and "downward-clearing wind" is based in the urinary and sexual organs and relates to the process of excretion.

Bile predominates in the centre of the body and has the qualities of heat, lubrication, oiliness and odour. It governs hunger and thirst, complexion and the functions of digestion, vision and temperament. It also has five types: "digestive bile" based between the stomach and intestines; "colour-transforming bile" based in the liver; "accomplishing bile" based in the heart; "visually adjusting bile" linked to the eyes and vision; and "complexion-clearing bile" linked with the skin.

Phlegm predominates mainly in the upper body and is cold, heavy and sticky in nature. It regulates sleep, joint mobility and mental awareness, and also affects digestion and excretion. Its five types are "supportive phlegm" based in the chest; "mixing phlegm" based in the upper digestive tract; "experiencing phlegm" based in the tongue and related to taste; "satisfying phlegm" based in the head; and "connecting phlegm" present in all the joints of the body.

These fifteen types of humour enable all the body's physical functions to be carried out. They also link with the subtle body that connects with the physical body but is made up of vibration, light, colour and sound rather than gross physical matter. It consists of a network of subtle energy channels, or "veins" (*rtsa*), that carry subtle energies, or vital forces, also known as "airs" or "winds" (*rlung*). The channels intersect at energetic centres – the *cakra* (*chakra* in Sanskrit) – which contain subtle essences (*thig-le*) that relate to consciousness. The physical body is also made up of seven basic constituents: nutritional essences,

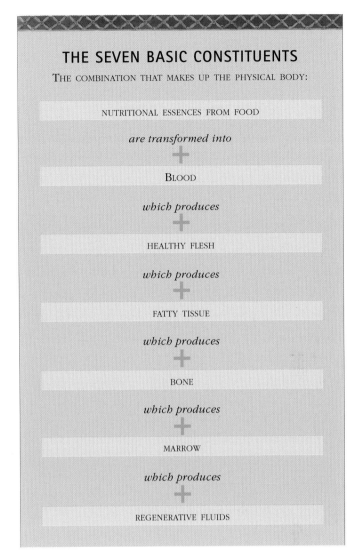

THE SEVEN BASIC CONSTITUENTS

THE COMBINATION THAT MAKES UP THE PHYSICAL BODY:

NUTRITIONAL ESSENCES FROM FOOD

are transformed into

BLOOD

which produces

HEALTHY FLESH

which produces

FATTY TISSUE

which produces

BONE

which produces

MARROW

which produces

REGENERATIVE FLUIDS

blood, flesh, fats, bone, marrow and regenerative fluids. Each one of these leads to the successful formation of the other. For example, food provides the nutritional essences from which blood is derived, leading to the production of healthy flesh. Good health also depends on effective excretion of waste products via urine, faeces and perspiration.

When the three humours, five elements, seven basic constituents and excretions are all well balanced in the physical body, and the flow of energy in the subtle body channels is unimpeded, a person can enjoy longevity and freedom from serious disease and can experience the benefits of the "three fruits of good health", namely successful religious practice, prosperity and happiness.

THE CAUSES OF DISEASE

In line with Buddhist philosophy, Tibetan medicine considers the root cause of all disease to be basic human ignorance about the true nature of reality. Because we fail to appreciate that everything is impermanent and changing, human beings are subject to desires and attachment, uncontrolled emotions and mental confusion. These negative states of mind – which can be summarized as desire, hatred and delusion – are known as the Three Poisons, and it is their influence that is said to cause disturbance in the balance of the humours in the body, leading ultimately to disease.

THE THREE POISONS
THE PRIMARY CAUSES OF DISEASE

The poison of desire is represented by a bird (*bya*), often a cockerel. Characterized by greed and pride, it causes restlessness, aggravating the wind humour and triggering mental and respiratory problems.

The poison of hatred is symbolized by a snake (*sbrul*). It is characterized by anger, dislike and aversion and disturbs the bile humour, leading typically to visual and digestive problems.

The poison of delusion is symbolized by a pig (*phag*). Characterized by mental dullness and faulty thinking, it leads to disturbance of the phlegm humour associated with stiff, heavy joints and indigestion.

The "poisons" are symbolized by three animals. The bird (normally drawn as a cockerel or peacock) symbolizes the mental poison of desire. It is characterized by attachment, greed and pride. Desire can cause feelings of dissatisfaction with what one has and constant material cravings. The snake symbolizes hatred, which refers to aversion and anger, and feelings of dislike for individuals, events or situations. Because of aversion we are unable to treat all situations and people with equanimity. The pig symbolizes delusion, characterized by mental confusion, slow thinking, mental dullness and bewilderment.

Desire creates restlessness, leading to a disturbance in the wind humour and ultimately causing "wind" diseases, such as mental illness. Hatred disturbs bile, which leads to digestive problems and other bile disorders. Delusion is linked to phlegm disorders, which include chronic joint stiffness and pain. In this way, negative mental states are seen as the underlying cause of illness, yet they can also provide the path to salvation – the suffering of illness often prompts an individual to resolve to adopt more healthy attitudes, to gain greater insight and to begin questioning the nature of human existence.

In addition to the internal causes of disease, there are also external causes related to the seasons, weather and environment; behaviour and lifestyle (including diet); or the influence of spirits. Living in harmony with the seasons by wearing suitable clothing, eating seasonal foods and behaving appropriately can play a large part in the prevention of disease. Inappropriate behaviour can cause humoral imbalances. For example, allowing oneself to get too hot in summer or too cold in winter can precipitate bile and phlegm disorders respectively. Eating cold foods in winter, rather than warming ones, can also cause phlegm disorders.

Behavioural causes of disease relate to body, speech and mind. A lack of physical activity, such as staying in bed late every day, can cause phlegm disorders, which are associated with drowsiness and being withdrawn. Talking too much, or worrying excessively about something, can cause a wind disorder such as nervousness or mental instability. The sense organs may also be involved – humoral balance can be affected negatively, for example, if the individual witnesses a horrific event, or positively, through activities such as listening to beautiful music.

As well as considering various mental "poisons", Tibetan medicine also takes account of actual poisons and the diseases caused by their toxicity. The medical texts list poisonous plants and explain the harmful effects of eating stale or rotten food and bad food combinations, such as milk and radishes (the acid in the radishes causes the milk to curdle in the stomach). Modern Tibetan physicians also warn of the possible harm which might be caused by food additives, chemicals, preservatives and genetic modification.

The most dramatic examples of external influences are those which involve spirits and demons (see box, right). Many Tibetans today still believe in their existence: they are thought to include water and mountain spirits, ancestral gods, demons who masquerade as spiritual masters, tormented spirits, cannibal ogres, flesh-eating demons and vampire ghouls. These elemental spirits are thought to be formed from natural energies in the environment but become malevolent when aroused. Alternatively, they can be conjured up through a variety of magical rituals and their formidable powers used to harm enemies. Tibetans are very careful to prevent accidental mishaps or actions that may disturb them.

The influence of spirits or deities can also be benevolent. Some goddesses and types of Buddhas are thought to be endowed with protective powers that can contribute to good health. Such deities are invoked in rituals used to consecrate elixirs for rejuvenation and longevity (see pages 86–87) and in practices for restoring fertility and virility.

A dance in Samye recollecting how demons tried to interfere with the building of Tibet's first monastery. Spirits can displace an individual's consciousness by invading the life-sustaining channel in the heart.

THE DEMONS OF DISEASE

The *Instructional Tantra* (see page 51) describes eighteen elemental demon types. These range from ogres to ancestors to mountain spirits and may be disturbed through certain behaviours, such as breaking or interrupting offerings being made to deities; frequently engaging in non-virtuous actions; remaining alone and in a fearful state for too long; or by being tormented by sorrows.

There are also said to be demons causing plague and skin-complaints who can be disturbed by impure actions, such as boiling over milk or digging up earth in places inhabited by spirits. Other diseases thought to be precipitated by demons include insanity, epilepsy and strokes. Poor diet and previous misdeeds may weaken the individual, enabling demons to gain a foothold of influence.

In Tibetan cosmology the "hungry ghost spirits" are thought to be the most likely to cause mental illness. However, while the Bon tradition views spirits as actual animated forms, the Buddhist view is that they are projections of the mind due to negative mental states (thus it is the mind itself that makes the mind "sick").

PATHWAYS OF DISEASE

In Tibetan medicine, diseases are classified according to their point of entry into the body, their location in the body, the pathways they follow within the body, the time at which they occur and the stage of the actual disease.

Once the causes of illness have arisen the disease is said to enter the body by one of the "entrances": the skin, flesh, channels, bone, solid (or vital) organs and hollow (or reservoir) organs. As in Chinese medicine, the solid organs are the heart, lungs, liver, spleen and kidneys, while the hollow organs are the stomach, small and large intestines, gall bladder, seminal vesicle (or female equivalent) and urinary bladder. Depending on the imbalance that exists, disease may start superficially and then gradually settle in the internal organs, where it is much harder to treat.

After entering the body, disease localizes itself in one of the three main sections: the upper (head and brain), middle (diaphragm and chest) or lower (hips and base of spine) part – the particular location depends on the predominance

of one or other of the humours in the disease. From there, the disease progresses through the body by means of "pathways". The pathways of disease relate to five factors: the vital constituents of the body, the sense organs, the functions for excretion, and the solid and hollow internal organs. Wind disorders tend to affect bone and the ears and are reflected in perspiration and the functioning of the heart and intestines. Bile disorders affect blood and eyesight, cause bodily excretions to become pungent, and pass to the liver, gall bladder and small intestine. Phlegm disorders pass from the nutritional essence of food via the flesh, bone marrow and sexual fluids to the lungs, spleen, kidneys, stomach and urinary bladder. Early in its formation a disease may not produce external symptoms, but as the illness begins to accumulate and spread via the pathways, symptoms begin to occur. If it is not treated at this stage, the disease will go on to manifest fully; it may do so at a particular time in the patient's life or in a certain climate or season.

CONDITIONS FOR DISEASE

Disorders depend on an interrelationship of humoral disturbance, influential factors and disease pathways

HUMOUR	INFLUENTIAL FACTORS	PATHWAY	DISORDER
Wind. Resides in the abdomen and lower body.	Windy weather (cool or warm), excess of tea/coffee, mental agitation and lack of sleep. Old age.	Moves in the bones, joints, heart, large intestine, skin and ears. Rapid onset and quick moving.	Forty-two types of hot and cold disorders. Worst before dawn and early evening. Example: arthritis.
Bile. Resides in the centre of the body.	Hot weather, overeating, excess of spicy foods, stress, competitiveness and hatred. Adult life.	Passes via blood, to liver and gall bladder, causing smelly excretions, fever and sweating.	Twenty-six types of hot disorders. Worst in the middle of the day and night. Example: indigestion.
Phlegm. Resides in the upper body.	Damp or humid weather, excess of cold or raw foods and daytime sleeping. Childhood.	Via the flesh and bone marrow to lungs, throat, nose and stomach. Slow onset and slow moving.	Thirty-three types of cold disorders. Worst in the morning and at dusk. Example: chest infections.

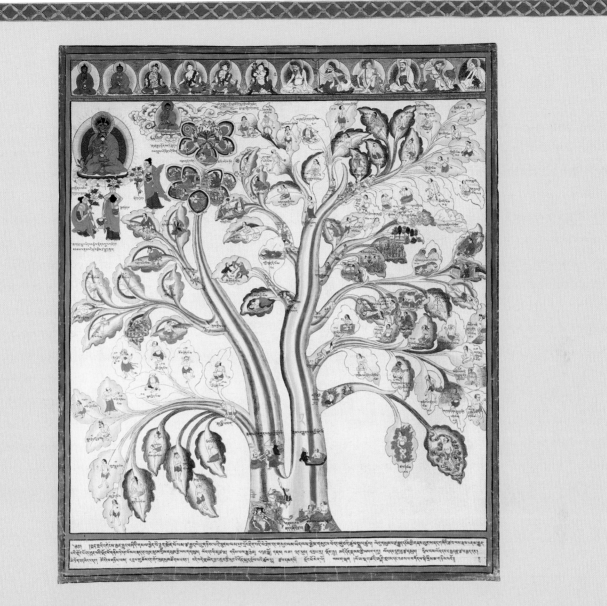

TREES OF MEDICINE

The study of Tibetan medicine is facilitated by traditional illustrations used as memory aids. These intricate drawings of tiny figures with accompanying text explain both pictorially and in words the key aspects of theory and practice. A number are in the form of trees, with the trunks and branches representing particular medical topics such as physiology or treatment, and the leaves and fruits containing outcomes.

One such "tree" (above) outlines medical teaching on the subjects of physiology and pathology. In the top corner is the Shakyamuni Buddha in his blue form as the Medicine Buddha (see page 49), imparting the medical teachings. The tree's left trunk represents the physiology of the body and has three branches describing the humours, bodily constituents and the excretion of impurities. It is topped with two flowers representing good health and longevity and two fruits representing well-being (material and spiritual) and enlightenment (symbolized by a person taking on a body of rainbow light). The right trunk represents pathology. It has nine branches showing the primary and secondary causes of disease, the starting points, locations and pathways of diseases, the causative conditions, types of fatal disease and humoral imbalances and a summary of hot and cold diseases.

TYPES OF ILLNESS

The Tibetan medical texts state that there are 84,000 negative mental states that produce the same number of different types of disease. To make these more manageable they are condensed by type, reducing to 1,616, then 404 and, finally, 101 types of humoral disturbance. Of these, 42 are wind disorders, 26 are bile disorders and 33 are types of phlegm imbalance.

The 101 diseases are organized into four classes, according to their original cause. Those of the first class originate in early life – pre-natally, in infancy or early childhood – and may be due to congenital factors, the health of

An 18th-century dagger used in exorcism rites by a lama *to drive away illness. The subjugation of evil influences through the use of a ritual dagger (*phur-bu*) has its roots in Tibetan shamanism.*

the mother during pregnancy or diet as an infant or young child. With careful treatment over time this type of illness can be improved. The second class contains diseases caused by factors in the patient's present life, including diet and behaviour. These are the easiest disorders to treat if the patient is willing to change his or her habits under the guidance of a physician.

Diseases in the third class are those that are considered to be due to karma from a previous life. It is thought that non-virtuous actions in a past life accumulate and then "ripen" in the form of a disease in this life. These

THE FOUR CLASSES OF DISEASE

CLASS OF ILLNESS	POSSIBLE CAUSES	TREATMENT
The diseases of the first class have their origin in the patient's early life.	Congenital. Due to the health of the mother during pregnancy, or diet as an infant or young child.	With careful treatment over time this type of illness can be improved.
Diseases of the second class are caused by factors in the patient's present life.	Lifestyle. These maladies are directly affected by diet and behaviour.	The least difficult forms of disease to treat, provided the patient is willing to change his or her daily habits under the guidance of a physician.
The third class of diseases is considered to be due to karma from a previous life.	Past lives. Non-virtuous actions from a former life are believed to "ripen" in the form of a disease in this life.	The best way to cure such diseases is to renounce worldly life and dedicate oneself to virtuous action in order to try to purify one's karma.
The fourth class of disease is believed to be due to the influence of spirits.	Spiritual. Disturbance of the spirit- through accidental or disrespectful actions and/or lack of due reverence.	Medical intervention is insufficient. A *lama* must be called in to carry out spiritual cures, such as an exorcism.

diseases are very difficult to treat, as they are rooted in the past, and may be fatal. The best cure is said to be through virtuous action, confession of misdeeds and spiritual practice in order to try to purify and dissolve the karma – all combined with the appropriate medication.

The fourth class of disease arises from spirit influence. In such cases, the disease will not respond to medical treatment. Instead, a *lama* (a Buddhist teacher) is required to carry out spiritual therapy, such as exorcism. The patient may also be required to perform certain rituals and make offerings in order to appease the malevolent spirit.

Diseases are further categorized according to the type of humoral imbalance and its corresponding disease. Disturbance of the five types of wind (see pages 56–57) leads to disorders of speech and memory, respiratory function, mental function and the gynaecological organs. Disturbance of the five types of bile leads to disorders such as eye disease and visual problems, skin diseases, digestive problems and mental indecisiveness. Disturbance of the five types of phlegm is associated with disorders of the joints, weight problems, impaired digestion, appetite and taste.

Diseases are also classified according to gender (male and female), their time of onset, the season and locality. During childhood, phlegm diseases are most common as children are thought to be relatively weak and vulnerable to that humour. During adult life, bile diseases predominate as adults are generally more active and assertive. In old age, wind diseases are most common due to physical frailty. In terms of the seasons, wind disorders tend to occur in the rainy season, bile disorders in the late summer and autumn and phlegm disorders in the spring. Windy environments trigger wind imbalance, hot and dry climates cause bile disorders and damp or humid places lead to phlegm disorders.

Ultimately, all diseases can be defined as either hot or cold disorders. Wind and phlegm disorders are generally "cool", while those of bile and blood are normally "hot". Categorization is based on symptoms such as the colour of the skin of the extremities and their temperature.

Giving alms and engaging in other altruistic behaviours are ways of generating merit. The combination of accumulated merit and good karma sustains physical life and determines whether a disease is treatable.

NINE INCURABLE MALADIES

Tibetan medicine recognizes nine types of incurable conditions that are due to negative past deeds (karma) and which are usually fatal. They cannot be treated by medicine. The only recourse is for the patient to devote themselves fully to religious and altruistic activities. Through divine intervention the person may be saved.

The first two types of fatal disease are due to hot disorders (fevers) and cold disorders that have passed beyond the stage of effective treatment. The third type is due to the severance of the life-supporting wind in the central channel of the body. The fourth type is due to severe depletion of the constituents of the body, meaning that life can no longer be supported. The fifth type is due to life essences and life-force being stolen away by a spirit. The sixth type is due to the exhaustion of life-span and merit earned from carrying out good deeds. The seventh type is due to a fatal humoral imbalance. The eighth type is where the remedy given is contraindicated by the causes of the disease. Finally, the ninth type is due to a fatal wound to one of the vital organs of the body, rendering it unable to sustain life.

CHAPTER 7

DIAGNOSTIC PROCEDURES

In the nineteenth century, a visitor to Tibet observed physicians at work and noted that they rarely spoke, preferring to diagnose by means of pulse-taking, urinalysis and observation. Even today, it is said that the best Tibetan doctor relies on pulse-taking alone, the next best utilizes urinalysis and other diagnostic techniques while the least accomplished of physicians has to resort to asking questions. Modern physicians use questions mainly to confirm their diagnosis. Normally, the physician first takes the pulse, which allows him or her to determine the patient's constitutional type and to investigate the balance of the humours and internal organs. Certain conditions are necessary for the pulse to be read accurately and the physician needs years of practice. Pressure points on the body and pulses on the feet and neck may also at times be palpated for diagnostic clues.

Like pulse-taking, urinalysis is a highly developed art in which the physician examines the patient's fresh urine in detail. Observational diagnostic techniques include looking at the tongue, face, body shape and posture, eyes and ears, and complexion. Astrological charts may also be calculated as a diagnostic tool. Either during or after the diagnostic procedures the physician may ask questions about diet and behaviour, the functioning of the sense organs including taste, and the presence of particular symptoms, such as aches and pains or fevers and chills. The patient's responses are used to confirm the diagnosis and to determine what advice, such as recommendations for dietary change, may be necessary.

CONSULTATION AND QUESTIONING

The Tibetan physician's first priority is care of, and compassion towards, the patient. The doctor is interested in the whole person, and not just their symptoms, and needs to understand their disease in the context of their general health and well-being.

Although questioning plays a more minor role in diagnosis than other techniques, such as pulse-taking or urinalysis, it may be used to make the patient feel at ease and to obtain additional diagnostic information. The physician's questions are aimed at building up a picture of the relative balance of the humours affecting physiological and psychological function.

The Trees of Medicine medical illustrations (see box, page 61) have different branches and leaves representing the humours, the diseases caused by their imbalance, and associated symptoms and remedies. The physician can use these as a basis for questioning.

To determine the conditions that may underlie the imbalance, the physician asks about environment, diet and behaviour. For example, if pulse and tongue diagnosis yields signs of a wind disorder the physician would ask about likely causes: recent exposure to cool breezes, sitting in windy places, drinking a lot of tea or coffee, or eating meats such as pork can all trigger a wind disorder.

Questions about symptoms cover those typically associated with each humoral imbalance. Wind imbalance is characterized by chills, yawning and stretching, aches and pains that move around the body, and mental disturbance. The physician may also ask the patient whether he or she eats

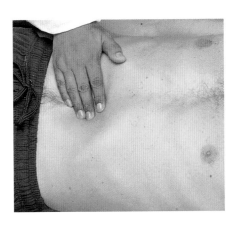

A practitioner palpating a patient's abdomen, feeling for any signs of lumps and blockages. This is an important diagnostic technique in Tibetan medicine.

warm, oily foods and has access to a warm place away from draughts – these are traditional remedies for wind disturbances.

To confirm diagnosis of a bile disorder the physician may enquire if the patient has experienced symptoms of excess body heat, such as sweating and flushes, a bitter taste in the mouth and digestive problems. He or she might also investigate whether the patient has been overheated recently or has consumed many spicy, hot foods and drinks, the antidotes to which are staying in cool places and consuming cool and bitter foods and drinks.

Phlegm disorders are characterized by feelings of cold, heaviness and dullness, bloating, loss of appetite, nausea and vomiting and a sour taste in the mouth. The physician may enquire about these symptoms and their causative conditions, such as staying in a damp, cold place or eating unripe or rotten food. Remedies, such as staying in a warm, dry place and eating light, easily digestible foods will also be discussed.

By talking about remedies as part of the diagnostic procedure, the physician can assess the patient's willingness to follow advice. This, combined with the diagnosis of the disease itself, enables the physician to assess the likelihood of a cure being successful and to decide whether the patient can be helped. The physician may also enquire about the progress of the disease in relation to time and its location in the body. Occasionally subterfuge may be employed to enhance patient compliance and the physician's credibility.

PULSE-TAKING

Pulse-taking is the most important form of diagnosis in Tibetan medicine. There have been many recorded instances of physicians providing a comprehensive and accurate diagnosis for patients by means of the pulse alone. In one study, a physician took the pulse of a woman who held her wrist out through a hole in a screen behind which she was hidden. Although the physician was not able to see the patient at all, he was able to make an accurate diagnosis.

Prior to taking the pulse, it is best if both the physician and the patient can take appropriate steps to ensure that the balance of the humours is stable. The medical texts state that, ideally, both should rise early and avoid strenuous activity, alcohol, meat and sex for at least twenty-four hours. The pulse should be measured early in the day, preferably on or soon after waking, and the patient should have an empty stomach. The physician's hands must be smooth, warm and flexible, and the patient's pulse should be held for at least 100 beats on each wrist.

To take the patient's pulse, the physician places three fingers on the radial artery. The forefinger presses on the skin, the middle finger presses a little deeper onto the muscle and the ring finger presses down onto the bone. The fingers are close together but not touching and each picks up messages from the various internal organs. The qualities of the pulses are described in lyrical terms, such as "bulky and long like the song of a cuckoo". On small children, the pulse is taken by examining the blood vessels behind the ear instead of palpating at the wrist.

A patient having her pulse taken during a consultation. Pulse-taking is the vital element in Tibetan diagnostic procedures and there are special pulses for determining pregnancy or the influence of spirit entities.

The Tibetan system of pulse-taking developed from Traditional Chinese Medicine. However, in the Tibetan tradition, the pulses are measured slightly higher up the wrist, some of the organ positions are different and the emphasis is on detecting the relative balance of the humours. There are also some additional pulses in the Tibetan system, which are known as the three "constitutional pulses" and the seven "astonishing pulses".

The constitutional pulse may be male, female or neutral (the latter is also called the *bodhisattva*, or *bodhicitta*, pulse). This pulse, however, does not depend on the sex of the patient but on the constitutional balance of the humours. The male constitutional pulse is governed by wind and is rough and bulky, the female one is thinner and faster and dominated by bile, and the neutral constitutional pulse is smooth, soft, flowing and conditioned by phlegm. Constitutional pulses play a role in fertility and determining the likely gender of offspring. It is said that if a couple both have male constitutional pulses they will produce boys, if they both have female constitutional pulses they will have girls and if they have one of each they will have a child of each sex. If both partners have a neutral constitutional pulse (which is rare) they will be childless but they will enjoy long lives. If one person has a neutral pulse but the other has a male or female pulse they will have one boy or girl respectively.

A healthy, normal pulse is smooth and flowing and beats five times to each cycle of inhalation and exhalation by the physician. If the pulse beats more than five times this indicates a hot disorder, whereas less than five beats points to a cold disorder.

The pulses vary according to the seasons, of which there are five in the Tibetan calendar (see page 75). During each season, one of the five elements and their corresponding internal organs predominates. By taking account of the seasonal changes, the physician can determine not only the balance of the humours, but also the exact functioning of each of the internal organs.

Other, more intriguing, pulses can be used to determine life-span and death, while the so-called "astonishing pulses" (see box, below) perform a divinatory function. The ability to determine these pulses requires great skill and specialist spiritual training, and because of this they are mainly used only by physicians who are also monks or *lamas*. Younger, lay physicians use these pulses only rarely nowadays, with the exception of the pregnancy pulse, which is still used quite often.

A detail showing practitioners assessing their patients' pulses, taken from a manuscript plate describing the detailed preparation required prior to a pulse examination and the conduct expected of the participants during it. Through pulse readings alone a practitioner can determine the physical, emotional and spiritual health of a patient.

THE SEVEN ASTONISHING PULSES

Also known as the "wondrous" pulses, these are divinatory pulses used by highly accomplished *lama* physicians. By attuning themselves deeply to the consciousness of the patient by means of the pulses, physicians can detect information about the family's condition, the likely outcome of significant events and the influence of spirits.

The "family pulse" gives information about family fortunes and prosperity, and potential problems such as the likelihood of quarrels or difficulties. The "guest pulse" helps determine the proximity of a visitor, while the "enemy pulse" can be used to predict the likely outcome of a fight. The "friend pulse" determines the number and quality of friends and the "evil spirit pulse" can reveal possession by spirits or

the effects of sorcery. The physician can take the "substitutional pulse" of a loved one in place of a sick patient who is unable to visit the doctor, using it to diagnose and treat *in absentia*. Taking the "pregnancy pulse" can confirm pregnancy and suggest the likely gender of the child.

The pulses are taken on the wrist of the individual most significant to the issue being determined, such as the head of the family for the family and friend pulses. Certain qualities are looked for in different pulse positions, for example, if the physician taking the "evil spirit pulse" finds a disturbance in the kidney pulses, this may indicate the influence of a water snake spirit. When examining the "guest pulse", a strong heart pulse indicates that the guest's arrival is imminent.

OBSERVATION

The two main forms of visual diagnosis employed in Tibetan medicine are urinalysis and tongue diagnosis. Urinalysis is such a broad subject that it is dealt with separately (see pages 70–71). Tibetan tongue diagnosis, which is relatively simple compared to its counterparts elsewhere, concentrates mainly on the colour and coating of the tongue in relation to the predominance of the humours.

A healthy tongue is said to be red, soft, moist and supple. A white or yellow coating and either excessive dryness or moisture indicate an imbalance. A tongue that is dry, rough and red is typical of a wind disorder. If the tongue is really parched, especially towards the throat, then the wind disorder is severe and urgent treatment must be sought. If the tongue is parched and also shrivelled up then fever has overtaken the wind disorder and the patient is becoming very dehydrated. If the tongue is parched and black the wind disorder and fever are present in equal measures.

A tongue thickly coated in yellow phlegm indicates a bile disorder. If the tongue is also parched this is a sign of a combined wind and bile disturbance, a not uncommon event since many illnesses involve the disturbance of more than one humour. A pale and moist tongue that is soft and lustreless is indicative of a phlegm disorder. If the tongue is also parched, the disorder involves wind disturbance as well. A pale, thickened tongue suggests a turbid fever.

The condition of the tongue can also be used to diagnose impending death. In such a case, it appears black, parched and cracked, rendering the patient speechless.

Observation of the eyes and ears is also used in Tibetan medicine, but this generally involves just looking for gross signs, such as yellowing of the eyes (indicative of jaundice or liver problems) or checking for obstructions or wax lodged in the ear that may be affecting hearing. However, the principle of searching for signs of humoral imbalance can still be applied: for example, a yellowing in the whites of the eyes is indicative of a bile disorder.

Posture, movement and body shape can also provide the physician with a lot of information. People suffering from a wind disorder tend to be thin and wiry, slightly stooped and unable to sit still for long. People with a bile imbalance are often medium-sized but may make quick, aggressive movements. A phlegm disorder can cause individuals to become overweight, slow-moving and very listless. Anatomical proportions may be considered, too: the medical texts describe a healthy body in terms of the optimum proportions of each body part or constituent.

A manuscript detail depicting tongue observation. The colour of the skin, or of any discharges such as mucus, are also looked at. Listening to the patient's pitch of speech can also be important.

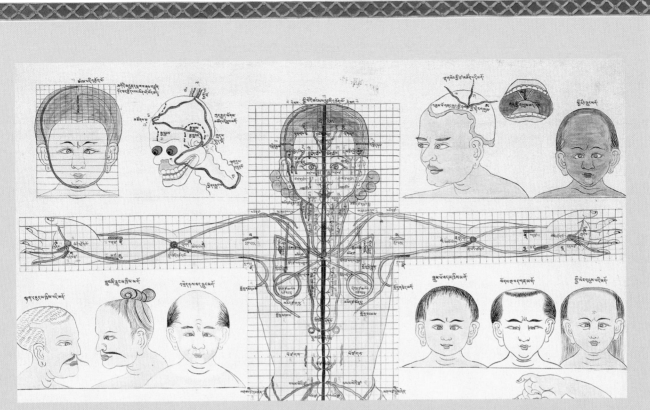

Depictions of the cranial types recognized in Tibetan medicine. Clockwise, from top right (the blue face): a high forehead (indicating wind predominance); a flat head (combined humoral predominance); a triangular head (phlegm predominance); a round head (phlegm and bile predominance); a broad or wide head (phlegm and wind predominance); a square head (wind and bile predominance); and a prominent occiput (bile predominance).

THE SEVEN CRANIAL TYPES

According to Tibetan medicine, the shape of a person's head is determined by the balance of their humours. Seven different cranial types are identified in the *Four Tantras*. A high forehead indicates wind predominance, a prominent occiput bile predominance and a triangular head phlegm predominance. The humours combine to form "square heads" (wind and bile predominance), "wide heads" (wind and phlegm predominance), "round heads" (phlegm and bile predominance) and "flat heads" (which combine all three humours).

Each type of cranium is also associated with a different type of brain. The "wind" head has the brain of the densest consistency, and is known as a "meat brain". The prominent "bile" head has a "butter brain" while the triangular "phlegm"

head has a "honey brain". The other cranial types are associated with a "cottage cheese brain", "milk brain", "curd brain" and "water brain" respectively. Brains of denser consistency are considered to be more receptive to treatment.

As with the pulse (see page 66), the cranial bones are classified as either male, female or neutral. This relates not to the sex of the patient but to the hardness of the cranium. The "male" cranium is the hardest and the "neutral" cranium the softest. The physician may observe the shape of the head and feel the hardness/softness of the cranial bones as part of the overall diagnosis of the patient, all the time building up a more and more detailed and accurate picture of the balance and function of each humour in the body.

URINALYSIS

Like water in a pond, urine can act as a mirror of its surroundings and it provides an invaluable diagnostic tool. Urinalysis, which probably derives from Greek or Persian influences, has been developed into a very precise science in Tibetan medicine. Traditional Chinese Medicine does not include urine analysis at all, while in Indian medicine the diagnostic use of urinalysis was introduced much later than it was in Tibetan medicine and is more rudimentary.

Urine is in a constant state of change and can give a very accurate picture of the condition of the digestive and excretory systems, as well as an indication of the individual's overall health. For up to twenty-four hours before the urine sample is taken, patients should avoid tea, coffee, alcohol and any strong foods that might affect the colour and smell of the urine. They should also get sufficient rest, have a good night's sleep and abstain from sex.

The urine should ideally be taken early in the morning, but after 5:00AM to avoid any strong influences from the

A Tibetan manuscript illustration depicting just some of the range of colours of urine to be found among patients. The odour of the vapours emanating from the urine is also an important factor in any diagnosis. Samples collected at dawn are thought to be best because lunar and solar energies are in equilibrium at that time.

previous night's meal. It should be collected in a clean container, preferably white or clear so that it can be studied easily. The physician makes a three-stage observation of the urine: when it is fresh and hot, when it is lukewarm and after it has gone cold. Visually, he or she checks the colour, vapour, sedimentation and the size of the bubbles produced when the urine is stirred. The odour is also tested for signs of humoral balance and clues as to the nature of any disease.

Healthy urine possesses a light golden colour, said to be "like the butter on top of a female yak's milk", with only a slight, musty odour. It produces an average amount of vapour and no unusual bubbles or froth are evident. After having cooled down, healthy urine becomes light yellow in colour and very clear. In contrast, the urine of a person suffering from a wind disorder is light blue and clear, like spring water, and has little odour but large bubbles that move and "pop" easily.

A person with a bile disorder typically produces urine that is dark yellow in colour or may even have an orange hue. It has a strong burnt odour, a lot of steam and small bubbles that disappear quickly. The urine from someone with a phlegm imbalance is white and cloudy with a stale

smell and white sediments. Stirring it produces medium-sized bubbles that stick together and stay for a long time.

As the urine cools the physician looks at the albumen content and the chyle, which are the cloudy sediments and the oily layer that rises to the surface during the cooling process. A lot of albumen and chyle indicate a heat disorder. A small amount of sediment and only a thin oily layer indicate a cold condition. Once the urine is cool, the final analysis can be made, and this includes noting how much time it took for the changes to occur. Very often this is, in fact, the only analysis that can be performed as urine samples brought along to the physician have usually already cooled down.

In general, heat disorders are reflected in urine that is yellow or red in colour, thick with sediment, with a lot of vapour that stays for a long time and contains small vanishing bubbles. Many of these characteristics are produced by bile and blood. In contrast cold disorders are reflected in pale blue or white urine that is very fluid and has no strong odour or vapour, but contains large bubbles.

Urine may also be used to diagnose impending death. If the urine is blood red with a strong odour, and medication produces no change, the hot disorder is likely to be fatal. If the thick, white, odourless and vapourless urine of a severe cold disorder does not respond to treatment the outcome will be the same. Finally, the urine might be examined to identify harmful spirits (see box, right), which must then be pacified with prayers and rituals.

The physician normally examines the properties of the patient's urine to ascertain their physical health but it can also be done for divinatory purposes or to identify spirits.

DIAGNOSING SPIRIT INFLUENCES

A special type of urinalysis can be used to determine the influence of different types of spirits on a person, their family and ancestors. A sample is left overnight and great care is taken not to disturb it. As the urine cools, patterns form in it and these are interpreted by the superimposition of a diagnostic grid represented as a tortoise shell.

Men are asked to urinate from the east side and a female divination chart, represented by the belly of a tortoise, is then used. Women must urinate from the west and a male chart, represented by the shell of the tortoise, is utilized. The divination grid has nine sections, representing the different areas of influence for a spirit, including the home, descendants and ancestors. A further grid is used to determine the type of harmful spirit.

DREAMS AND OMENS

*Auspicious dreams signifying good health and longevity include those which feature lakes
and the climbing of mountains. Should a dream also include other positive signs – such as
a holy man, a fire or riding on an elephant – it indicates even greater good fortune.*

Tibetan medicine places great significance on dreams and omens, which are incorporated into the diagnostic process. The dreams of both the doctor and the patient may be considered, alongside portents suggesting the likely outcome of an illness and the potential success of a particular form of treatment.

During sleep, the conscious mind is said to be carried along the energy channels and to enter the dream state by means of the movement of the wind humour originating in the heart centre. Consciousness may move from the heart centre along channels in different directions, determining the type of images perceived in dreams. For example, if the consciousness ascends the channel to the crown, dreams are likely to include images of deities, whereas if it descends the channel to the navel, the dreams may feature animals, spirits and dark places.

Dreams may be stimulated by what one has seen, heard, sensed intuitively, aspired to in prayer, or thought consciously. They may also be triggered by imbalances in the humours, giving rise to different images in the dream state. If the dreams are caused by an imbalance of the wind humour, for example, they are characterized by the appearance of black, blue and green objects and sensations of flying. Such dreams have a transitory, fleeting quality. Dreams linked to bile disturbance contain red and yellow objects and generally feel more slow-moving and solid. Phlegm imbalance results in dreams of a fixed nature featuring white substances or objects, such as snow, water, pearls and white flowers. This type of imbalance may also give rise to dreams about physical contact and blissful sensations.

The physician may interpret certain dream sequences to give an indication of the patient's fortunes. Dreams about falling, fighting, losing skin and even tax evasion are all described in the Tibetan medical texts as inauspicious. Other dreams may indicate the presence of specific diseases. Skin complaints, for example, may be symbolized by dreams about a lotus emerging from the heart centre. Tumours may be revealed in dreams in which thorny plants grow out of the body. Dreams featuring drunken dancing can portend epilepsy and images of the sun and moon falling down may precede blindness.

The time at which the dream occurs is also considered to be significant. Dreams caused by phlegm imbalance tend to come during the deep sleep states of the late evening, whereas bile-related dreams occur in the middle of the night and dreams linked to wind disturbance occur towards dawn. It is the dawn dreams that are regarded as the most significant for diagnosis and – because the wind humour is also the vehicle for higher consciousness – such dreams are often prophetic.

Fortunately, it is thought that the outcome of inauspicious dreams can be mitigated if the patient follows the physician's advice and performs certain offerings, prayers and rituals.

Omens can be seen in the person who comes to fetch the physician, the activity being performed by the physician when the caller arrives, signs that the physician may notice en route to the patient and the activity being performed by the patient when the physician arrives. If the person calling on the physician acts nobly or is a monk this is taken as a good sign, but if the person is a woman, disabled or riding a beast of burden the ancient texts suggest that the prognosis may not be so good. If when the person arrives the physician is in bed or is having an oil massage, this is a bad omen, as are certain phenomena that the physician may see while he or she is on the way to visit the patient, such as a snake, a cut rope, a person lamenting or a corpse. In contrast, circling animals, images of deities, ringing bells and singing larks are all considered to be good omens for recovery and health.

THE IMPERMANENCE OF LIFE

Tibetan physicians feel it is important to be able to diagnose impending death accurately so that patients may be helped to prepare for it. Diagnosis may be made using special pulses (see box, page 67), with the aid of divination grids used in urinalysis (see box, page 71) or through dreams and omens.

The pulse of a person who is dying shows abnormal changes in its beats and becomes erratic like "a bird eating worms" or a "flapping flag". The pulses of certain organs such as the heart may disappear altogether and there may be abnormal accompanying signs, for example a black coating on the tongue and a glazed look in the eyes. Alternatively, there may be pauses in the pulse points for particular organs, indicating that the organ is fatally afflicted, or indicating the presence of fatal spirits. By tuning into these pulses carefully, and also by taking them on other parts of the body, such as the ankle, a skilled physician can predict quite accurately when death is likely to occur.

Urinalysis allows the physician to predict imminent death. If the patient's urine is an abnormal colour, such as black or red, this indicates fatal poisoning or blood disorders, respectively. Fatal wind disorders are revealed in blue, thread-like patterns on the surface of the urine. If the surface is yellow or orange it indicates a fatal bile disorder; if it is white and sticky it indicates a fatal phlegm condition. Death is also reflected in an increasingly strong, rotten odour and urine characteristics that do not change in spite of treatment.

Depending on the diagnosis, it may be possible to avert death by accumulating merit through good deeds, or by practising longevity techniques (see pages 84–85).

A skeletal "lord of the funeral pyre", or citi patti, *one of the attendants of the Tibetan god of death, Yama.*

CHAPTER 8

HEALING IN TIBETAN MEDICINE

Tibetan healing emphasizes a balanced and harmonious life. In the early stages of any imbalance, self-care, through modifying diet, behaviour and daily habits, can be sufficient to effect a cure. Even in the later stages, such alterations can make a big difference to the efficacy of other treatments because of their direct effect on the humours, and so they are almost always recommended by physicians.

As an illness develops, more radical intervention is required and this generally takes the form of herbal medicine in conjunction with appropriate external treatments, such as moxibustion, massage or bone-setting. Surgery is used only rarely. Herbal medicines are usually in the form of pills, powders and ointments.

Divine healing is regarded as being just as important as all the other forms of healing. If the patient is religious this may take the form of Buddhist rituals, but even if the patient has no religious belief the physician will pray on their behalf and invoke the power of the Medicine Buddha to facilitate healing.

Both the physician and the patient are encouraged to live virtuous and altruistic lives in order to accrue merit. It is believed that this can, in turn, help to prevent or alleviate disease. Some practices focus on rejuvenation and longevity, the belief being that by accessing subtle energy the organs of the body can be revitalized and the aging process can be delayed. As always, the focus is on healing the whole person – body, mind and spirit – and treatments are targeted at both physical and subtle levels via the humours and the subtle energy channels.

MODIFYING LIFESTYLE AND BEHAVIOUR

Having diagnosed a humoral imbalance, the Tibetan physician recommends any appropriate lifestyle and behaviour changes to facilitate healing. Some may be for permanent changes in behaviour, while others are based on the seasons and "occasional behaviours".

Physicians advocate strongly that the ten "non-virtuous behaviours" be avoided. Of these, some are physical – killing, stealing and sexual misconduct; some are verbal – telling lies, divisive speech, talk that harms others and useless chatter; and some are mental – covetousness, having harmful intent and holding wrong views. In place of these, virtuous behaviours such as service, compassion and altruism are encouraged.

Tibetan medicine advocates that clothing be appropriate to the climate. Gems, including turquoise, may be worn for protection from evil.

Dietary intake is best regulated according to the seasons and the nature and qualities of particular foods (see pages 76–77). In general, physicians suggest that foods be consumed when they are in season and selected according to the individual's constitutional balance. Sleep is also best regulated according to humoral balance – people with phlegm problems should never sleep immediately after eating as this encourages more phlegm to form, but those with wind problems may benefit from a short rest after meals.

Appropriate sexual behaviour includes refraining from committing adultery or performing sexual acts with animals and taking care over the frequency of sexual activity in order to preserve the life essences. Sexual contact can be frequent in winter but is best limited to twice a week during spring and autumn and fortnightly in summer to prevent energy loss. Bathing and warm oils help maintain vitality and vigour.

In order to use the senses in a healthy way, patients are encouraged to look at beautiful things, to smell pleasant odours and listen to beautiful music. Precious gems or blessed threads may be worn to protect against harmful influence.

The Tibetan year is divided into five seasons – spring, early summer, late summer (the rainy season), autumn and winter – and each one is associated with a predominance of certain humours and particular climatic conditions. Correct seasonal behaviour includes wearing appropriate clothes (warm ones in winter and cool in summer), taking vigorous exercise in spring to move any stagnant phlegm in the body (but avoiding over-exertion in the summer that may stir up bile) and eating warming foods in winter and cooling foods in the summer.

Recommendations may be based specifically on the humours. People with wind disorders should keep warm, stay with friends, take plenty of rest, limit sex and moderate consumption of food or drink. Those with a bile imbalance should stay quietly in a cool place and avoid strenuous activity. Those with a phlegm disorder are encouraged to keep warm, take exercise and avoid damp places.

"Occasional behaviours" are natural functions, such as yawning, belching and sneezing. These should be neither suppressed nor forced but allowed to occur naturally.

FOOD AS MEDICINE

Tibetan physicians are well trained in dietetics and consider not only what is eaten but also the amount that is eaten and the combinations of different foods and drinks. Nourishing food is seen as life-sustaining while stale, rotten or "fast" food is believed to be detrimental to health.

There are five categories of food (grains, meats, oils and fats, vegetables and herbs, and cooked dishes), classified by their properties as well as their tastes (see pages 78–79).

TIBETAN BUTTER TEA

Tibetans believe that tea helps to sharpen the mind. Their butter tea or *solja* is made with clarified butter and salt, giving it a rich, oily texture thought to enhance the complexion, cleanse the body and increase life-span.

Place three cups of water and one or two teaspoons of tea leaves (or a tea bag) in a small pan and bring to the boil. Reduce to a simmer, remove the leaves (or bags) and stir in half a cup of milk and half a teaspoon of salt. Add one tablespoon of butter (clarified is best, but ordinary butter will do). Stir until the butter is melted, remove from the heat and whisk for a minute to make a light froth. Pour and serve immediately (makes four cups).

Grains include the Tibetan staples of barley, buckwheat and rice and also legumes, such as lentils and beans, and seeds, such as sesame. Certain foods can alleviate specific conditions, such as rice for diarrhoea.

Meat is further classified according to the type of animal it is taken from and where and how they live. The consumption of cooling meats, such as beef, ,pork or venison, is used to treat heat disorders. In contrast, mutton and yak meat are thought to warm the body and ease cold disorders. (Although most Tibetans are Buddhists, many eat meat.)

Oils and fats are held in high regard, as they are essential for keeping the body warm and nourished in the country's cold, mountainous regions. Rubbing the body with sesame oil is believed to relieve phlegm and wind disorders, while mustard oil can be used to generate bile.

Vegetables and aromatic herbs are classified as warming or cooling according to whether they grow in dry or damp places. They can be used medicinally in their own right, but all greens are to be avoided when taking herbal medicine as they may interfere with the medicine's potency.

Cooked foods help to improve digestion and build strength by warming the body through digestive "fire". As elsewhere in the East, rice gruel, sometimes with meat or vegetable stock, is a favourite medicinal food.

Drinks are sometimes used to help balance the humours. Milk generates phlegm but clears wind; water generates wind but clears bile; and beer and wine generate bile but clear phlegm. Milk may be from the cow, goat, sheep or *dri* (female yak) and water from various sources such as rain, glaciers, rivers and wells. Each have their own properties, but fresh, warmed dairy milk and fresh, clean rain water are considered the best for health. Tibetan butter tea is thought to benefit all the humours (see box, left).

AND FATS

d fats include milks, butters and cheeses, seed and plant oils, and
narrow. All are thought to improve vigour, complexion, menstrual
n and joint mobility, as well as promoting longevity.

right: butter, sesame oil, cheese and milk.

GRAINS

Grains divide into podded and unpodded types and include cereals,
legumes and seeds. Rice and buckwheat are considered cooling,
whereas barley and sesame are warming and vitality-boosting.

Clockwise, from top left: barley, millet, lentils and rice.

ETABLES AND HERBS

that grow in dry places have light and warming properties, while
from damp places are more heavy and cool in nature. Young leaves
ighter, more warming properties; older ones, heavier and cooling.

right: yam, onion, garlic and radishes.

MEATS

There are eight classes of meat and three types of animal: wild or
domestic, birds of prey and aquatic creatures. Fresh, raw meat is cooling, while sun-dried meat is warming and generates digestive fire.

Clockwise, from top left: beef, pork, sun-dried beef and lamb.

COOKED DISHES

Both rice and barley are
prominent, with the latter
favoured for its warming
qualities. Roasted barley
ground into flour (*tsampa*)
is a staple and is mixed
with tea into a porridge.

Left: Mo-mo *dumplings, a
traditional Tibetan cooked
dish, contain either meat or
vegetable fillings.*

HERBAL MEDICINE

The Tibetan materia medica is extensive, listing more than 1,000 plants, herbs and other ingredients. Traditionally, Tibet was known as the Land of Remedies, both because of the abundance of plants, minerals and gemstones that could be found there and due to the Tibetans' deep-rooted belief that everything in nature can be used medicinally provided its properties and actions are fully understood.

A Tibetan woman selling medicinal herbs at a street market. Knowledge of the potencies of the many medicinal plants that grow in Tibet's remote hills and valleys is extensive.

Tibetan medicines are made from plants and herbs (the flowers, stalks, leaves, fruits and grasses), trees (roots, bark, sap, leaves, flowers and fruits), types of earth (sand, saltpeter and bitumen), nectars (from grasses, trees and animals), metals, minerals and precious gemstones. Some medicines also contain animal and human products. Medicines are classified according to their taste, potency and the way in which they are combined together and then used to treat specific humoral imbalances.

The pharmacology of Tibet is based on six digestive and post-digestive tastes – sweet, sour, salty, bitter, hot and astringent – each made up of two elements (see page 56).

For example, the elements of earth and water, found in certain roots and aquatic plants, have a sweet taste. Each element also has its own properties – earth is heavy, dull and stable, whereas water is cool, fluid and supple. Wind disorders are treated with medications that are sweet, sour, salty and hot. Bile disorders are treated with bitter, sweet and astringent medicines, and phlegm disorders are dispelled by hot, sour and salty remedies.

In addition to taste and elemental make-up, medicinal ingredients are further classified according to four pairs of potencies: heavy/light, smooth or oily/rough, hot/cold and dull/sharp. Heavy and oily combinations are used to reduce wind, cool and dull properties decrease bile and those that are light, rough, hot and sharp clear phlegm. This concept of tastes and their correspondence with the elements and potencies was derived from Ayurveda (see pages 32–33).

The potencies subdivide into those that are tranquilizing and capable of restoring balance to the humour and those that are cathartic and used to expel a pathogenic humour. The tranquilizers are generally used first and consist of decoctions, powders, pills, pastes, medicinal butters, medicinal wine, concentrates, medicinal ash, gemstone or herbal compounds. The cathartic ones are used in the more advanced stages of disease as purgatives for expelling bile in the lower body, emetics for expelling phlegm in the upper body, nasal medications for expelling pathogenic factors in the nose, head and neck, mild and strong enemas for clearing the intestines and medicines for clearing the channels when all else has failed.

Other factors taken into account in the classification of ingredients is the place where they grow (sunny, shady, high mountain or plateau), the time when they are collected (day or night) and the manner in which they are preserved. Medicines are then compounded according to their tastes and potencies and many contain more than twenty primary and secondary ingredients to create overall balance. Mantras are recited during the collection and preparation of herbs, for this is believed to enhance their potency.

Rinchen ribu, or Precious Pills, wrapped in silk. To make the seven different types of pills, minerals and gems are first washed and crushed before being mixed with herbs and formed into round, dried medicinal pills.

PRECIOUS PILLS

Some Tibetan medicines contain prized metals and gems, including gold, silver, lapis lazuli, turquoise, quartz, pearls and coral, and are known as Precious Pills. These valuable ingredients were originally sourced from gem- and mineral-rich mountains in Tibet, or obtained in trade conducted with Mongolian, Chinese and Indian merchants. Copper and various types of iron ore are also occasionally used in the preparation of medicines.

Each mineral or gem is classified according to its properties and its effect on specific disorders. Gold is considered to be cooling and is used to increase longevity and to expel harmful spirits. Silver is thought to help to dry out pus from infected wounds. Copper and iron are used to relieve liver diseases. Extracts from fossils and stalactites are believed to repair bones, ligaments and tendons respectively. Certain toxic substances, such as arsenic and mercury, were once used in traditional formulations but are rare today.

EXTERNAL THERAPIES

If changes in diet and conduct and the use of remedies fail to produce a cure, then the Tibetan physician resorts to the use of external therapies. These may be gentle, strong or drastic. Gentle therapies include burning and inhaling incense to relieve wind disorders, the use of compresses for phlegm disorders and bathing with herbs to treat bile conditions. (Tibet has many hot springs suitable for such hydrotherapy treatment.) Massage using medicinal butters and oils, such as sesame oil, is also used in order to invigorate the

"Golden needle" therapy is a uniquely Tibetan technique. The doctor has arranged the ball of dried herbs on top of the needle and placed it on the crown of the patient's head where it has been lit.

burning of small amounts of dried herbs on or close to the patient's skin to provide heat. In China the herb *Artemisia vulgaris* is used (see pages 116–117), but in Tibet gerbera and other herbs, including nutmeg and ginger, are favoured. The dried moxa herb is rolled into a small cone and placed on one of more than seventy moxibustion points on the body. It is then lit and burned either just until heat is felt or right down to the skin. Moxibustion is ideal for treating cold and wind disorders, especially joint stiffness, fatigue and pallor, and mental imbalance.

body and reduce joint stiffness. Stronger forms of external therapy include blood-letting (although it is rarely used today), moxibustion, cupping and acupuncture. More radical external treatments, rarely used by physicians today, were cauterization – applied using a red-hot iron rod – and surgery.

Blood-letting, also widely used in Japan and China until recently, was frequently used in Tibet to treat bile and blood disorders. Three days before treatment, herbs would be given to the patient to purify the blood and separate the "good" and "bad" constituents. On the day of the therapy, tourniquets would be applied to isolate veins at any of more than seventy points suitable for blood-letting. The isolated vein would then be nicked with a small blood-letting knife and a little blood extracted. This procedure was often performed on patients suffering from fever or gout.

Moxibustion, cupping and acupuncture were brought to Tibet from China, but in Tibetan medicine interesting variations have been developed. Moxibustion consists of the

One distinctly Tibetan application of moxibustion is "golden needle" therapy, which is said to invigorate the body and restore nervous balance. A thick, gold needle is placed over the meeting point of the channels at the crown of the head. A ball of dried herbs is placed on the top of the needle and lit. As it burns, the needle heats up and heat is transferred into the point at the crown. It is not known how or where this treatment originated – it does not appear in the Tibetan medical texts, nor is it performed in precisely this manner in other Eastern medical traditions.

Cupping is believed to increase the circulation of blood and fluids in the skin and can provide dramatic relief for shoulder, back and joint pain. The treatment involves placing a lighted match or piece of paper inside a small copper bowl in order to burn up the oxygen and then immediately placing the cup onto the affected part of the patient's body. The cup will be held in place for some time by the resultant vacuum before it is released. Other cups may be placed

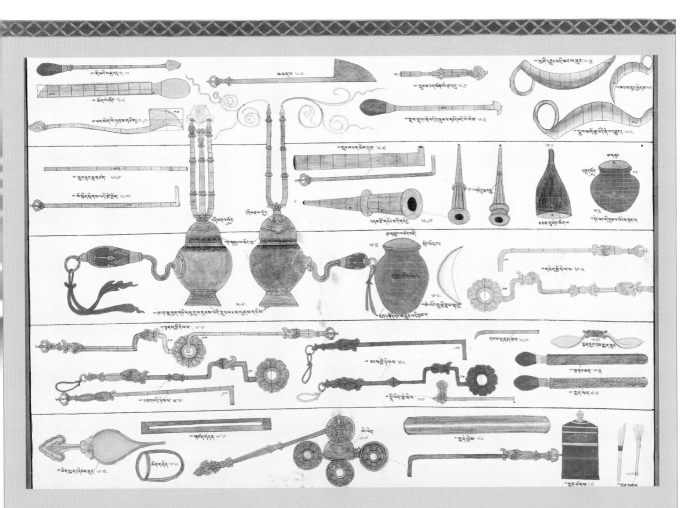

SURGERY IN TIBETAN MEDICINE

In early Tibetan medical practice, surgery was used, although only as a last resort. Ideas about surgery were probably brought from India, where surgical techniques were quite advanced (see pages 14–15), but met with only limited enthusiasm because of the Tibetan belief that cuts and incisions can damage the flow of vital force in the channels. It also lost favour after the mother of King Trisong Detsen died in the eighth century following major surgery.

However, many types of surgical instruments (above) were developed, especially for minor surgery. They included diagnostic instruments, used to locate swellings, piles and the presence of foreign bodies. Sometimes shaped like animals, pincers were used to perform extractions. Sharp tools were made for blood-letting and spoons were used to remove tumours, pus and collected fluid. Other implements were designed for clearing various bodily passages.

simultaneously. Cupping can be combined with blood-letting by making a small incision in the skin before putting the cup onto the body. This causes blood and pus to be drawn out of the skin into the cup.

Only a small amount of acupuncture is performed by Tibetan physicians, most of it having been learnt from Chinese acupuncturists, but a more limited number of points are used. Some Tibetan physicians, however, do use adjunct acupuncture therapies. One of the most commonly used is the "plum blossom hammer" – a small hammer with a head consisting of many little spikes – to stimulate circulation in the channels (see box, page 116).

EXERCISE, MEDITATION AND RITUAL

According to the principles of Tibetan medicine, physical exercise should be performed according to the season and the humoral balance of the individual. In spring, vigorous exercise is essential to dispel phlegm accumulated in the body over the winter. However, exercise should not be performed on an empty stomach, as this can stir up the wind humour in the body and lead to disease. Instead, nourishing food should be consumed and exercise should be integrated into daily life. In Tibet this takes the form of walking, running, horse-riding, kite-flying, prostrating before holy images and going on pilgrimages.

Over-exertion is seen as harmful, especially in summer, when exercise should be reduced due to the heat. In particular, care should be taken to maintain regular breathing – holding the breath or straining during exercise detracts from its benefits and can lead to heart problems.

In Tibetan healing it is believed that exercise can also affect the flow of subtle energy. Certain exercises combining posture, breathing and visualization, known as *kum nye*, have been devised in order to relax the body and promote the flow of subtle energy (see pages 84–85).

Meditation is also seen as a valuable healing tool, as it can promote feelings of relaxation and inner peace as well as help transform the negative emotional states that are

A simple, cross-legged position is comfortable and suitable for meditation. Placing a pillow under the buttocks will help to keep the back straight. Prayer beads are useful for counting mantra recitations.

linked to disease. It is especially useful in the healing of wind disorders, as it helps to calm the wind humour and still the mind. Meditation can also produce autonomic changes, affecting heart rate, respiratory function and so on, as shown in modern research trials where its use appears to speed up healing and helps to alleviate common ailments such as headaches.

Meditation practice typically requires a quiet place, good posture (comfortable but with a straight back), a relaxed, passive attitude of detachment and a point of focus. This point of focus may be an object, a visualization, the use of sacred sounds (mantras), prayers or sacred hand gestures (*mudras*). The recitation of healing mantras during meditation is thought to generate vibrations conducive to healing. The mantra of the Medicine Buddha is very commonly used, as is the best-known mantra from Tibet: *"Om mani padme hum"* ("O jewel in the lotus"). Many Tibetans also take the Medicine Buddha initiation in order to link closely with the healing deity. The *mudras* are used to convey symbolic messages and also to connect subtle energy channels in the body and stimulate awareness.

Objects used for meditation may be real, such as a religious statue or painting, or symbolic, such as sacred shapes (*yantras*) and designs (mandalas) (see box, page 53).

INITIATIONS AND PILGRIMAGE

Many of the most important physicians in the history of Tibetan medicine were saints, spiritual practitioners and religious scholars. This illustrates the close link between medicine and Buddhism and lends credence to the Tibetan concept of seeing one's physician as guru and guide. Because Buddhist practice is seen as the ultimate panacea, both the healthy and the sick are encouraged by their spiritual teachers and physicians to take part in religious rituals. These may be internal and personal – in the form of meditation, visualizations and the recitation of mantras – or external, such as taking initiation from accomplished teachers or undertaking pilgrimages.

In tantric practice it is not sufficient simply to read and perform rituals, they must first be transmitted by a qualified spiritual teacher who can confer empowerment by initiation, increasing the potency of the ritual. The ritual practice most associated with healing is known as "the Medicine Buddha empowerment", which most Tibetans endeavour to perform at least once in their life. This ritual involves several hours of visualization and recitation, during which the participant identifies with the Medicine Buddha and receives healing energy. Spontaneous healings are known to occur during this practice.

Pilgrimages are thought to generate merit for both the pilgrim and all sentient beings and are performed regularly. Favourite destinations in Tibet are Mount Kailash, the holy mountain (known to Tibetans as Kang Rinpoche, the Great Ice Jewel), and the Potala Palace, the former seat of His Holiness the Dalai Lama. Pilgrims are willing to endure extreme hardships, often walking vast distances. Some pilgrims perform full-length prostrations at regular intervals along their route or around the sacred site. During the pilgrimage many mantras and prayers are said and it is thought that a close connection can be formed with the relevant deity.

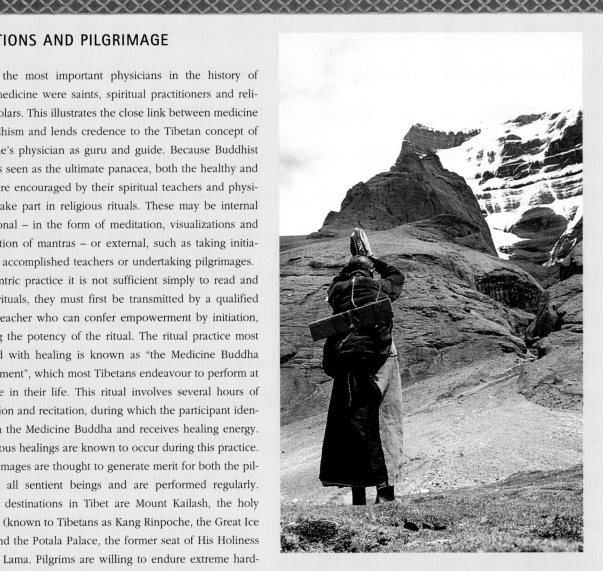

Pilgrim prostrating in the foothills of Mount Kailash, the most sacred mountain in Tibet. Any pilgrim who is physically unable to undertake a pilgrimage can either be carried or must pray and enact rituals at home instead. Generating merit is a way of ensuring good health and longevity.

Visualizations for healing often centre on the Medicine Buddha – the patient may imagine healing rays emanating from the Buddha, or from the physician as his representative, into the affected part of the body.

Meditation can be combined with exercise by synchronizing a mantra and breathing with movements, such as steps taken while running or walking or with each bend of a prostration. In tantric meditation practices the aim is to transform oneself into the body, mind and speech of the Buddha and other deities, first through visualization and then through identification. Ultimately this is not only for one's own benefit but for the benefit of all sentient beings.

THE SUBTLE BODY

The channels, winds and essences of the subtle body (see page 57) can be brought under conscious control and purified through the practice of Tibetan yoga – that is, through breathing exercises, meditation practice, visualization, mantra recitation and subtle energy exercises (see also *kum nye*, right).

There are said to be 72,000, or more, subtle energy channels of the body that correspond with, but are not the same as, the nervous and venous systems. The three main ones are the central channel or "vein" (*dhuma*), the right channel (*ro-ma*) and the left channel (*rkyang-ma*). (These correspond to the *sushumna nadi* and the *ida* and *pingala* channels in Ayurveda – see box, page 21.)

The "vein" is said to be thin, straight, hollow, luminous and blue in colour. It corresponds with, but is not the same as, the spine. It runs from the top of the head through the body to a point level with four finger-widths below the navel. The side channels are thinner than the central one but also hollow and luminous. The right one is red in colour (representing the feminine and menstrual blood) while the left is white (representing the masculine and semen).

Certain tantric practices from Vajrayana Buddhism (see page 53) are thought to enable vital energy to be collected in the side channels and dissolved into the central channel leading to a state of pure consciousness totally free from mental negativity. The side channels criss-cross the central one and their meeting points are energy centres – the *khor-lo* (*chakra* in Sanskrit). The point where all three channels meet, below the navel, is the seat of the esoteric *gtum-mo* fire.

In the Tibetan system there are six major *chakras* (as opposed to the seven described in India; see box, page 21). Most visualizations and meditations concentrate on just three *chakras* – the brow (representing the Buddha's body), the throat (His speech) and heart (His mind) – or on five *chakras* where the fourth is the navel *chakra* and the fifth the root *chakra* (the genitals). The crown *chakra*, at the top of the head, is the sixth and is often counted as one "head" *chakra* in combination with the brow *chakra*.

KUM NYE EXERCISES

Place the right arm over the left, with palms on the shoulders and the right leg over the left with feet adjacent. Hold it for a moment, breathing slowly and deeply, then reverse the position. Note the sensations and the flow of energy on each side. This posture balances body energy and brain function.

In addition to mantras, subtle body functioning can be affected by physical treatments such as acupuncture and massage. The medical texts describe a form of massage known as *kum nye* (pronounced "koom nyay"), which literally means "ointment massage" but which encompasses self-massage and relaxation techniques designed to work on both the physical and subtle bodies. But the textual references are sparse and *kum nye* has been passed down mainly as an oral tradition and taught directly by physicians to their patients. For this reason, it has been open to modern interpretation. Tarthang Tulku, the son of a lama physician, now living in the United States, has developed many exercises based on *kum nye* principles taught to him as a child. Some Tibetan physicians have taught *kum nye* to their Western patients and students and in this way the tradition has begun to spread outside Tibet. The exercises use breathing, relaxation and mental concentration to help balance the humours in the physical body and thereby clear blockages in the subtle energy channels. The upright or seated postures involve little movement, as awareness is focused on subtle energy flow. Regular practice is said to promote inner radiance and mental calm.

Begin this two-stage exercise by holding the arms out to the sides. Focus on the heart centre, imagining your energy is radiating out and along the arms. Then draw the arms in and lightly touch the heart centre. Repeat, radiating energy out and then drawing it into the body. Note the sensations balancing the heart centre.

REJUVENATION AND LONGEVITY

In the Tibetan tradition, the desire to extend longevity is based less on the simple desire to live longer than on the recognition that human life is a precious chance to undergo spiritual development that should not be wasted – a longer life gives more opportunities for spiritual practice and the accumulation of merit.

The speed of the aging process is linked to impurities of body and mind – that is, imbalances of the humours and negative emotions, mental stress and exhaustion. To combat this, Tibetan medicine advises that the person alters their lifestyle and behaviour (see pages 74–75), changes their diet and balances the humours (see pages 76–77), relaxes the body and mind (see pages 82–85) and focuses all the energies on cultivating merit through virtuous behaviour.

In addition, certain medicinal elixirs of rejuvenation have been formulated that are designed to restore youthful appearance, increase vigour and extend life-span. These elixirs are said to be particularly effective for those aged over sixty. Before taking an elixir, the patient should purify his or her diet, cleanse the body with purgatives, bathing and oil massages, abstain from sex and vigorous activity, spend time in meditation and make offerings to their favourite deities. The elixir should then be taken at dawn on an empty stomach on an auspicious day that is also the

An assortment of gems used in Tibetan healing and more commonly ground down and included in various elixirs or pills.

first day of a waxing moon cycle. Once effects such as new hair growth, restoration of hair colour, increased lustre of the skin and increased vitality are observed, the treatment is regarded as successful and is discontinued.

The greatest of these medicinal elixirs is made up of minerals, gems, honey, molasses, aged garlic, plant nectars, types of bitumen and stimulant herbs, which include ephedra and tansy. A "lesser elixir" is made from limestone ash, butter, nectars, bitumens, honey and molasses, while inferior remedies are simply made from various plants and minerals.

Even more important than the actual ingredients is the consecration of the remedies. This is done by the physician who, while compounding the ingredients, visualizes deities from the families of Buddhas or Amitayus, the Buddha of longevity, and other deities delighting in sexual union. This union of the deities is believed to produce the subtle equivalents of seminal fluids combined with cosmic elements and essences from different realms to produce a nectar of immortality. The deities are said to merge into the nectar, which is transformed into light and in this form passes directly into the medicine.

Tibetan medicine also incorporates the practice of "inner" alchemy – that is, the transformation of the elements of the body and the energy in the subtle channels and the

A UNION OF BLISSFULNESS

In Tibetan medicine, sexual health is clearly linked to physical, mental and spiritual health. On a mundane level, sexual ability is seen as important for procreation, physical pleasure, vitality and vigour. On a higher level the bliss of sexual union, whether real or sublimated as in the case of celibates, is seen as a vital tool for accessing higher states of consciousness.

In medicine the elements, humours and nutritive essences of the body make up the white (male) and red (female) seeds that form the essence of the reproductive fluids. Thus techniques for restoring sexual potency in men and ensuring fertility in women concentrate on restoring these essences by means of balancing the humours, purifying the body and harnessing the mind.

To improve virility, a male patient is advised first to purify his body and then build up his strength with nutritious foods. He should then carefully select a young and attractive female, spend time romancing her and engaging in foreplay in beautiful surroundings. Finally, he can make use of medicines which enhance potency and act as aphrodisiacs.

For women, the medical focus is on fertility rather than sexual enjoyment. Infertility is seen as a result of humoral disorder, post-natal retention of placenta, or amenorrhea (absence of periods) due to contraceptive medicines, sterility or spirit possession. Treatment involves herbal medicine, prayers and rituals.

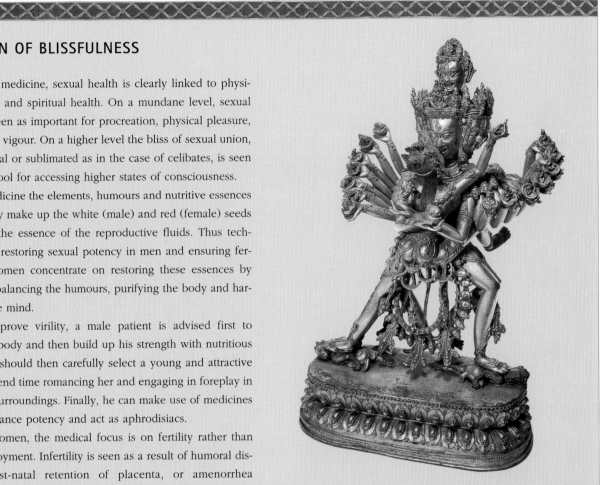

A bronze gilded statuette of the powerful god Yidam Hevajra (Eternal Thunderbolt) in yab-yum *or sexual embrace with his consort who symbolizes wisdom.*

psychic centres into spiritual essences. These essences can be used not only to restore health and extend life-span but also to transform spiritual consciousness.

Certain practices aim to stimulate the heart centre, in which the life-essence of the body is said to reside. From this centre there is said to be a "vein" of transcendental consciousness that can then be accessed and vitalized, leading to the creation of a "rainbow light" body and a state of enlightened awareness and bliss. It is at this point that body, mind and spirit become truly integrated. Precious gems and jewels are also used to adjust the vibrations of the subtle body and energy centres.

According to the *rGyud-bzhi* (see box, page 51), one of the most potent forms of healing and rejuvenating is to constantly visualize oneself as the Medicine Buddha, to regularly recite his healing mantra and to visualize his rays of healing light entering one's body. These rays can be directed at a diseased organ or area, or can be used to bathe the body as a whole. This practice is said to generate tremendous healing power both for self-healing and for healing others. The Medicine Buddha symbolizes the attainment of *buddha* nature – the ultimate aim of all healing and spiritual practice. By identifying with the Medicine Buddha one obtains the means to recognize one's own *buddha* nature.

C H I N A

The origins of Chinese medicine date back more than 2,000 years. Extensive early literature has survived and the texts extol the wisdom of following a moderate and balanced lifestyle in order to promote good health.

The energy of the universe is conceptualized as a creative interplay between two mutually dependent forces – *yin* and *yang* – and the body is thought to be a microcosmic representation of this. Vital energy (*qi*, pronounced "chee") is described as flowing in the body via a network of channels, called the meridians, that contain active points used for both diagnosis and treatment. An abundant and free flow of *qi* is the key to the maintenance of health and the prevention of disease.

Treatment modalities include acupuncture, moxibustion, massage and herbal medicine. The main emphasis is on self-care through good diet and a wide variety of supporting approaches. Traditional Chinese Medicine has survived many upheavals at home and is now taught and practised worldwide.

A tiled dragon frieze in Beijing, China's capital city and home to the imperial Forbidden City, once occupied by the emperor of China who sat upon the Dragon Throne. In addition to being the most important of all imperial symbols, dragons were associated with fertility and strength, and were an embodiment of the yang *principle.*

CHAPTER 9

THE ORIGINS AND HISTORY OF CHINESE MEDICINE

China, like Tibet (see pages 48–51), has a blend of myth and fact to account for its system of medicine. Legendary Chinese emperors are thought to have begun the tradition of combining a universal philosophy of life with practical applications for maintaining health, alleviating disease and promoting longevity.

Philosophy and religion have long had close links with Chinese medicine, and the concept of living in harmony with the laws of the universe by following the path of Dao (see pages 92–93) is seen as all important. Derived from Chinese agrarian culture, which sought to find a formal expression of its dependence on nature, Daoism was seen as a way of maintaining harmony between heaven and earth. The interdependent creative forces that make up the physical universe were described as *yin* and *yang* (see pages 92–93). Supernatural powers were also seen to be the origin of the concept of five basic phases or elements. This concept was used to describe and comprehend changes in both the physical world and the human body (see pages 94–95). Both *yin* and *yang* and the Five Phases, as they became known, were believed to be subject to certain rules and Daoism proposes that living according to these laws can ensure longevity and good health. These ideas have been retained in the theoretical principles of Traditional Chinese Medicine to the present day. Western medical practice was formally adopted in China in the twentieth century, but ancient knowledge has survived alongside it.

LEGENDARY EMPERORS AND ANCIENT TEXTS

The earliest Chinese medical knowledge dates back to two ancient emperors, Shen nong and Huang di. According to legend, the latter – also known as the Yellow Emperor – lived 2697–2597BCE. Both were reputed to have great wisdom, medical knowledge and even supernatural powers. Some modern scholars regard these emperors as mythical figures.

Shen nong is held to be the "father of agriculture and herbal medicine". Portraits always show him dressed in leaves and chewing or holding medicinal plants. It is said that he tasted every herb in order to determine its medical function and that he was responsible for the first comprehensive Chinese materia medica. Huang di is thought of as the "father of medicine" and was reputed to be the author of one of the most important medical texts, the *Huang di Nei jing (The Yellow Emperor's Inner Canon)*.

Although the *Huang di Nei jing, or Nei jing*, has been dated to the first century BCE, it refers to knowledge that is considered to be much older and it is now agreed that it is a compilation of a number of texts accumulated over a period of time. The *Nei jing* has been revised and adapted several times over the centuries and, because of the ambiguities of the wording, has given rise to literally hundreds of commentaries and interpretations.

Written in the form of questions and answers between the Yellow Emperor and one of his ministers, Qi Bo, the *Nei jing* includes philosophical ideas, the concepts of the Dao, *yin* and *yang*, and the Five Phases, the origins of disease,

Ivory figurines of the legendary emperors Huang di (left) and Shen nong (right), who introduced to China knowledge of medicine, agriculture and healing and the secret of eternal life.

methods of treatment – especially acupuncture and moxibustion – and lifestyle recommendations. It is such an important text that it still forms the basis of Traditional Chinese Medicine practices. Other important early texts also exist. The *Nan jing (The Classic of Difficult Issues)*, dated to the second century CE, explains difficult passages from the *Nei jing*. The *Shang han lun (Treatise on Cold Damage Disorders)* concerns the symptoms and herbal treatment of febrile diseases. The earliest complete text of herbal remedies, the *Shen nong ben cao jing, (Shen Nong's Materia Medica Canon)*, was reconstituted c.500CE.

Surgery and anesthesia are said to have been practised as early as the second century CE by the famous physician, Hua Tuo. Both, however, fell into disuse due to a preference for herbal medicine and acupuncture.

Throughout the history of Chinese medicine, there have been many strands of practice and treatment. Most doctors learned medicine as their family trade and worked rurally, though there were also tutored physicians who practised at the imperial court or for high-ranking families. In the seventeenth century, Western medicine was introduced by Jesuit missionaries and in the centuries that followed, Western hospitals and clinical training institutions were set up. However, the traditional skills were still needed to provide care for much of the population and modern-day politicians have been keen to preserve this important and clinically effective part of China's heritage.

THE UNIVERSAL PRINCIPLES

According to Daoist belief, the universe exists as a unified whole, symbolized by a circle, which is made up of two great opposing yet interdependent creative forces known as *yin* and *yang*. *Yin* characteristics are passive, contracting, cold, dark, soft and feminine, whereas *yang* characteristics are active, expanding, hot, bright, hard and masculine. All aspects of the universe, including all the material things in it, can be described in terms of these two forces: from the environment and natural phenomena (plants, trees, the weather, and so on) to the physical body and its constituents – even the human mind and emotions.

Yin and *yang* are mutually interdependent and each is constantly in a state of change. For example, day (*yang*) becomes night (*yin*), which again passes into a new day (*yang*). *Yin* and *yang* can thus be seen as complementary opposites that interact as agents of change to make up the unified whole – in this case, the cycle of day and night.

Every phenomenon or thing can be divided, subdivided and divided further still according to the interplay of *yin* and *yang*. The outside of the human body may be seen as *yang* and the inside as *yin*, but it can be subdivided as the front of the body (*yin*) and the back of the body (*yang*), and the upper body (*yang*) and the lower body (*yin*). Similarly, each of the body's inner organs may be described as *yin* or *yang*, according to its properties and function. This theory is used to explain not only the working of the body itself but also the course of disease and the appropriate treatment for the malady.

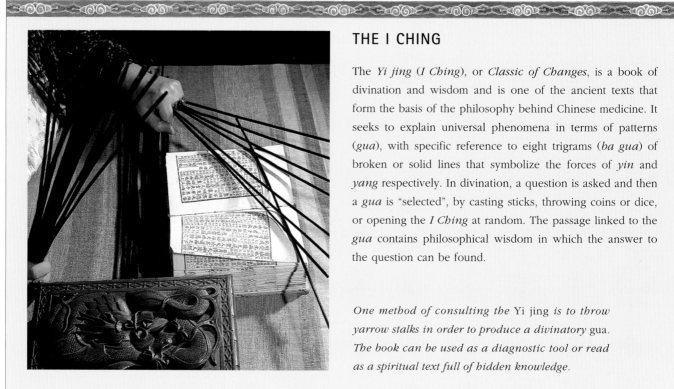

THE I CHING

The *Yi jing* (*I Ching*), or *Classic of Changes*, is a book of divination and wisdom and is one of the ancient texts that form the basis of the philosophy behind Chinese medicine. It seeks to explain universal phenomena in terms of patterns (*gua*), with specific reference to eight trigrams (*ba gua*) of broken or solid lines that symbolize the forces of *yin* and *yang* respectively. In divination, a question is asked and then a *gua* is "selected", by casting sticks, throwing coins or dice, or opening the *I Ching* at random. The passage linked to the *gua* contains philosophical wisdom in which the answer to the question can be found.

One method of consulting the Yi jing *is to throw yarrow stalks in order to produce a divinatory* gua. *The book can be used as a diagnostic tool or read as a spiritual text full of hidden knowledge.*

As *yin* and *yang* are constantly in a state of flux they affect one another – too much of one will produce the other. For example, salt is considered *yang* because of its power to contract and shrink, as demonstrated by its water-retentive effect in the body. An over-consumption of salt, however, affects the tissues and heart function and will eventually cause the body to enter a weakened *yin* state. Sugar, on the other hand, is considered *yin* because of its sweetness and dissipating properties, yet an excessive sugar intake can create an imbalance in the blood which can produce hyperactivity and aggression, which is a *yang* state.

In ancient Chinese thought, the human body was often conceived as the universe in microcosmic form. Some Daoist drawings show the body as a landscape in which hills, valleys, lakes and peaks are used to represent body structure and the vital inner organs, which are classified according to their *yin* and *yang* qualities. This "country" – the human body – is ruled by a "regent" (the heart) assisted by various "ministers" (the other inner organs); he communicates with the "country" via a network of channels (the blood vessels, nerve pathways and meridians, see pages 98–99). The smooth running of the "country" may be influenced by external, or pathogenic,

An amulet adorned with the eight trigrams (ba gua), representing the balanced energies of nature, and the yin *and* yang *symbols (in the centre). At the top is the trigram for heaven, three solid lines epitomizing* yang; *at the bottom is the trigram for earth, with three broken lines epitomizing* yin.

factors (see pages 100–101) or by the existence of "disharmony" among the inner organs and their important connecting channels.

As in the function of systems elsewhere in the universe, the forces of *yin* and *yang* within the body must work in harmony for there to be internal balance and good health. The "regent" must possess wisdom and insight and be able to coordinate the "ministers" so that they can all work together effectively. The Chinese concept of the heart encompasses not only the physical heart, but also the home of the spirit and consciousness. Thus, for the body to function to optimum effect, the mind must be illuminated. In this way, it is believed that inner alchemy can be achieved and a long life can be cultivated – a process known as *yang sheng* (see pages 122–123).

The all-pervasive energy that powers the universe is known as *qi* (or *ch'i*). It suffuses every living thing – and even non-organic matter – and changes its qualities according to the interplay of *yin* and *yang*. In the human body, the transformations and the flow of *qi* affect every stage of growth and development from conception – when it aggregates to form the body – and birth, through to death – when it dissipates. The concept of *qi* is central to Chinese culture, language and medicine (see pages 97–99).

THE FIVE PHASES

The theory of the Five Phases, also known as the Five Elements, draws on observations of the world and was developed, like the theory of *yin* and *yang*, as a way of explaining the relationships between all natural phenomena and between humans and their environment. The Five Phases is believed to be Chinese in origin, as it is described in detail in the ancient Chinese text, the *Nei jing* (see page 91). The five elements are wood, fire, earth, metal and water. They are more accurately called "phases" since they describe changes and relationships within and between living things rather than actual substances or elements. Their relationships may be, among others, productive, supportive, nourishing and promoting, like that of a mother to a child, or counteractive, inhibiting and destructive, like an enemy attacking its foe. In their cycle of production (see diagram, below), wood feeds fire, ash from fire nourishes the earth, the earth provides the constituents from which precious metals are formed, metals melt to form or exude liquids (water), while water enables trees and plants to grow. In their destructive cycle wood (through roots, for example) can break up earth, earth absorbs water, water extinguishes fire, fire melts metal and metal cuts wood.

The theory of the Five Phases helps to explain the mutually productive, supportive and potentially destructive

THE CYCLE OF THE PHASES

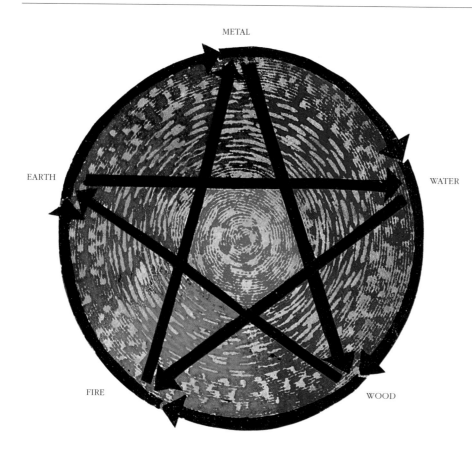

All life results from the interaction of the Five Phases, or wu xing. *The five are thought to promote and control one another in a dynamic and unending cycle of creation (the external arrows) and destruction (internal arrows). Water supports wood but quenches fire, and so on. Early Chinese philosophers felt that the interaction of* yin *and* yang *was the very process of life itself, and that the building blocks of the universe were patterned by these interactions and were themselves aspects of* yin *and* yang *fluctuation. History and the universe can therefore be explained as a cycle of the Five Phases or Elements. Humans, too, through their* qi *can have an imbalance of these elemental constituents: too little water, for example, will cause dry skin and kidney ailments.*

THE FIVE PHASES SYSTEM OF CORRESPONDENCES

The organization of the Five Phases into a system of correspondences can provide the practitioner with vital clues for diagnosis. The hue of a person's complexion, their food preferences and taste in the mouth, the time of year in which their disease manifested or worsened, and so on, are all taken into account. For example, a liver disorder – which may be triggered in spring – is sometimes characterized by eye problems, aching tendons, angry outbursts, a sour taste in the mouth and a preference for sour foods, a yellow/green hue to the skin and over-sensitivity to draughts and wind.

THE FIVE PHASES	THE HUMAN BODY					NATURE					
	YIN (ZANG ORGANS)	YANG (FU ORGANS)	FIVE SENSE ORGANS	FIVE TISSUES	EMOTIONS	SEASONS	ENVIRONMENTAL FACTORS	GROWTH AND DEVELOPMENT	COLOURS	TASTES	ORIENTATION
WOOD	Liver	Gall bladder	Eyes	Tendons	Anger	Spring	Wind	Germination (birth)	Green	Sour	East
FIRE	Heart	Small intestine	Tongue	Vessels	Joy	Summer	Heat	Growth	Red	Bitter	South
EARTH	Spleen	Stomach	Mouth	Muscles	Worry	Late summer	Dampness	Transformation	Yellow	Sweet	Middle
METAL	Lungs	Large intestine	Nose	Skin and hair	Grief and sorrow	Autumn	Dryness	Reaping (decline)	White	Pungent	West
WATER	Kidneys	Urinary bladder	Ears	Bones	Fright and fear	Winter	Cold	Storing (rebirth)	Black	Salty	North

relationships between the inner organs of the human body. The organs are paired according to their *yin* or *yang* characteristics (see also pages 98–99), and each pair is ascribed a phase or element. Their relationships are then described according to the cycle of the Five Phases. For example, the mother–child relationship between the different organs is the same as that of the productive cycle of the Five Phases: thus the liver is the mother, or nourisher, of the heart, the heart the mother of the spleen, the spleen the mother of the lungs, the lungs the mother of the kidneys and the kidneys the mother of the liver, which gives nourishment to the heart and receives nourishment from the kidneys.

These relationships form the basis for both diagnosis and treatment. For example, if a person is displaying symptoms associated with liver dysfunction, the diagnosis will include an assessment of kidney and heart function in order to determine whether the disorder originates in the liver itself, has been caused by an imbalance in the kidneys or is affecting heart function. On the basis of this analysis, treatment may be directed at the kidney and/or heart as well as, or instead of, the liver.

The Five Phases have correspondences both inside and outside the body: within, they are used to classify the vital organs, sense organs, body tissues and even emotions; outside, in the natural world, seasons, climate or environmental factors, stages of growth and development, colours, tastes and orientations may all be understood in terms of the relationships between the Five Phases (see box, above).

When the elements act in harmony with one another the body is healthy; when one or the other element predominates, however, imbalance occurs and eventually disease results. By diagnosing and treating according to the theory of the Five Phases, disease can be prevented from spreading to other parts of the body and may be cured.

CHAPTER 10

CONCEPTS OF THE BODY AND DISEASE

In Daoist thought, the body's physical, mental and spiritual health are seen as being integrally connected. It is considered important to live a life of moderation and balance in harmony with the seasons and prevailing conditions. These concepts have been absorbed into medical theory and practice.

In Traditional Chinese Medicine, the body is described in terms of twelve vital organs linked via channels, or meridians (see pages 98–99), which contain hundreds of points at which the health of the organs can be gauged.

Traditional Chinese understanding of the organs was based on observation of their living function, and although modern texts have been adapted to incorporate Western medical anatomy, certain concepts remain exclusive to China; one such is that of the triple burner, which relates to the functions and qualities of the organs in the three sections of the torso – upper, middle and lower (see pages 98–99).

The Three Treasures – *qi* (energy), *jing* (essence) and *shen* (spirit) – form the basis of both physical function and alchemical transformation. *Qi* flows through the channels to vitalize the organs, but it also affects *jing* and *shen* and thereby consciousness. If the *qi* is blocked, both physical and mental illness can result. Disease may also be caused by external factors, such as extreme heat or cold, which disrupt bodily functions, or by having an irregular lifestyle rather than a nourished body regularly regenerated through exercise (see pages 124–125).

QI, BLOOD AND FLUIDS

The character for *qi* (pronounced "chee" and sometimes written as *ch'i*) has two parts. The lower part represents rice, a nutritive energy from the earth, while the upper depicts flow and water's transformation into vapour; the character thus encompasses both that with form (earth) and that without (the heavenly and the cosmic) and can represent the union of the heavenly and earthly. This paradox hints at the indefinable nature of *qi* – it is both substance and non-substance, present yet moving, real yet elusive. It can be transformed and it can cause transformation.

There are thought to be many types of *qi* in the body, some of which appear to be material and others which can be grasped more easily in terms of function. "Congenital *qi*" (*yuan qi*), also known as "source *qi*", is inherited from parents; it determines the individual's vitality and life-span, as well as his or her reproductive capacities. "Nutritive *qi*" (*ying qi*), which is *yin* in nature, is obtained from digested food and is essential for nourishing the body. It is paired with "defensive *qi*" (*wei qi*), with *yang* aspects, which protects the body from the harmful external pathogens that can trigger disease. "Gathering *qi*" (*zong qi*) collects in the chest and encompasses the various *qi* inside the body and the *qi* obtained through breathing.

Each organ also has its own *qi*, sourced from "congenital *qi*" and the *qi* from digestion and respiration, which regulates its function. If an organ is "*qi* deficient" it is weak and functions poorly – spleen *qi* deficiency, for example, leads to indigestion and diarrhea. On the other hand, an excess of *qi* causes its own problems – *qi* repletion in the liver leads to intense heat in the body, irritability and anger.

Qi is closely related to other body fluids. The most important of these is *xue*, which is generally translated as "blood" but has a wider meaning than that. *Xue* comprises "nutritive *qi*" and a transformation of the essences in the kidneys that also produce bone marrow and all other body tissues and fluids. *Xue* circulates via the veins and arteries, nourishing the tissues and organs. Its relationship with *qi* is interdependent: *qi* plays a role in *xue*'s formation and circulation, while *xue* affects the amount and flow of bodily *qi*. Medical texts also mention other body fluids (*jin ye*): thin, clear ones such as sweat and tears, known as *jin*, or "dews", moisten the skin and nourish the muscles; thicker ones known as *ye*, or "juices", maintain joints and brain functions.

DIFFERENT TYPES OF QI

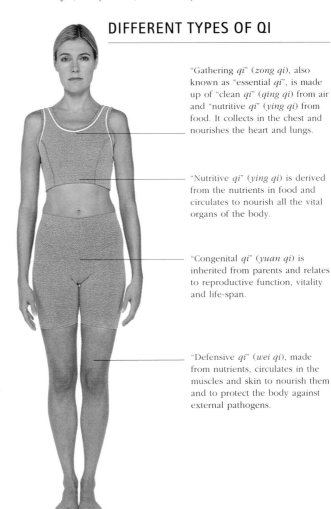

"Gathering *qi*" (*zong qi*), also known as "essential *qi*", is made up of "clean *qi*" (*qing qi*) from air and "nutritive *qi*" (*ying qi*) from food. It collects in the chest and nourishes the heart and lungs.

"Nutritive *qi*" (*ying qi*) is derived from the nutrients in food and circulates to nourish all the vital organs of the body.

"Congenital *qi*" (*yuan qi*) is inherited from parents and relates to reproductive function, vitality and life-span.

"Defensive *qi*" (*wei qi*), made from nutrients, circulates in the muscles and skin to nourish them and to protect the body against external pathogens.

THE ORGANS AND CHANNELS

The Chinese recognize twelve main organs of the body. These are divided into two principal "types" according to their function. "Solid organs" – the lungs, spleen, heart, kidneys and liver (also known as the *zang* organs) – create and store vital essences and fluids and are *yin* in nature. The sixth *zang* "organ" is the pericardium. "Hollow organs" – the stomach, small and large intestines, gall bladder, urinary bladder and triple burner (also known as the *fu* organs) – are responsible for receiving and transforming nutrients and excreting waste matter and are considered more *yang*. The sixth *fu* "organ" – the triple burner (*san jiao*) – maintains the balance between the upper, middle and lower parts of the body and relates to circulation, temperature regulation and sexual function.

Traditional Chinese Medicine describes not only the anatomy of each of these *zang* and *fu* organs, but also their close working relationships with one another. They are further subdivided into the *yin* and *yang* pairs of organs that

THE MERIDIAN SYSTEM OF ENERGY CHANNELS

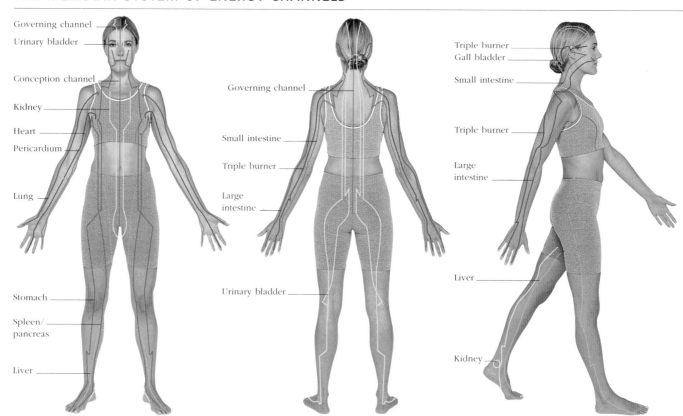

■ The governing and conception channels

■ The lungs (*yin*) and the large intestine (*yang*) channels
■ The spleen (*yin*) and the stomach (*yang*) channels

■ The heart (*yin*) and the small intestine (*yang*) channels
□ The kidneys (*yin*) and the urinary bladder (*yang*) channels
■ The pericardium (*yin*) and the triple burner (*yang*) channels
□ The liver (*yin*) and the gall bladder (*yang*) channels

work synergistically to ensure smooth body functions (see box, page 95). The body's organs are seen in a much wider sense than in the West. For example, the heart is not simply related to blood and blood circulation around the body – it also houses the mind and consciousness, controls mental function and emotional health, regulates sleep and dreams, affects the quality of the complexion and is mirrored in the colour, shape and agility of the tongue.

There is also an emphasis on the essences that are vital to growth and healthy development. The *fu* organs take up "nutritive essences" from food and these are combined with "constitutional essence", known as *jing*, which is derived from one's parents (and ancestors) and stored in the kidneys. *Jing* governs vitality and longevity and should be preserved rather than depleted through over-work, exhaustion or sexual excess.

The organs also house "spirit" or *shen*, referring to both consciousness and spirit entities. The second- or third-century CE Daoist book the *Huang ting jing* (*The Canon of the Yellow Court*) describes the body as being full of *shen* that lives in all the main organs and energy centres and influences their workings. *Shen* also enables a person to think clearly and use the power of the mind to attain higher mental states. *Shen* must be monitored as it can be inadvertently released by incorrect acupuncture or certain spiritual practices which can result in disturbance or even death.

Each organ is connected to an energetic pathway known as a channel or meridian. Although the channels are invisible, modern research has shown them to be electrical pathways located deep within the skin tissue. Traditional medical charts depict the twelve major channels as precise pathways that course the body from head to toe, connecting with the inner organs. The channels carry *qi* to each of the body's organs and modern researchers have been able to measure the flow and distribution of *qi* at various points (acupoints) along each meridian pathway. Stimulating or releasing *qi* at the acupoints is the basis of acupuncture treatment (see pages 114–115).

EIGHT "EXTRAORDINARY CHANNELS"

In addition to the twelve major channels there are eight "extraordinary channels", the *qi jing ba mai*, which help to regulate the circulation of *qi*. They also have their own functions that are said to relate to the body's formative energies acquired at conception and nourished during growth and development.

Three channels – the "conception" (*ren mai*), "governing" (*du mai*) and "penetrating" or "core" (*chong mai*) channels – originate in the lower torso and connect with two great energy sources

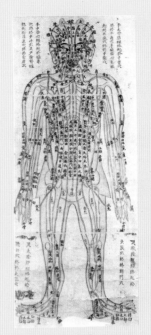

An ancient chart detailing the body's multiple energy channels for qi *circulation.*

– the *ming men* and the *dan tian*. The *ming men* is a gateway of moving energy between the kidneys, and is regarded as the *tai ji*, or centre, of the body from which all *yin* and *yang* originate. The *dan tian* is located in the lower abdomen.

The conception and governing channels, which run along the front and back midlines of the body, are the repository and regulators of all the *yin* and *yang qi* in the body. The penetrating channel, which runs through the middle of the trunk, links these two together and is sometimes referred to as the "sea of blood".

The girdle channel (*dai mai*) runs around the waist, uniting the vertical paths of the primary channels and their *yin* and *yang* functions. The other four channels – the *yang*-heel (*yang qiao*), *yin*-heel (*yin qiao*), *yang*-linking (*yang wei*) and *yin*-linking (*yin wei*) – begin in the feet or lower leg and run up the body's sides to link at the head. Link points are held to be particularly effective treatment points for various disorders. They also connect with the body's subtle energy centres.

HARMONY AND DISHARMONY

At the root of all harmony and disharmony in the body, mind and spirit are the forces of *yin* and *yang*. A healthy individual is seen as one who lives in harmony with the universe and nature's seasons, and who balances *yin* and *yang* in his or her diet, activities and lifestyle. Such a person has a calm mind and an energetic body.

It is thought that if *yin* and *yang* are allowed to become imbalanced then the inevitable result is disease. The causes of such an imbalance may be internal or external and disease is precipitated by a disturbance in the flow and functions of *qi*, blood and/or body fluids.

Internal causes of imbalance are often related to the individual's diet and may be triggered by excessive eating or drinking, poor or irregular eating habits, or the consumption of inappropriate foods. Other internal causes include over-exertion, over-work, mental strain, emotional imbalance and excessive sexual activity. External causes, other than those due to injuries or traumas caused by burns, stings or bites, are due to various environmental forces.

Chinese medicine classifies six major pathogenic factors (*liu yin*) that are environmental triggers for disease. These are wind (*feng*), cold (*han*), heat (*shu*), fire (*huo*), dampness (*shi*) and dryness (*zao*). Wind, heat and fire are generally *yang* pathogenic factors, while cold is a *yin* pathogenic factor and dryness and dampness can manifest as either *yin* or *yang*. As with all aspects of *yin* and *yang*, these factors are relative and can easily transform into their opposites. For example, if untreated, a cold, damp *yin* condition may develop into a hot, painful *yang* condition – this happens if joints that are stiff and aching from sitting on cold ground later become inflamed and swollen. These pathogenic factors cause imbalances of *yin* and *yang* in the body, either if they are experienced in excess or if the body is so weak that it cannot withstand their influence.

THE SIX MAJOR EXTERNAL CAUSES OF ILLNESS
Environmental pathogenic factors and disease

PREDOMINANTLY YIN	PREDOMINANTLY YANG
Cold (*han*) diseases occur in winter and are triggered by cold weather, inadequate clothing and exposure to cold after sweating. Symptoms are colds, chills and diarrhea.	Wind (*feng*) is most prominent in spring. Wind diseases occur after exposure to draughts and breezy weather. Wind attacks the upper body and causes colds, stiffness and transient joint pain.
Dryness (*zao*) diseases occur in autumnal weather when it is dry and indoor heating begins to be used. Symptoms are dry coughs, dry skin and sore throats.	Heat (*shu*) diseases occur in the summer due to an over-exposure to the sun or overheating. Fever, excessive sweating and mental delirium result.
Dampness (*shi*) diseases occur in the rainy season and are due to frequent drenching and exposure to water. Symptoms are lethargy, vomiting and rheumatism.	Fire (*huo*) diseases are the most severe type of heat disturbance. Symptoms are skin infections, boils, convulsions and even coma. The heat can also affect the mind.

Wind is seen as one of the major pathogenic causes of disease. External exposure to winds or draughts can disturb the body's natural balance of *yin* and *yang*, causing sudden symptoms such as headaches, joint pain or even a stroke. Wind interacts easily with the other pathogenic factors. A problem caused by a combination of wind and cold, for example, is mostly characterized by shivering, chills and colds. Disturbance caused by wind and heat produces symptoms of fever and thirst. A combination of wind and fire factors leads to severe heat symptoms, such as boils or abscesses. Extreme exposure to wind and heat may even lead to convulsions or loss of consciousness.

Dampness due to rainy or humid conditions, and dryness due to a dry climate or environment or internal dehydration, can become manifest in moist, smelly discharges or dry, itchy skin respectively.

The six pathogenic factors can also create disturbances of the organs inside the body. For example, the "fire" of the heart may rise, causing anxiety and irritability, or the spleen may become too "damp", leading to bloating or diarrhea.

As well as being classified according to the extent of excess (*shi*) or deficiency (*xu*) of the prevailing pathogenic factors, diseases are also classified according to the stage of *yin* and *yang* development, their degree of heat or cold, and the external or internal depth of the manifestation of the disease in the body. These guiding factors in diagnosis are known as the Eight Principles.

In addition to these, there are several more influences to be aware of. Chinese medicine sees a clear link between emotional and physical health. Under normal circumstances, emotions do not lead to disease; however, if an emotion is felt either excessively or very rarely, or arises suddenly, this can lead to disruption of the corresponding inner organ function and eventually to disease (see box, right). Finally, the ancient medical texts paid considerable attention to the celestial influences of the stars and planets. Today, however, this is generally found more in the realm of astrology and fortune-telling than in medicine.

It is normal to experience a full range of emotions, but if one emotion is experienced intensely and repeatedly – even if it is joy – this will lead to a disruption of the corresponding organ function and eventually to disease.

THE SEVEN EMOTIONAL FACTORS

There are seven main emotions (*qi qing*) that can play a role in disease: anger (*nu*), joy (*xi*), worry (*si*), sorrow (*you*), grief (*bei*), fright (*jing*) and fear (*kong*). They are linked to the internal organs according to the Five Phases system of correspondences (see pages 94–95). For example, anger (*nu*) is linked to liver function, so repeatedly allowing oneself to feel angry can damage the liver, or irritability can be attributed to liver weakness.

Emotions only become harmful when they are experienced to the extent that a person is either overwhelmed or subdued by them. Even a positive emotion can become pathogenic if experienced excessively.

Daoism advocates that one should avoid being at the mercy of uncontrolled emotions. An attitude of calm detachment is believed to be a prerequisite for longevity.

CHAPTER 11

DIAGNOSTIC PROCEDURES

The Chinese medical practitioner develops finely tuned observational and tactile skills for use in diagnosis and combines deductive logic with intuition in order to identify disease. There are four main types of examination, or *si zhen*: observation (*wang zhen*); listening (*wen zhen*), which includes smelling; questioning (also *wen zhen*); and palpation, or touching (*qie zhen*).

Observation involves an assessment of the patient's facial characteristics and expression, complexion, gestures, general appearance and also an inspection of the tongue, which includes detailed analysis of the body of the tongue and its coating (see pages 106–107). During the listening stage the practitioner notes the quality of the patient's voice and respiration, and the odour of the breath and the body. Questioning covers diet, sleep, excretory functions and details of the nature, duration and severity of the complaint. Palpation is a highly skilled practice and focuses on identifying different pulse patterns. Pulses are taken for each of the organs and channels, usually at the wrists, but they may also be taken elsewhere on the body (see pages 104–105). Six pulses can be taken on each wrist, one for each organ. The depth, pace, strength and quality of the pulse are all noted. Individual acupoints and areas of pain can also be palpated.

The Chinese practitioner makes a diagnosis by evaluating the findings in the light of the Eight Principles (see pages 100–101), the effects on the functioning of the *zang* and *fu* organs and the flow of *qi* through the channels or meridians.

OBSERVING, LISTENING AND QUESTIONING

The patient's face, body type, posture, movement and appearance are all observed closely by the medical practitioner. The lustre of the complexion and brightness of the eyes and expression give an indication of the patient's overall health and the likelihood of recovery. Different hues of the skin can indicate a disturbance affecting particular organs. For example, a greenish tinge suggests liver disturbance, while paleness signifies lung problems. Certain physical signs and the proportions of both the face and body are also closely linked to internal organ function and may indicate a predisposition to certain diseases. A well-lined forehead, for example, may indicate current or future intestinal problems.

The quality of the voice and breathing provides information about the patient's constitution. A feeble voice and shallow breathing indicate a weak constitution and suggest that the individual's illness may be serious and protracted. A loud voice and heavy breathing can denote heart problems. The practitioner also listens carefully to the patient's cough and any intestinal gurgling in order to determine which inner organ is most disturbed.

The smell of the patient's breath is classified according to the taste correspondences of Five Phases theory (see pages 94–95). Traditionally, the urine and stools were also smelled (sometimes even tasted) and then classified according to the theory. Today, although urine and stools are

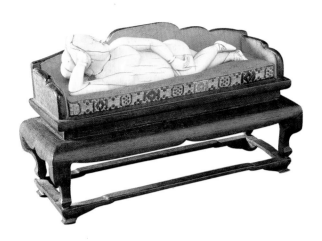

It was once common practice in China for patients to make use of diagnostic dolls, such as this 19th-century ivory female figure, to indicate where they felt discomfort, thus obviating the need to undress in front of the doctor.

always discussed during questioning, when their frequency and colour are enquired about, they are rarely examined.

Questioning puts the patient at ease and is used to confirm the diagnosis already obtained on the basis of signs and symptoms. Queries about the onset of the symptoms and the time of day, or season, when they are most severe are interpreted in terms of the Eight Principles (see page 101) and the Five Phases (see pages 94–95). The progression of symptoms and the areas involved also provide vital information about the balance of *yin* and *yang*, the channels or organs affected by the disturbance and the likely prognosis.

Physicians also enquire about the presence of chills and fever; the presence or absence of sweat; food and drink intake; appetite and sense of taste; the nature and location of pain; and sleeping habits. Women are asked about their menstrual cycle. Chills and fever indicate the predominance of cold or heat in the body and point to the organ that is likely to be affected. For example, a cold abdomen and undigested food in the stools can indicate a weak spleen, while a fever with hot soles and minimal sweat may indicate kidney infection. Practitioners know that preferences for certain foods and drinks can be caused by, or affect, the balance in particular organs. For example, people with a sweet tooth tend to suffer from poor spleen and stomach function, whereas excess salt weakens the kidneys.

PULSE-TAKING

Pulse-taking has a central role in diagnosis in Traditional Chinese Medicine. Because, historically, it was considered indecent in China for a patient to undress, physicians developed refined diagnostic skills on the basis of external signs and the examination of accessible parts of the patient's body, such as the wrists, ankles and face. Even today, patients rarely undress when visiting a traditional Chinese physician.

The pulse is examined in the region of the radial artery on the wrists. The patient is asked to rest each wrist, with the palm facing upwards, on a cushion placed on a desk or table and the physician then uses the tips of his or her index, middle and ring fingers to apply pressure in three different positions on the wrist – the front (*cun*), middle (*guan*) and rear (*chi*). Each point corresponds to one of the *yin* and *yang* pairs of inner organs. Pressure is applied at three different levels on the skin – superficial, medium and deep – and comparisons are made. Each pulse is analysed according to its depth, frequency, rhythm, strength and other qualities. Factors that can affect the patient's pulse, including gender, age, activity prior to pulse examination and even the time of day, are all taken into account.

PULSE POINTS ON THE WRIST

Six pulses are identified along the radial artery on each wrist and three different pulse positions are palpated at different levels on the skin.

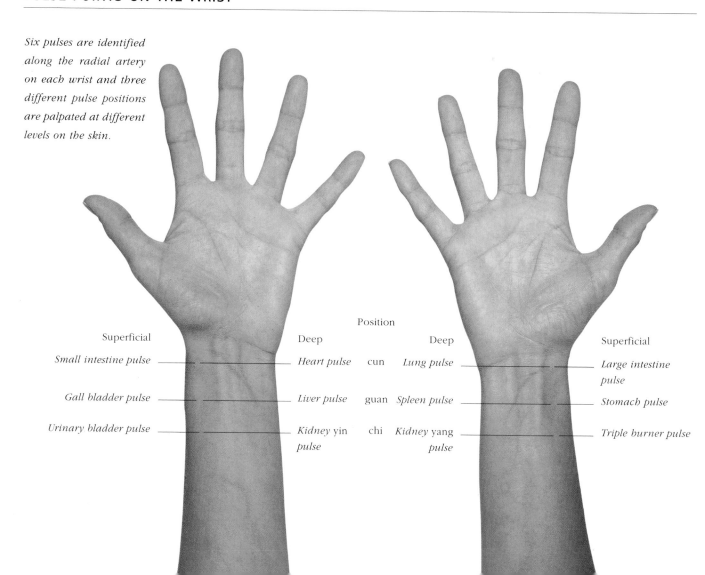

Superficial	Deep	Position	Deep	Superficial
Small intestine pulse	*Heart pulse*	cun	*Lung pulse*	*Large intestine pulse*
Gall bladder pulse	*Liver pulse*	guan	*Spleen pulse*	*Stomach pulse*
Urinary bladder pulse	*Kidney* yin *pulse*	chi	*Kidney* yang *pulse*	*Triple burner pulse*

A normal pulse pattern is smooth, even and strong, and beats four or five times per breath. An abnormal pulse pattern has qualities that reflect internal dysfunction. Superficial pulses tend to indicate the early stages of disease, while deep, weak pulses can be indicative of more serious conditions. Cold disorders are generally reflected in slow, heavy pulses, whereas hot disorders, such as fevers, create rapid pulses. Certain pulse patterns in each organ position can yield important information about the organ's condition. For example, a tight, wiry pulse ("like the drawn string on a bow") in the liver position (see diagram, left) occurs when the liver is in a *yang* state, which can lead to headaches, epigastric pain and irritability. A very thin, weak pulse in the kidney positions can indicate weakened kidney function due to stress, overwork or excess intake of caffeine or nicotine.

Certain pulses can indicate pregnancy and the likely sex of the unborn child. The pulse pattern of a pregnant woman is said to be rolling "like pearls on a plate". A strong kidney pulse on the left wrist is believed to indicate a male child, while a strong kidney pulse on the right side is thought to show that the baby is female.

There are many different combinations of pulse pattern, and considerable practice, experience and skill are required to diagnose correctly using this technique. The focus in Chinese pulse-taking is specifically on the relative functioning of the *zang* and *fu* organs (see pages 98–99) and the effects of any pathogenic factors, differentiated according to the Eight Principles (see pages 100–101). Nowadays in China there is no mention of spirit influence in connection with pulse analysis (unlike in Tibet where the concept of "astonishing pulses" persists, see pages 66–67). Rather, the focus has recently been on scientifically verifying the accuracy of pulse-taking by using electrodermal measuring techniques to record pulse differences accurately and to link these to organ functions. Skilled physicians have demonstrated the high accuracy and clinical validity of this technique, although variations in interpretation exist.

A practitioner palpating points on the patient's back, along the urinary bladder channel that runs parallel to the spine. This investigation can reveal whether or not the patient is suffering from an imbalance of some kind.

PALPATING POINTS AND CHANNELS

Each channel has a specific internal pathway that connects to its corresponding inner organ. Pressure on major points reveals the state of the organ. If the application of pressure on a specific point is painful, this indicates an excess (*shi*) condition, linked to a blockage of *qi*, blood and body fluids. If the pressure feels comfortable and relieving this indicates a deficiency (*xu*) condition in the organ. This procedure is often carried out on the urinary bladder channels, which have important points (the *shu* points) that relate to each of the inner organs.

Palpating major points along a channel can also tell the physician which organ is the source of the imbalance responsible for the patient's symptoms. For example, if the patient feels tenderness when the practitioner presses acupoint Liver 3 (*taichong*) on the foot, this indicates an imbalance in liver function. Similarly, if a person has a headache, gentle pressure on various points along the channels of the head can reveal the underlying cause.

The abdomen may also be palpated, and it is felt for hard masses (indicative of constipation or tumours), soft masses (*qi* blockages), gurgling (fluid retention and digestive problems) and distention. Abdominal palpation techniques have been further refined in Japanese medicine, see pages 138–139.

TONGUE DIAGNOSIS

In Traditional Chinese Medicine, tongue diagnosis ranks second only to pulse diagnosis in importance. The system of analyis used in China is much more detailed than elsewhere (for example, in Tibet; see page 68). In China, the tongue is seen as a mirror of the body as a whole and different parts of the tongue are taken as indicators of the function of each of the corresponding internal organs. As with the pulse patterns, Chinese practitioners recognize that the tongue's body and coating vary widely depending on the individual's constitution and other factors. Observation of the body of the tongue will indicate the condition of the inner organs, while the coating gives information about the effect on the organs of the pathogenic factors (see pages 100–101). Examinations should be done in natural light to enable the colours and coating to be seen clearly.

Analysis of the body of the tongue takes into account its shape, colour, size and movement. A healthy tongue is said to be of normal size, pink or light red in colour and capable of free and easy movement. A pale tongue is generally indicative of a cold condition, while a red tongue shows the presence of pathogenic heat in the body. If the tongue is a very dark red this may denote that fever has gone deep into the body and that the condition is serious and threatens the health of the inner organs. A purple tongue indicates blood stagnation and this can often be seen in women suffering

Tongue examiniation offers important information about the patient's health, even early indicators of illness. Care must always be taken, however, to rule out false information caused by the residue from particular foods or drinks.

from painful menstruation. An enlarged and flabby tongue that shows the imprint of teeth marks at the sides indicates the presence of phlegm and damp in the body and is typically linked with digestive problems. A very dry and cracked tongue with deep ridges signifies a loss of body fluids and dehydration. If the body has been affected by pathogenic wind, the tongue usually shows signs of a tremor and the person may not be able to point it straight forwards.

Analysis of the tongue's coating – the word for which translates as "fur" or "moss" – is based on its colour, consistency and the area on the tongue in which it predominates. On a normal tongue, the coating should be thin and clear or white and neither too moist nor too dry.

Abnormal coatings – reflecting problems in the digestive organs – vary in colour, thickness, consistency and precise location on the tongue (see box, right). A white coating indicates cold conditions, while yellow indicates heat in the body. Thick white coatings generally suggest an invasion of wind, whereas sticky white coatings indicate dampness. Thin yellow coatings denote an invasion by wind-heat, and thick yellow coatings suggest the long-term influence of damp and phlegm.

Occasionally the tongue coating may be grey – even black – or peeling. Depending on information from other signs and symptoms, this can indicate serious conditions in

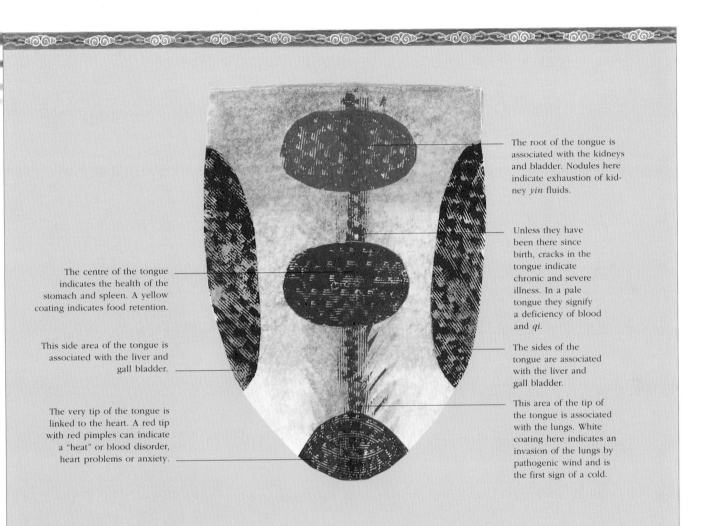

The root of the tongue is associated with the kidneys and bladder. Nodules here indicate exhaustion of kidney *yin* fluids.

Unless they have been there since birth, cracks in the tongue indicate chronic and severe illness. In a pale tongue they signify a deficiency of blood and *qi*.

The sides of the tongue are associated with the liver and gall bladder.

This area of the tip of the tongue is associated with the lungs. White coating here indicates an invasion of the lungs by pathogenic wind and is the first sign of a cold.

The centre of the tongue indicates the health of the stomach and spleen. A yellow coating indicates food retention.

This side area of the tongue is associated with the liver and gall bladder.

The very tip of the tongue is linked to the heart. A red tip with red pimples can indicate a "heat" or blood disorder, heart problems or anxiety.

SIGNS OF HEALTH ON THE TONGUE

Each part of the tongue is linked to particular inner organs and parts of the body. The tip and top part of the tongue corresponds to the upper body, the central part to the middle of the body and the root of the tongue to the lower body. The tip is linked to the heart, the top part of the tongue at the front to the lungs, the middle to the stomach and spleen, the sides to the liver and gall bladder and the root to the kidneys.

Diagnosis of the inner organs is made according to the colour and coating in each of these areas of the tongue. For example, a very red tip of the tongue usually indicates heart problems and over-anxiety, while nodules and white coating at the root of the tongue show all is not well with the kidneys, and a thick, yellow coating in the centre of the tongue indicates digestive problems.

which the body fluids have been used up and the patient is in a very weakened physical state.

Examination of the tongue can play a role in preventive medicine as changes in the coating often manifest before actual symptoms. For example, if one morning the tongue has an abnormally thick white coating it can indicate an

invasion by pathogenic cold. If preventive measures are taken immediately the cold may be arrested.

Tongue analysis also enables differential diagnosis to be made. For example, two people may display identical cold and cough symptoms, yet their tongues might reveal that the underlying causes differ, affecting the treatment.

CHAPTER 12

HEALING IN CHINESE MEDICINE

The *Nei jing* medical text (see page 91) relates that people once lived simple lives in harmony with their natural surroundings and so diseases were few and could be treated. Healing was by means of religious practices and invocations to beneficent gods to "treat the spirit", and one aim was to restore the individual to the way of Dao (see pages 92–93).

The Yellow Emperor's minister, Qi Bo, states that as people's lives became more complicated so did diseases, and new methods of treatment had to be developed. These included ways of nourishing the body, the correct use of appropriate medicines, needling techniques, and treating the inner organs, blood and breath. The aim was to expel pathogenic factors and toxins from the body and increase the supply and flow of *qi* and nutrients. This was achieved by eight therapeutic methods for purging and replenishing the body: sweating (*han*), vomiting (*tu*), evacuating (*xia*), eliminating (*xiao*), purifying (*qing*), harmonizing (*he*), warming (*wen*), and supplementing (*bu*) the supply of *qi* and blood.

Treatment selection depends on accurate diagnosis, which is seen as the most important part of healing. The *Nei jing* states that a superior physician is able to treat the body before disease manifests itself, whereas an inferior one only acts when the patient is displaying symptoms of the disease. The methods range from dietary and lifestyle change, exercise therapy and massage to herbal medicine, acupuncture and moxibustion, blood-letting and minor surgery. The emphasis is on self-care and individual responsibility first, and on medical intervention second.

LIVING IN HARMONY

A t'ai ch'i *exercise, making use of slow and graceful fluid movements – many
of them based on those of animals and birds – to regulate the flow of vital energy
or* qi *in the body and calm the mind.*

In ancient China, physicians were expected to keep themselves in excellent health and, by their example, to educate their patients in the correct way of living. It was thought that breath control was crucial to health – the physician learned how to control and regulate breath and was expected to teach patients these breathing techniques. Today breathing is still taught as the key to good acupuncture treatment and to ensuring the efficacy of therapeutic exercises such as *qi gong* (see pages 124–125).

Physicians also taught their patients how to live in harmony with the seasons. Traditional Chinese Medicine asserts that each individual should consume different foods and perform certain activities according to the season and the environment in which he or she lives (see pages 112–113). In cold weather, for example, vigorous exercise should be performed to warm the body; in warmer weather overheating should be avoided. Care must be taken to evade pernicious winds and draughts which may injure the body, and the body should not be cold or damp for long periods.

Treatment may also include advice in accordance with these principles and it is not unusual for the physician to recommend that the patient change workplace, the type of work being undertaken, or even move home if this is thought to be linked to their current health problems.

Ideally, the best environments for health are peaceful and secluded with lots of fresh air and sunshine, a temperate climate, minimal pollution and limited stress. Because such an environment is not readily attainable the science of feng shui was developed to modify one's surroundings in order to maximize the flow of beneficial energy (see page 123).

FOOD AS MEDICINE

Eating food according to the seasons and the constitution of the individual has long been held as the secret of good health in China. Foods may be classified according to their *yin* and *yang* nature and their essentially cooling or warming properties in the body. Foods that grow or live in water or cool places tend to have a cooling nature whereas meats, roots and certain vegetables have more warming properties. Cereals, grains and pulses are generally classified as neutral but they can be affected by the way in which they are cooked and the other ingredients that they are cooked with.

Foods may also be classified according to the pathogenic factors they may disturb or create in the body (see pages 100–101). Dairy produce, sugar, bread and cakes made from refined flour are said to produce damp and heat in the body, leading to digestive problems, while certain acidic foods, such as rhubarb and spinach, can increase internal wind, contributing to joint aches and pains.

In general, Traditional Chinese Medicine advises that the healthiest diet is *qing dan*, that is, "clear" and "light" (literally "bland"), consisting of fresh foods, lightly cooked and predominantly vegetarian in nature. Many texts extol the virtues of wholegrains and vegetables and proclaim the benefits of warming or cooking food lightly, in order to aid digestion and the assimilation of nutrients. "Harmful" substances, such as sugar, refined flour, red meats, animal fats, caffeine and alcohol, are considered best avoided or taken only in moderation.

A balanced diet contains all five of the tastes linked to the Five Phases (see pages 94–95 and box, page 113), thus harmonizing the functions of the internal organs. Sour foods stimulate the liver and gall bladder; bitter foods are said to help the heart and small intestine; sweet (although not necessarily sugary) foods harmonize the stomach and spleen; pungent foods balance the lungs and large intestine; and salty foods tonify the kidneys and bladder. This applies only when the five tastes are included in a balanced way – if too much of any one predominates in the food it will have the opposite effect. For example, an addiction to

A BALANCED STIR-FRY

Heat a teaspoon of sesame oil in a pan and add half a teaspoon of freshly grated ginger and a finely chopped clove of garlic. Add Chinese black mushrooms, cut into strips, and stir for a few minutes. Next add sliced lotus root, cucumber (cut into strips), a couple of leaves of chopped cabbage and a handful of beansprouts and shredded carrot. Stir all the ingredients for a few minutes then serve with a lettuce (*yin*) and spring onion (*yang*) salad.

WARMING FOODS

Warming foods are said to be *yang* in character. Carrots, garlic, Chinese chives, ginger, leeks, onions, shallots and spring onions (scallions) are all warming vegetables. Warming fruits include apricots, cherries, lychees and mangoes, among others.

Left to right: chopped apricot, leek, lychee, spring onions, sliced mango and black cherries.

COOLING FOODS

Cooling foods are *yin* in character. Commonly-used vegetable ingredients include beansprouts, water chestnuts, cucumbers, dandelion leaves, black Chinese mushrooms, lettuces, lotus roots and yam beans. Easily obtained cooling fruits include coconuts, mandarins, pears, pineapples and watermelons.

Left to right: celery, lettuce, mushrooms (top), star fruit (bottom), asparagus and a banana.

NEUTRAL FOODS

Good examples of neutral vegetables are broccoli, cauliflower, Chinese kale, fennel, lamb's lettuce, parsley, parsnips, pumpkins, sweetcorn and turnips. Neutral fruits include apples, grapes, papayas and plums.

Left to right: sweetcorn, broccoli, raspberries, papaya fruit and fennel.

sweet foods will seriously weaken the individual's spleen and stomach function. Food also follows the relationship between the Five Phases (see diagram, page 94). So, just as "water supports wood", eating water-rich foods – fresh fruits, seaweed and raw vegetables – helps to strengthen liver function.

Selection of appropriate foods is made on the basis of the constitution of the individual concerned and the nature of the disease. If there is a tendency to heat disorders then cooling foods and drinks such as cucumber, lettuce, celery, buckwheat, soya, mushrooms, fish, seafood, bananas, tropical fruits, yoghurt, fruit juices – pineapple, grapefruit or orange – and mint tea might be recommended. However, if the underlying cause of the heat is internal dampness then all cool and mucus-producing foods, such as tropical fruits and dairy produce, including yoghurt, would be removed from the diet. If the person suffers from cold and lethargy, warming foods such as oats, lentils, sunflower seeds, onions, carrots, chicken, ginseng, and ginger or cinnamon teas should be consumed.

The methods of cooking and the choice of cooking utensils are also important. Frying or grilling the food increases its warming properties more than boiling or steaming, while chilling or freezing foods makes them more cooling in nature.

Cast iron, enamel or stainless steel pots, pans or woks are considered best as the food is heated more evenly and gradually than it is with aluminium pans or microwaving – they are also less toxic. Food should be as fresh as possible and be eaten promptly after preparation, when its *qi* and essences, taste and aroma are all at their height.

A balanced meal may be obtained by combining cooling foods with a few warming ones and using a warming method of cooking (stir-fry, for example) with a neutral oil – such as sesame (see recipe, page 110), which will also have the effect of aiding digestion. Balanced meals should also ideally contain ingredients with all the colours associated with the Five Phases: green, red, yellow, white (or pale) and black (or dark).

Personal eating habits also affect health and digestion. Hunger and thirst should be avoided, but excessive eating or drinking are injurious to health by putting a strain on the digestive system and the internal organs. Eating at regular times in a calm environment and chewing food slowly are

A vast open-air food market in China, the produce all freshly harvested and brought into town from the surrounding countryside. China has long been self-sufficient in foodstuffs, vital given its vast population, and it is not difficult to obtain fresh fruit and vegetables anywhere in the country. The types available vary from region to region.

all thought to aid digestive function and the absorption of those nutrients essential to vitality and longevity.

The consumption of food is best adapted according to the seasons. In winter take lots of warming foods (heated soups and casseroles) and avoid cold and raw foods. In spring eat lots of fresh, young vegetables and avoid sour foods. In summer prevent overheating by consuming cooling foods and beverages (see page 111) and avoid spicy, hot foods. In autumn take light, easily digestible foods and lots of seasonal fruit and vegetables.

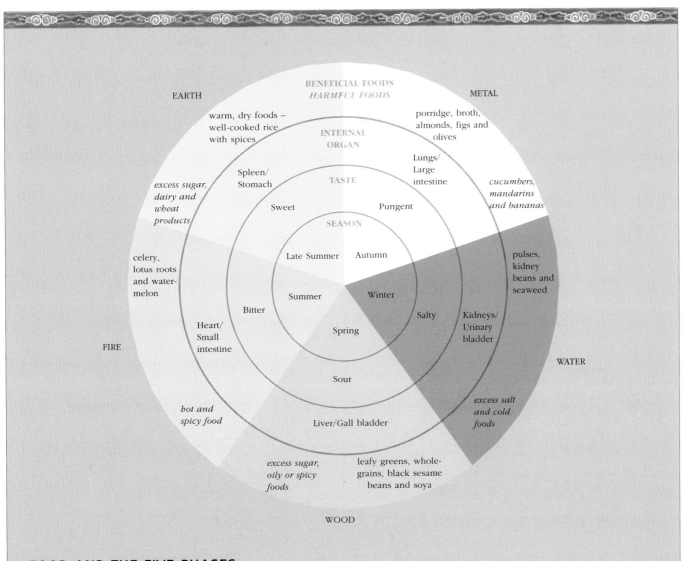

FOOD AND THE FIVE PHASES

The seventh-century CE physician Sun Simiao commented, "A good doctor first makes a diagnosis, and having found out the cause of the disease, he tries to cure it first by food. When food fails, then he prescribes medicine." The classification of foods accords with the Five Phases system of correspondences. Each season is associated with a specific taste, and for each season certain foods are beneficial and help to stimulate the corresponding organs, while others are harmful and inhibit their function. However, balance must be remembered and excesses avoided. For example, a sour food, such as a lemon, taken in moderation will stimulate liver function, but an excess would cause overactivity of the liver.

ACUPUNCTURE

The Chinese term for acupuncture, *zhen jiu*, refers to both the insertion of needles and the application of moxibustion (heat treatment) at precise points (*xue*) on the skin in order to facilitate the flow of *qi*, blood and fluids in the body. Needling techniques have been in use since ancient times and it is believed that stone needles (*bian*) were used in China before metal needles were first introduced in the Iron Age – iron needles subsequently giving way to gold and silver ones, which were superceded by high-quality, sterilized stainless steel, disposable needles. Acupuncture was banned during periods of political unrest in the nineteenth and early twentieth centuries, but in recent decades it has enjoyed a great revival in China and attracted growing interest in the West.

In Western medical terms, acupuncture is thought to work by blocking pain receptors, stimulating the nervous system and the production of endorphins, and promoting blood circulation. Although no one is certain exactly how acupuncture works, it is now widely recognized as an effective form of pain relief and the World Health Organization has published a list of disorders that acupuncture can treat effectively, including digestive complaints, respiratory diseases, gynaecological ailments and neurological problems.

Acupuncture needles vary in length from around half an inch (125mm) to five inches (12.7cm) and are of varying thicknesses. They are selected according to the part of the

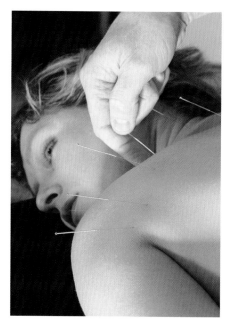

Acupuncture is an ancient Eastern discipline now practised widely in the Western world for a variety of ailments. Its use in anaesthesia is still mainly confined to China.

body being needled, the type of disease being treated and the age of the patient. Points located above bone are needled very shallowly using a short needle at an angle. Fleshy areas require longer needles inserted perpendicularly and to greater depths. Children, the elderly and the very frail are generally treated with small, very fine needles.

Acupuncture points are selected mainly from the 365 principal points on the channels, or meridians, according to the diagnosis made. They may be local points in the area of the pain or problem, or can be distal points lying along the associated meridian pathways. Additional points known to be effective for particular symptoms or known to have certain effects on the body may also be selected, or a combination of points known to work together in an effective way may be used. Points are carefully located either anatomically or proportionately and this must be done accurately for the treatment to be effective.

Needle insertion is quick and normally painless. Once the needles have been put in, various techniques are used to either sedate and disperse *qi* or to supply and tonify it. These techniques involve rotating, lifting and lowering, or perhaps even vibrating, the needle, and they may be synchronized with the patient's breath. The practitioner aims to achieve a needling sensation described as "a fish taking a bait" (known as *de qi*) and sometimes felt by the patient as numbness, tingling or a heavy sensation. Needles are kept in place for up to thirty minutes and then carefully withdrawn; various quantities can be used and they are inserted on either one or both sides of the body.

According to the *Nei jing*, it is also important to schedule treatment according to the seasons and the movements of celestial bodies, but less attention is paid to this today because of the volume of demand. Recent developments in acupuncture include electrical stimulation of the acupoints, the injection of drugs or herbal medicine into points and the use of lasers, sound vibrations and coloured light.

Some acupuncture-related adjunct techniques are also used, such as moxibustion, intradermal needles or "plum blossom" needle hammers (see pages 116–117).

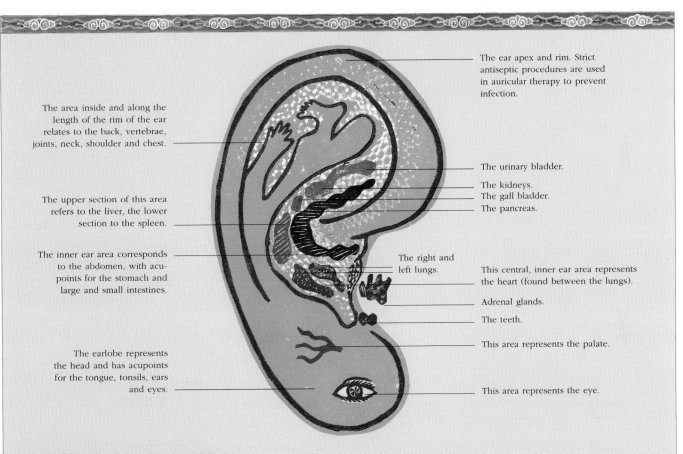

The ear apex and rim. Strict antiseptic procedures are used in auricular therapy to prevent infection.

The area inside and along the length of the rim of the ear relates to the back, vertebrae, joints, neck, shoulder and chest.

The upper section of this area refers to the liver, the lower section to the spleen.

The inner ear area corresponds to the abdomen, with acupoints for the stomach and large and small intestines.

The earlobe represents the head and has acupoints for the tongue, tonsils, ears and eyes.

The urinary bladder.

The kidneys.
The gall bladder.
The pancreas.

The right and left lungs.

This central, inner ear area represents the heart (found between the lungs).

Adrenal glands.

The teeth.

This area represents the palate.

This area represents the eye.

AURICULAR ACUPUNCTURE

Like the tongue, the ear can be regarded as a mirror of the whole body, with different areas equating to an organ or body part. The twelve channels connect directly or indirectly with the ear, and many ancient texts point to the relation between auditory function, the flow of blood and *qi*, and the health of the internal organs.

In auricular therapy, the body is represented as an upside-down fetus on the ear, with the lobe corresponding to the regions of the head and neck, the outer rim to the spine and the inner parts to the inner organs (see above).

Problems in the body can be identified by determining minute areas of sensitivity or discolouration in the ear. Illness can then be treated by needling these areas. Ear points can also be selected for treatment according to the diseased area of the body, the Five Phases correspondences and the theories of the channels (see pages 94–95 and 98–99).

ADJUNCT THERAPIES

Adjunct therapies such as moxibustion, cupping, supplementary needle techniques and acupressure, may be used in addition to, or in combination with, acupuncture.

Moxibustion is the burning of the herb *Artemisia vulgaris* (Chinese or Common mugwort) on acupuncture points and certain areas of the body to warm them and to stimulate the flow of blood and *qi*. The term "moxa" is actually a Japanese derivative (see pages 144–145) but has now been adopted in both China and the West. The Chinese term for "moxa" is *ai rong jiu*: *ai* refers to the plant *Artemisia*; *rong* refers to the down on the leaves, which is dried to make the moxa "wool"; and *jiu* means cauterization.

Moxa may be applied either directly or indirectly. In its direct form it is lightly rolled into a cone shape, placed on the skin and then lit. The size of the cone may vary from that of a wheat grain to approximately half a date stone. In the West, care is taken not to burn or scar the skin, but in many Chinese clinics the treatment is considered more effective if a blister is allowed to form. Indirect moxa treatment may involve the use of moxa sticks, which are lit and then gently rotated around the affected area in order to warm it without touching the skin; alternatively, moxa may be placed in a specially designed box and used to treat large areas, such as the lower back or abdomen; or it is often applied by placing it on the top of acupuncture needles, which then transmit the heat directly into the acupoint. Moxa treatment is especially helpful for joint pain and stiffness caused by cold and damp conditions.

A separate therapy for joint stiffness and pain is provided by cupping. This involves attaching small glass, or metal, jars to the skin by creating a vacuum inside. It is done by placing a lighted match or alcohol-soaked cotton ball inside the jar to burn up the oxygen and then rapidly placing it onto the skin. The suction created by the jars helps to improve the local circulation of blood and *qi*.

Acupressure is a method for using finger pressure instead of needles to treat the body via the acupuncture points (see box, right).

Moxa is especially good for yin *and cold conditions. Moxa sticks are rolls of moxa "wool" in paper which are lit and rotated gently around the affected area to warm it.*

ADDITIONAL TECHNIQUES

Moxibustion can also be applied by placing a cone of moxa onto a slice of ginger or garlic to release the therapeutic effect of the herb, or onto a pile of salt.

Acupuncture techniques include the use of three-edged needles, tapping needles and intradermal needles. Three-edged needles are used for blood-letting to relieve fevers and sore throat. A tiny incision is made and a few drops of blood squeezed out. Tapping needles have seven or five ("plum blossom"-type) short needles attached to a handle, like a hammer. They are used to tap the skin and treat headaches and baldness. Intradermal needles are like tiny thumbtacks, which are retained on the skin in the treatment of chronic diseases.

*Located in the space between the thumb and index finger, Large Intestine 4 (*hegu*) is a very potent point. It stimulates energy flow in the upper body, aids digestion and helps to improve the complexion.*

*Located in the groove above the upper lip, just below the nose, the acupoint "governing channel" 26 (*renzhong*) is useful for stimulating mental alertness, concentration and memory.*

ACUPRESSURE

The application of fingertip pressure on acupoints of the body in order to aid the flow of *qi* and blood in the channels is known as acupressure. With reference to the appropriate instructions, acupoints may be located anatomically or proportionately using the measurement of *cun*: one *cun* is the distance between the two middle creases of the middle finger and three *cun* is the breadth of four fingers.

Acupressure is effective and easy to learn. First, locate the relevant acupoint correctly, then apply gentle pressure using the tip of the ring or index fingers or the thumb. Initially, the pressure can be used diagnostically, for if the point feels tender it indicates an excess condition, whereas a lack of sensation signifies a deficiency. Continue to apply pressure evenly or use small rotations for about thirty seconds, then repeat the process for the acupoint on the opposite side of the body.

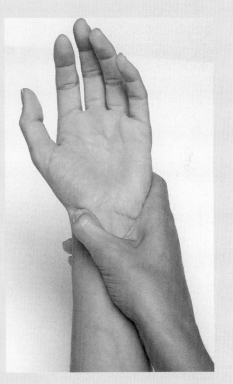

*Located two finger-widths inside the wrist crease in line with the thumb, Lung 7 (*lieque*) is in the hollow behind the wrist bone. It strengthens respiratory function and treats coughs, asthma and sore throat.*

MASSAGE

escriptions of both massage and self-massage techniques that have been found on ancient oracle bones and in the writings of the Yellow Emperor (see page 91), are clear evidence that massage techniques have been used for millennia in China. The various types of massage used in Chinese medicine aim to promote circulation and the flow of blood and *qi* internally and ease muscle stiffness or even realign bones externally.

The range of techniques known as *Dao yin*, meaning "to lead" and "to guide", includes massage, self-massage, breathing and exercises to redistribute and balance the flow of *qi* in the body (see box, right).

There are eight main massage techniques. *Tui* involves a combination of vigorous methods, grasping or pushing with the palms, thumbs and elbows all over the body to stretch the muscles and vibrate the joints in order to relieve common ailments, heal injuries and ease stress. *Na* is a technique of pinching the skin between the finger and thumb or the interlocked fingers of both hands, and is especially useful in relieving pain. *Ning* involves pinching, lifting and then releasing the skin and is often used to ease tension in the neck and shoulders. *Nie* is a twisting and pulling movement, ideal for use on the back. *An* techniques use rhythmical pressing and pushing with the palms and knuckles especially to the back, abdomen and chest. *Tao* involves strong pinching that is mainly used for first aid revival. *Ma* is a light rubbing technique using the hands to promote

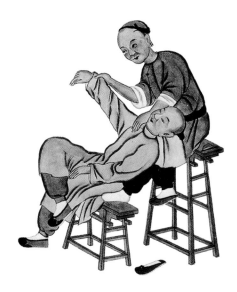

A patient receiving a massage to ease shoulder pain. The treatment improves circulation and qi *flow and increases mobility; 19th-century watercolour.*

circulation, while *pai* involves percussive tapping with the palms or fingertips. Manipulative techniques involve shaking, vibrating and rotating the joints, extending and flexing the limbs and stretching exercises. They may be used in combination with acupressure (see pages 116–117).

All of the body can be treated, with gentle techniques used for the face and other sensitive areas. The massage is performed mainly with the hands and fingers, but the elbows and feet can also be used. Oils and herbs may be utilized in conjunction with massage techniques; wooden rollers and balls are popular for self-massage.

In a typical massage treatment the client is first made warm and comfortable. The massage is usually performed while the person remains clothed, but the upper body may be exposed to enable techniques to be used on the skin of the back, chest and abdomen. Whole body treatment may be given or just local symptomatic treatment – for example, on the neck and shoulders. Acupressure points may be selected to help relieve particular symptoms and combined with stretching and invigorating techniques. These massage techniques are therapeutic and suitable for all age groups.

Massage may also be used diagnostically as changes in skin colour and sensitivity indicate the functioning of the channels and organs within. Skin that turns dark red or purple during pinching or grasping techniques indicates conditions due to heat and repletion, while skin that remains pale suggests conditions resulting from cold and depletion.

1 *Ear rubbing: Clear the mind and breathe deeply. Place the heels of the palms over the ears and then rub vigorously back and forth seven times. This will stimulate the flow of blood in the ear and the auricular acupoints relating to the entire body.*

2 *Then rest the palms over the ears and tap with the fingertips on the back of the head. The tapping should be light and rhythmical, rather than pressing down hard into the head. This exercise will improve the hearing and stimulate mental function.*

DAO YIN SELF-MASSAGE

A simple *dao yin* self-massage routine can be performed daily in less than ten minutes to stimulate the senses and regulate body functions. The steps are as follows:

Eye exercise: Sit upright and look straight ahead. Slowly roll the eyes up and down, to the left and right and clockwise and anti-clockwise repeating each movement three times and resting the eyes on a fixed point in front of you between each movement. Finally, rub the palms together and rest them over the eyes for a few seconds. This is said to improve vision and brighten the eyes.

Ear rubbing: See the simple, stimulatory exercise pictured above and the box, page 115.

Teeth exercise: With the mouth gently closed and the jaw relaxed, tap the teeth together forty times. This strengthens the teeth, stimulates mental function and improves digestion.

Mouth rinsing: Close the mouth and move the tongue around to produce saliva and use it to rinse the mouth.

Swallow it slowly in three parts and repeat forty times. This improves gum health and digestion.

Nose massage: Put the tips of the index fingers on either side of the bridge of the nose, placing the thumbs under the chin. Massage gently down as far as the nostrils and then back up, and repeat three times. This will clear the nostrils and relieve the sinuses.

Kidney massage: Make the hands into loose fists and rub the small of the back forty times. This warms the kidneys, relieves backache and helps regulate menses.

Abdominal massage: Place your palm above your navel and rotate five times clockwise for men or anti-clockwise for women. This stimulates digestion.

Foot massage: Apply pressure with the thumbs to the kidney source point, *yongquan*, located under the ball of the foot. Continue applying small rotations to the point for some minutes. This improves vitality and vigour.

HERBAL MEDICINE

Herbal medicine, a principal part of Chinese healing, is thought to have developed from the Daoist alchemists' search for the "elixir of life". The ancient literature records emperors requesting their physicians to find herbs to promote longevity and maintain good health.

There is a vast body of literature on herbal medicine – including manuscripts dating back 2,000 years – which describes many thousands of medicinal ingredients. The

HERBAL REMEDY FOR COLDS

The following cinnamon remedy can be effective when used to treat the early stages of common colds, chills, fevers and cold-related headaches.

Take ¹/₈ oz (3g) each of dried, chopped cinnamon stick, peony, jujube and ginger roots and ¹/₁₆ oz (1.5g) of dried, chopped liquorice root. Add six cups of water to the herbs and boil for forty-five minutes, or until the liquid has reduced by half. Strain and drink cold within one day.

Shang han lun (see page 91), compiled around the second and third centuries CE, includes 113 herbal formulas and discusses the use of herbs in curing febrile disease. A large number of formulas in use today come from this text. The *Shen nong ben cao jing*, compiled by the great pharmacologist Tao Hong jing (456–536CE), describes 730 herbs according to their actions, toxicity and so on, and identifies three broad categories of herbs that are still in use today.

The first category is that of the upper or "ruler" (*jun*) herbs, which boost vitality and nourish life. These are non-toxic, widely used herbs, such as ginseng, that stimulate *qi* and blood production and can be taken by anyone. The second category is that of the middle or "ministerial" (*chen*) herbs, which are used to nourish the body and treat minor diseases and mental problems. These commonly used herbs, such as Bupleurum, are mainly non-toxic but should be taken on prescription from a qualified herbalist because of their powerful effects. The third category is lower or "assistant" (*zuo shi*) herbs, which are toxic curatives used to expel serious diseases. Given that ingredients such as arsenic and euphorbia are included, these herbs must only be taken under careful supervision.

Herbal medicines are made from plant, mineral and animal products and include: grasses, vegetables, nuts, berries and fruits; precious gems, such as jade; types of earth; and insects, fish, birds and wild-animal parts – although the latter are becoming less common because of international attempts to preserve endangered species. Various parts of plants and animals may be used, such as roots, stalks, branches and bark, leaves and fruits, as well as dried bone, bile and placenta. Vegetarians can use plants in place of the animals, but the Chinese have traditionally considered animal ingredients to be more potent.

UPPER HERBS

Upper or "ruler" (*jun*) herbs constitute the basic ingredients of longevity formulas. They are thought to assist the smooth flow of *qi* ("vital energy") and blood around the body.

Left to right: ginseng root (ren shen), *peony root* (bai shao yao), *cinnamon* (gui zhi), *sweet gum fruit* (lu lu tong), *Sichuan pepper, leaves and fruit* (hua jiao), *ginger* (gan jiang).

MIDDLE HERBS

Middle or "ministerial" (*chen*) herbs are quite strong and may have side effects, therefore professional advice is recommended before they are taken. They are used to treat minor diseases and relieve psychological problems.

Left to right: field mint (bo he), *loquat* (pi pa ye), *clerodendrum* (chou wu tong), *euonymus or spindle fruit* (chi gen), *wormwood or mugwort* (ai yi), *fossil bone* (long gu).

LOWER HERBS

Lower or "assistant" (*zuo shi*) herbs are toxic and require the skills of a qualified herbalist. These herbs treat serious disorders and the category encompasses substances such as arsenic and euphorbia.

Left to right: opium poppy (ying su ke), *ephedra* (ma huang), *persica* (above, tao ren), *forsythia* (below, lian qiao), *evodia* (wu zhu yu), *Japanese honeysuckle* (qin yin hua), *dried ephedra* (ma huang).

Herbs are classified according to their nature, taste, use and effectiveness, and this includes reference to their source, toxicity, and methods of harvesting and preparation. Traditionally, herbs were gathered according to the season that was related to the organ or the condition to be treated, sometimes even according to celestial movements, but nowadays commercial pressures dominate harvesting regimes.

The "nature" or "temperature" of a herb is classified according to four types of *qi* (*si qi*): hot (*re*), warm (*wen*), cool (*liang*) or cold (*han*). Herbs that do not fall into these categories are classified as neutral (*ping xing*). Herbs of different natures are selected in order to counteract the effects of particular pathogenic factors – for example hot or warming herbs would be used to treat cold conditions, while cooling and cold-inducing herbs would be used to treat hot conditions.

Herbs are also classified according to the Five Tastes (see pages 94–95 and pages 110–113). Sour (*suan*) herbs have a gathering effect, bitter (*ku*) herbs a strengthening effect, sweet (*gan*) a retarding effect, pungent (*xin*) a dispersing effect and salty (*xian*) a softening effect. These effects operate according to the Five Phases (see pages 94–95). Herbs that do not fall into these categories are classified as tasteless (*dan*) or rough, also called astringent (*se*).

Herbs are compiled into medicinal formulas according to their effects and compatibility, and the prescriptions take into account the relative quantities required of each herb, the method of use and any contra-indications. Raw herbs, obtained from herbal pharmacies, are generally sold dried and then boiled into teas or made into decoctions to be

Modern herbal tonics are now available in pill form, and many people prefer them to the unpleasant-tasting teas made from raw herbs – teas which are also laborious to make .

taken internally or into pastes and ointments to be applied externally. The smell and taste can sometimes be unpleasant, so a huge market has developed in more palatable ready-made "patent remedies" available over the counter. These pills, capsules, powders and plasters are widely used as general tonics and in the treatment of various digestive, respiratory and gynecological disorders.

The early alchemists believed that herbal formulas could play an important role in delaying the aging process and ensuring longevity. By combining essences of heaven and earth – in the form of exalted and base substances combined in exact proportions and made into medicinal elixirs – it was thought that blood and *qi* could be nourished and inner organ function enhanced. Even today, herbal formulas for promoting longevity are extremely popular, especially among the over-sixties age group and accounts of active, vital people in their eighties, nineties and even 100-plus are legendary.

Longevity formulas often contain a number of animal ingredients, such as deer antler, gecko lizard, donkey skin gelatin, the penis, kidneys and testes of various animals and even human placenta. Objection to the use of such animal ingredients is growing in most countries and many of these items – particularly those, such as rhinoceros horn, tiger parts or seahorses, that are derived from protected species – are scarcely used today. Common herbal ingredients used in longevity formulas are *Angelica*, *Astralgus* and ginseng – the latter considered to be a supreme *yang* and *qi* tonic.

The ingredients selected are generally designed to increase the production and flow of *qi* and blood and to promote the function of the liver, kidneys and spleen. They may be taken daily or seasonally in the form of wines or liquid tonics, or as pills. It is believed that these tonics boost energy levels, prevent disease, improve digestion and vital function, and strengthen the bones.

Texts on longevity advocate that these herbal formulas should be combined with a moderate lifestyle. Overtaxing or overworking the body should be avoided, but so too should overly comfortable, leisurely or idle lifestyles. It is considered vital to keep both body and mind active and alert by means of careful nutrition, regular health exercises, self-massage, meditation and contemplation, and practice of the arts, such as calligraphy.

Sexual activity is also covered in the texts. Certain herbs are used to promote virility and fertility, but sexual conduct is important, too. Frequent sex leads to a depletion of *jing* essence in the body, resulting in lethargy and weakness and ultimately disease and chronic ailments, including impotence and infertility. On the other hand, moderate sex and the conservation of sexual fluids is seen as life-enhancing.

The ultimate aim of the pursuit of longevity, known as "the cultivation of life", or *yang sheng,* is to achieve "immortality" through spiritual transformation. In addition to the herbal formulas, there are within the Daoist tradition a number of spiritual exercises which facilitate progress towards this goal. These exercises are designed to increase vital energy (*qi*), essence (*jing*) and spirit (*shen*), and to transform physical energy into more subtle energy for spiritual purposes (see pages 124–125).

FENG SHUI

Feng shui is the art of creating auspicious placement and a harmonious flow of *qi* in the home or working environment in order to promote health and healing. Every room and building is believed to have its own flow of *qi* and the correct placement of furniture, doors and objects is thought to have a profound effect on physical, mental and spiritual health. If the *qi* flow becomes trapped or blocked it can cause difficulties in sleeping or concentrating, and can provoke discord and physical ailments.

Spaces are analysed by means of a chart based on the eight *yin* and *yang* trigrams (see pages 92–93). The eight segments are orientated to the compass and cover health, prosperity, fame and future prospects, lovelife, children, helpful friends, career, and education or knowledge. If any segment contains clutter or unhelpful objects likely to inhibit the flow of *qi* there may be problems in the corresponding area of the person's life.

Corrections are made by moving furniture, adding mirrors and chimes and burning herbal incense. These are thought to clear "bad" energy and promote the flow of *qi*. It is claimed that feng shui leads to increased efficiency, improved health and mental calm.

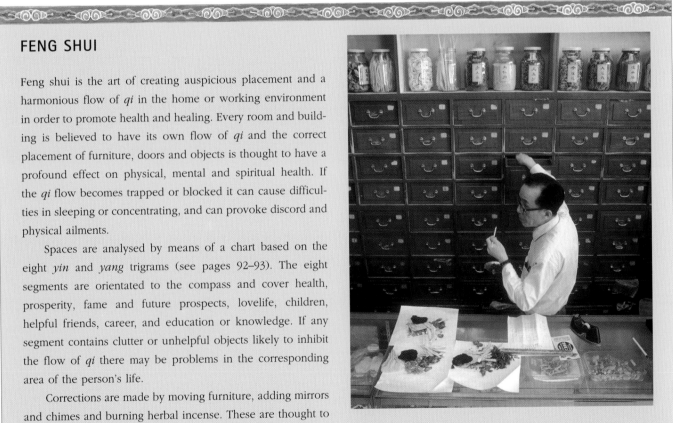

More than 500 herbs are used today by Chinese herbal practitioners. Dried herbs and herbal incense are used in feng shui to purify rooms and ward off evil spirits.

HARMONIZING ENERGY FLOW

Exercises for the improvement of health have always been an important element of Chinese medicine. It is firmly believed that a sedentary lifestyle and lack of exercise can contribute to disease and that exercises designed to promote the flow of *qi* and blood can ensure vitality and longevity (*yang sheng*).

Writings about the benefits of exercise date back to the Western Han dynasty (206BCE–23CE). Silk scrolls from *c.*168BCE depict men and women undertaking various bending, stretching and breathing exercises – these exercises are collectively referred to as *dao yin* (see also pages 118–119). The physician Hua Tuo, who lived several centuries later during the Eastern Han dynasty (25–220CE), is thought to have made an in-depth study of exercise to create a famous sequence that still exists in various forms today. The five-stage exercise, known as the *wu qin xi* or "five animal play", was based on observations of the stances and movements of five animals known for their strength, versatility and longevity: the deer, tiger, bear, monkey and bird.

Many different traditions of therapeutic exercise exist in China, with the three major religions – Daoism, Confucianism and Buddhism – each developing their own distinct forms. These include medical exercises to prevent and treat disease, and the martial arts – the *wu shu* traditions – designed to enhance physical performance and promote strength and health.

The term *qi gong*, meaning "working with", "directing" or "mastering" *qi*, was coined in the 1930s to cover therapeutic breathing, postural and moving exercises designed to promote the flow of *qi* in the body. There are thousands of these exercises and they have been practised for centuries; they aim to regulate the body by means of both moving and stationary poses, to regulate the breath by means of breathing exercises, and to regulate the mind by means of visualization and concentration techniques. The intention is not merely to exercise the physical body but also to stimulate the energy systems of the body, enhance mental function and, ultimately, develop higher consciousness.

Even the simplest *qi gong* exercise (see right) can improve relaxation and strengthen the body. It need only take a few minutes but should be repeated regularly and the duration of practice should gradually be increased. In any posture, always touch the roof of the mouth with the tip of

THE CINNABAR FIELDS

Daoist illustrations show the existence of three major energy fields in the body, including the upper, middle and lower *dan tian*, also known as the Cinnabar Fields. These are located between the eyebrows, between the nipples and three centimetres below the navel, respectively. They have their equivalents in the *chakras* described in the Indian yoga system (see box, page 21) and the energy centres of Tibetan medicine (see page 57).

Many subtle energy exercises exist for building energy in these "fields" and circulating it through specific "orbits" in the body. A commonly practised one, the "microcosmic orbit", circulates energy from the lower *dan tian* across the perineum and up the governing channel to the upper *dan tian*. Cosmic energy is drawn in through the crown centre at the top of the head during this part of the cycle. Energy is then lowered through the conception channel and middle *dan tian* back to the lower *dan tian* where earth energy is absorbed. This is said to regulate *yin* and *yang* energies in the body and to unite physical and cosmic or "heavenly" energies. Such exercises balance health and promote longevity and are part of the process of spiritual transformation.

the tongue in order to connect the governing and conception channels (see page 98). Research has shown that *qi gong* can produce profound physical and mental changes, including lower pulse rate and blood pressure, increased oxygenation of the tissues and greater mental alertness. In a medical context *qi gong* is used for rehabilitation in clinics throughout China and in the treatment of serious illnesses such as heart disease. In the martial arts the "soft" forms of *qi gong* developed into *t'ai ch'i* while "harder" forms developed into disciplines such as *kungfu*. Each has its own style but all aim to harmonize body, mind and spirit, and all produce benefits in terms of mobility, flexibility, improved physical functions, such as digestion and sleep, greater mental clarity and inner tranquility.

QI GONG EXERCISES

2 *Inhaling through the nose, slowly begin to raise the hands up the front of the body, imagining that you are cradling this "energy ball" in your palms and moving it upwards past the torso.*

3 *At the top of the breath, slowly rotate the hands around the ball, turning the palms over. As you exhale, start to move the hands downwards, pushing the "energy ball" as you go.*

1 *This exercise helps build qi in the lower* dan tian. *Position the hands in front of the abdomen with the palms facing upwards and the fingers nearly touching. Imagine that you are holding an "energy ball". Relax and breathe softly.*

4 *On completion of the exhalation the hands should be below the navel. Slowly rotate them and, inhaling, start to lift the "energy ball" once more. Repeat rhythmically for several minutes. End by placing both hands on the* dan tian *point and focusing energy within.*

JAPAN

THE PATH OF PURITY

Early Japanese medical practices emphasized purity and involved cleansing rites, ritual exorcisms and herbal therapy. Ideas from Korea, China and Europe have all influenced medicine in Japan but there are also many uniquely Japanese refinements and innovations.

Disease is seen as the disruption of normal bodily processes due to an imbalance of *ki* ("vital force", pronounced "kee" and equivalent to *qi*) energy that may be either deficient (*kyo*) or excess (*jitsu*). Diagnostic techniques for assessing this imbalance include abdominal examination and micro-diagnosis, which involves examining individual parts of the body to obtain information about the whole.

Treatment aims to purify the body and to restore normal health balance. The approaches most widely used are herbal medicine (*kanpo*), acupuncture and moxibustion, and massage and manipulation, but there is also great emphasis placed on spiritual health and mental well-being.

At the entrance to every Japanese shrine is a water basin used for ritual cleansing. Bamboo or metal cups are used to pour water for the washing of the hands and rinsing of the mouth. The person is then considered to be purified and ready to approach the holy site. Similar ritual cleansing takes place before the consumption of Japanese tea (chanoyu) in teahouses (chashitsu), some with gardens similar to that shown here.

127

CHAPTER 13

MYTHOLOGY, INSPIRATION AND PURITY

Japanese myth relates how two deities, Izanagi and Izanami, who represented the male and female principles respectively, made the islands of Japan and all its natural phenomena such as water, wind, mountains and vegetation. While purifying himself, Izanagi also produced three divine offspring in the form of the sun goddess Amaterasu, the moon god Tsukiyomi and the storm god Susano.

According to the *Kojiki* (*The Record of Ancient Matters*), compiled in 712CE, Amaterasu was said to have gained control over the Central Land of the Reed Plain, as Earth was known. In time the sun goddess came to be seen as the supreme deity in Shinto (see page 131) and she was revered as the direct divine ancestor of Japan's emperor, the protector of the entire Japanese race.

Since early Japanese society was primarily agricultural, it was dependent on sunlight and reasonable weather conditions to ensure good harvests and sufficient food for health and survival. People revered and made offerings to the deities thought to control such natural phenomena as sun, water, wind and grains. Gradually, ceremonies evolved to offer ritual thanks for abundant harvests and to serve as purification rites guarding against disease to crops or humans.

THE HISTORY OF JAPANESE MEDICINE

The earliest healing traditions in Japan centred around exorcism, purification and herbal therapy. Old accounts of Japanese life describe individuals, often women, thought to have shamanistic or occult powers and the ability to facilitate healing. Illness was attributed to malevolent spirits, physical impurity or to deities who had been neglected or mistreated. Accordingly, the healer would recommend exorcism of the evil spirit or cleansing rituals, such as bathing, or offerings to appease the deity. The *Kojiki* contains an early mention of herbal therapy, detailing native plants and fruits used in healing, such as *momo* (peach) and *kuzu* (arrowroot).

Foreign influences on Japanese medicine began in the fifth and sixth centuries with physicians and monks visiting from Korea and then China. The Korean physician Kon-mu arrived in 414CE and was invited to serve as the emperor's physician. In 552CE Korean monks introduced Buddhism, which took root after a difficult start. The Chinese envoy Zhi Cong arrived in 562CE and brought with him medical texts, including ones on acupuncture and moxibustion, which were studied avidly at court.

During the sixth and seventh centuries, diplomatic and scholarly exchanges between Japan and China increased and many Chinese medical, scientific and religious texts were introduced into Japan. Two Buddhist monks, Enichi

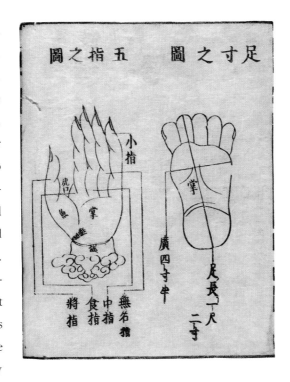

A late 17th-century print denoting the acupoints in the hand and foot, from a Japanese commentary on a Chinese medical text first printed in 1341.

and Fukhuin, spent fifteen years studying in China and, upon their return in 623CE, they advocated that Japan adopt the Chinese system of medicine.

In a series of reforms introduced just prior to and during the Nara period (710–794), Japan was given a new bureaucratic structure based on that of China. According to the Taiho and Yoro codes, each prefecture was to establish a medical school and three new institutes were founded in the capital at Nara. Courses at the Institute of Medicine included those for the use of herbs, diet, acupuncture and moxibustion, *anma* massage and bone-setting, and complex rituals for spiritual cleansing.

These new practices were largely restricted to royalty and the social elite. Rural people relied on Buddhist monks and Shinto priests to attend to their medical needs. The formalization of medical training led to increased interest in medicine among scholars and physicians and to the creation of the first Japanese texts – including the *Ishinpo (Prescriptions at the Heart of Medicine)*, compiled in 984 by Tamba Yasunari. Most other texts at this time were commentaries on Chinese writings. From this point onwards, with the rising power of Japan's warlords and their inward-looking policies, there was restricted foreign contact and Japanese medicine began to develop in its own right.

PRINCIPLES AND PRACTICE

Between the ninth and twelfth centuries the Japanese imperial court weakened, causing a decline in those medical institutions the court had favoured. Buddhism flourished nevertheless and monk-scholars, who were still allowed to travel, continued to bring medical texts into Japan, stimulating interest in medicine. Physicians began to develop original Japanese approaches and to incorporate folk remedies and native herbs into their treatments alongside tradi-

A 19th-century woodblock print of a Tokugawa-period pharmacist chopping plants, which he will later use in herbal medicine – kanpo.

tional Chinese practices. Writing in about 1368, the Zen monk Yurin devised a new method for classifying diseases and around the same time another monk, Majima Shigetsune, developed special techniques for treating eye diseases. New forms of moxibustion treatment by monks also became popular at Buddhist temples.

From the mid-sixteenth century onwards, the arrival in Japan of European merchants and missionaries led to the introduction of Western anatomy and surgery. Portuguese Jesuit Francis Xavier and trader Luis d'Almeida both introduced some medicines and simple practices. By the end of the sixteenth century, Spanish Franciscans and Dutch and German traders and physicians had arrived too.

Japan's ruling powers initially welcomed these influences, as they had need of good medical treatment for their battle-wounded warriors. However, the Europeans and their religion were soon seen as a threat, and persecutions of Christians began. Some physicians remained, though, and one Portuguese doctor, Fereira, who took the name

Sawano, wrote a book on surgery. There were, however, more edicts to expel foreigners and the country was closed to foreign influence after 1639. The only exceptions to this were a few Dutch and German traders and physicians permitted to remain on the island of Deshima in Nagasaki Bay. They continued to trade and to teach, and in 1665 a Japanese student attained a Dutch surgery certificate for the first time.

During the era of Tokugawa rule (1603–1868) and the expulsions, Japanese medicine really began to flourish. Three new schools arose, absorbing influences from China and Europe – the Gosei school, started by herbalist and acupuncturist Manase Dosan, was based on new ideas from China; the Koho school favoured the classical Chinese texts; and the Rampo school incorporated Western ideas. At the same time, more uniquely Japanese approaches were developed. Sugiyama Waichi, a blind acupuncturist, devised a guide tube for simple and painless insertion of acupuncture needles. This is still a defining aspect of Japanese acupuncture (see pages 144–145). Sugiyama also advocated fine needles and established acupuncture schools for the blind.

Another medical innovation that occurred during the period was abdominal diagnosis and treatment (see pages 138–139). Mubunsai, a monk, refined diagnosis by palpation and then treatment through needling the abdominal area.

Other physicians continued to study both Western and oriental medicine and achieved some major medical breakthroughs. Early in the eighteenth century, Fuseya Soteki discovered that urine is produced in the kidneys rather than the intestine, as was the Chinese belief at that time. This preceded Western physician William Beaumont who was credited with it in 1842. Similarly, in 1805 the physician and herbalist Hanaoka Seishu succeeded in developing a herbal anaesthetic that he used during a breast tumour removal. Anaesthesia was not used in the West until 1846.

With the end of the feudal era in 1868 the Meiji period commenced and Japan's modernization began. All medical practitioners were now required by law to study Western medicine. Traditional practices such as acupuncture lost status and became mainly the realm of blind practitioners. The Dutch and German medical systems were formally adopted and in 1911 the first licensing law for acupuncturists was introduced, whereby acupuncturists were required to study Western medical principles and practice.

In the 1920s, however, a classical revival began, initiated by journalist Nakayama Tadano and acupuncture and moxibustion practitioner Sawada Ken. This was continued by the prominent acupuncturist Yanagiya Sorei and his students into the 1930s. The war years intervened and in the ensuing American occupation General MacArthur tried to stamp out traditional medical practices, deeming them to be primitive and unhygienic. As a result practitioners from all the different schools joined together and, after a protracted legal battle, secured the right to practise under a new law that introduced new licensing procedures.

Today many forms of medicine exist side by side in Japan. Western medicine is practised both by doctors and in hospitals and is used widely for most conditions. Many doctors freely practise herbal medicine or *kanpo* (see pages 152–153). Acupuncture and moxibustion (see pages 144–145) as well as massage and manipulation (see pages 146–147) thrive in private clinics and are often used for chronic and painful conditions. There is also a large industry in self-help therapies, from over-the-counter herbals to massage aids, and the Buddhist temples and Shinto shrines offer elaborate spiritual charms and offer healing rituals.

The straw rope and paper cuttings encircling this tree at a Shinto shrine signify that the tree is to be treated with reverence. The white of the paper symbolizes purity and the rope protects the tree from external "pollution".

SHINTO – THE WAY OF THE GODS

The indigenous religion of Japan, Shinto (meaning "The Way of the Gods"), is a form of nature worship and animism. It is based on the idea that all things, both animate and inanimate, possess a spirit. Accordingly, anything from rocks, mountains, waterfalls, trees, animals and plants to natural phenomena such as storms or winds may be revered for their spirit. A whole pantheon of heavenly deities are also revered and thought to exert a direct influence on the health and welfare of the nation, including powers over agricultural harvests and human fertility. These deities, or *kami*, are accorded special shrines and festivals where they are celebrated with offerings and rituals.

Daily practice of Shinto in the home involves first washing, as a form of purification, and then a brief ritual in front of the family altar, the *kamidana*, or "shelf of the gods". This is a small, wooden shrine on a high shelf that contains offerings, Shinto symbols and memorial tablets for deceased relatives. The person bows to the shrine, claps hands twice to draw the attention of the gods, and then makes a brief, silent prayer. This is usually an expression of thanks and a request for blessings and protection during the day ahead.

CHAPTER 14

CONCEPTS OF THE BODY AND DISEASE

The concepts of *in* and *yo* and of the Five Elements – wood, earth, fire, metal and water – in Japanese medicine came directly from China (see pages 92–93 and 94–95). In order to live happy and healthy lives, the Japanese have always regarded it as essential to live in harmony with these universal forces, which manifest themselves in nature, the food we eat, and so on. Next to cleanliness and purity (see page 128), the keys to remaining healthy have always been seen as the correct way of eating (see pages 142–143), appropriate breathing and exercise (see pages 146–159) and correct lifestyle (see page 141).

Life is conceptualized in stages from pre-conception to foetal development, birth and infancy, childhood, adulthood, old age and post-human life in which we reassume our energetic or spiritual form. The belief in reincarnation, or some sort of life after death, is widespread. The thread linking all these stages together is thought to be *ki* energy, which is said to create vortices of energy during foetal development that contribute to the creation of the meridians, internal organs and structures of the body.

Central to the Japanese view of the body and the natural world is the concept of *ki*. Good health is described as *genki*, meaning "to have a good supply of source *ki*"; disease is *byoki* and means "blocked" or "sick" *ki*; *tenki* (weather) means the "*ki* of heaven"; *kuki* (air) is "empty *ki*"; and the word *iki* (breath) is also used to describe mental phenomena. *Ki* is thus the link between body, mind and spirit.

THE MERIDIANS

The body is sustained by *ki*, the "vital force" or life energy, which courses through the main acupuncture meridians. In modern Japanese medicine, the twelve main meridians and the eight extra channels are the same as in the Chinese system (see pages 98–99). However, some practitioners also add one further meridian in the feet (the stomach branch meridian, linked to the middle toe and associated with the oesophagus, stomach function and digestion) and one in the hands (the diaphragm meridian, linked to the outer edge of the middle finger and associated with the lungs and breathing function). The twentieth-century practitioner and *shiatsu* master Shizuto Masunaga also developed an extended system for the twelve main meridians (see pages 148–149), after having located pathways for all of these meridians in both the arms and legs.

Along the sides of the spine, on the urinary bladder meridians, are a series of "entering" points known as the *yu-ketsu* or *yu* (called *shu* points in Chinese medicine). These are places where energy is said to "pour in" to the body and which are held to have a direct association with specific internal organs. Having "charged" the internal organs, *ki* energy is then said to stream out to the front of the body where it collects in the *bo-ketsu* or frontal "gathering" points (frontal *mu* points in Chinese medicine). These major points are widely used for treatment in both Japanese and Chinese medicine; in Japan, however, they are also often used for palpation diagnosis and for rice grain moxa treatment (see page 145).

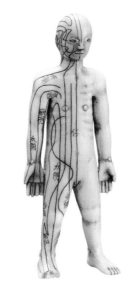

A 19th-century Japanese netsuke *carved in ivory and inscribed with the major acupuncture meridians.*

The *ki* energy is then dispersed through the arm and leg meridians, ending at the *sei-ketsu*, or "well" (*jing-well* in Chinese), points on the tips of the fingers and toes. The term "well" is used to suggest the bubbling and issuing forth of water at a well or spring. The *ki* flow is balanced by the *gen-ketsu*, or "source" points, (*yuan* points in Chinese medicine) at the ankles and wrists.

In Japanese acupuncture, the *sei-ketsu* points have been used to develop diagnostic systems to determine the amount of *ki* in their corresponding meridians. Two twentieth-century examples of this are the *akabane* method and the Apparatus for Measuring the Meridians and their Corresponding Internal Organs, better known as AMI. The *akabane* method, named after the practitioner who developed it, is a system in which a lighted moxa stick is rapidly passed across the *sei* point until a sensation is felt (see page 138). AMI, devised by Dr Hiroshi Motoyama, involves the placing of electrodes on each of the *sei-ketsu* points and then a form of electrical measurement to determine polarization effects in the skin. The measurement before polarization (BP) indicates the amount of *ki* energy in the meridian and corresponding internal organ.

The points along the meridians are named according to their character and effects. They may be described in terms of certain natural landscape features, such as hills or hollows, or with reference to their effects. Generally, these Japanese names correspond in meaning to the Chinese point names.

PATTERNS OF DISEASE

Disease patterns can be described in terms of the relative balance of *kyo* (deficiency or depletion) or *jitsu* (excess or fullness). *Kyo* conditions are associated with weakness, fatigue and incapacity, while *jitsu* conditions are signified by overactivity, tension and discomfort. The character for *kyo* (*xie* in Chinese) means a hollow or a mound that is hollow inside, while the character for *jitsu* (*shi* in Chinese) represents a house filled to capacity. *Kyo* is generally *in* (*yin*) in nature while *jitsu* is generally *yo* (*yang*). Thus, just as *in* and *yo* are relatively interdependent and give rise to

one another, so *kyo* gives rise to *jitsu* and within every *jitsu* condition there is an underlying *kyo*. However, while *in* and *yo* describe opposing and interdependent tendencies, *kyo* and *jitsu* describe the actual condition and function of *ki* energy in the body.

Kyo conditions are harder to detect as they are less visible and often located deeper within the body, while *jitsu* symptoms appear more prominently on the surface. However, it is essential to diagnose and treat the *kyo* in order to successfully treat the *jitsu*. Inexperienced practitioners are led towards the *jitsu* signs and symptoms because of their prominence but the more experienced are able to accurately detect and treat the underlying *kyo*.

The two can be determined according to the type and nature of symptoms, diagnosed through observation and questioning, pulse-taking or through palpation of the meridian pathways, acupuncture points and body parts such as the abdomen (see pages 136–139). *Kyo* meridians or areas are felt as flabby, weak and hollow; movement is loose, limp and unrestricted; and the person feels tired and empty. *Jitsu* meridians or areas are felt as tight, hard and prominent. There is often muscular tension and there is an uncomfortable sensation when the relevant area is touched.

In meridian diagnosis (see pages 144–147), the most *kyo* and the most *jitsu* areas must be determined so that both may be treated simultaneously. Often these form a meridian pair; for example, if the *in* spleen meridian is the most *kyo* then its corresponding *yo* meridian, the stomach, is likely to be the most *jitsu*. Such a *kyo/jitsu* pattern would manifest as a digestive disturbance, such as indigestion.

All the meridian lines will demonstrate some degree of *kyo* or *jitsu* imbalance because the body is in a constant state of dynamic change, but it is only when these become

KYO AND JITSU CONDITIONS

A stiff neck and shoulder tension are signs of a *jitsu* condition.

A *kyo* condition of the stomach results in lack of appetite and a feeling of coldness in the abdomen. A *jitsu* condition results in overeating, acid indigestion and sometimes vomiting.

A *jitsu* bladder condition causes painful urination, as with cystitis. However the underlying *kyo* condition is weak kidney function. This manifests as low backache and cold limbs.

Kyo conditions cause feelings of lethargy, fatigue and weakness in the limbs.

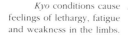

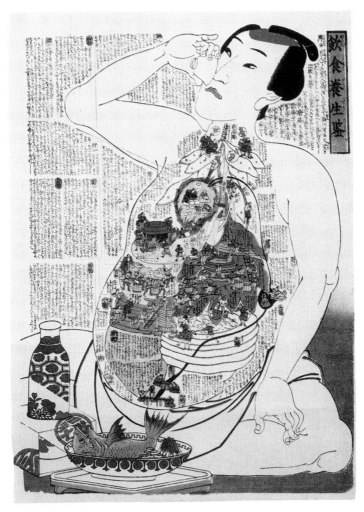

The Rules of Dietary Life, *a 19th-century print by Kunisada*
Utagawa suggests how eating the wrong foods, or an excess of
the right ones, can upset the digestive system.

pronounced or prolonged that disease results. The degree of distortion between *kyo* and *jitsu*, known as *ja-ki*, is affected by constitution, healing ability and mental attitude.

Once the pattern of *kyo* and *jitsu* has been identified the primary aim of treatment is *kyo-jitsu-ho-sha*, meaning to reinforce (*ho*) the *kyo* and disperse (*sha*) the *jitsu*. *Kyo* conditions are treated with tonification. In acupuncture this means painless, superficial needling and the application of heat, such as moxa. In massage and *shiatsu* it means gentle, comfortable pressure and touch. The aim is to replenish the *ki* in the meridian or area that is deficient and empty.

Jitsu conditions are treated with acupuncture needle techniques that disperse energy and by massage techniques using light, brief movements and pressure. These allow the *jitsu* to normalize. If the person's healing force is strong, *jitsu* conditions will correct quickly. *Kyo* conditions often take longer to treat because they are associated with chronic fatigue in the body and a depletion of the healing force.

With the main imbalances treated, homeostasis will correct lesser ones naturally. Exercises can also help, as can the mind. The phrase *kibun-o-kaete* means "a change of attitude", but its literal meaning is "to redirect" one's *ki*.

CHAPTER 15

DIAGNOSTIC PROCEDURES

I n Japan the diagnostic emphasis is on observation and palpation. Observational diagnosis (*bo-shin*) is regarded as a primary method and practitioners make use of many visual indications in diagnosis, including the gait, body size and proportions, skin, nails and hair through to facial features and expression. Diagnosis using touch (*setsu-shin*) includes pulse diagnosis, which differs slightly from the Chinese method. In addition, abdominal palpation has developed to such an extent that it is used as a form of diagnosis and treatment in its own right. Palpation of pressure points on the channels is also used diagnostically (see pages 138–139).

Listening and smelling (*bun-shin*) encompasses the voice and breath, as well as any gurgling from the intestines, which may indicate digestive disturbance. Body odour is noted, and the smell and appearance of body waste is considered. Questioning (*mon-shin*) is used to glean information about the patient's constitution, preferences, family medical history and so on, and also to confirm the diagnosis and determine the best treatment. Questioning plays a lesser role than in other traditions; in Japan, practitioners emphasise observation and palpation.

Whatever the method of diagnosis, the practitioner is determining the bodily imbalance of *in* and *yo*. Great significance is attached to the concepts of *kyo* ("deficiency") and *jitsu* ("excess") – measures of the amount of energy or vitality in the different channels (see also pages 98–99) and their corresponding organs. It is considered essential to identify the underlying deficiency in order to determine the root cause of the disease and thereby initiate appropriate treatment.

DIAGNOSING THROUGH OBSERVATION

The first thing a Japanese practitioner looks for in a patient is *shin* or "spirit". The renowned acupuncturist Okabe Sodo described how this could be identified according to the luminescence around the body, sparkle in the eyes, lustre in the skin, clarity in the voice, liveliness in behaviour, and depth and evenness in breathing. These factors are observed from a slight distance and the greater the *shin* the better the prognosis is.

As the patient approaches, his or her gait is also noted. If the toes are turned out, the posture stooped and the movement lethargic this suggests that *in* energy predominates (the equivalent of *yin*). If the toes are turned in and the gait is upright and forceful this suggests a predominance of *yo* energy (as *yang* is called in Japan).

Next, attention may be paid to the face, tongue, ears, hands and feet, nails and hair. The tongue and ears may be observed micro-diagnostically, whereby each is thought to correspond to the body as a whole (see pages 106–107). This also applies to the face, hands and feet and is combined together with a diagnosis of meridian imbalance through the palpation of points (see page 138).

In facial diagnosis, the shape of the face and the arrangement of its features are used both to determine the balance of *in* and *yo* and also to detect signs of meridian imbalance. A face shaped like a downward pointing triangle – with a large forehead, pointed chin and features spaced apart – indicates an *in* constitution. A face with a square jaw, small forehead and features set close together is indicative of a *yo* constitution.

A late-19th-century netsuke *of a practitioner pulse-taking. Taking the pulse at the wrist enabled the physician to obtain information about the whole body while the patient remained clothed.*

The eyes also reveal vital information: large eyes mean a big intake of *in* foods, while small ones suggest a diet dominated by *yo* foods. Sparse eyebrows indicate an excess of sugar and short eyelashes a predominance of animal products. Puffiness or dark rings under the eyes mean problems with kidney function and fluid retention. Eye-white under and around the iris, a condition called *sanpaku* ("three whites"), indicates poor health linked to bad diet and lifestyle.

Narrow noses with small nostrils indicate weak lungs while bulbous, red noses are linked to overindulgence and possible heart problems. Long noses are consistent with an *in* constitution and short noses with a *yo* one. Similarly a small mouth with thin lips is *in* while a large mouth and thick lips is *yo*. Dark lips indicate poor blood circulation; pale, dry lips poor stomach function.

Hands and feet can be assessed by size, colouring and texture. They also correspond with the standard meridians that start and end at the tips of the fingers and toes. Short, thick fingers and strong hands with a full palm indicate a strong constitution, while thin, long fingers and a flexible palm suggest a weaker one. If the palms are moist there is a problem with fluid metabolism; if they are hot and dry there may be an excess of *yo* and some "internal heat".

These and many more signs are stored mentally by the physician while further information is obtained using other techniques. Like clues in a detective mystery they are combined together using the processes of logic and instinct to produce a firm conclusion about the patient's illness.

THE MICRO-DIAGNOSIS SYSTEM

Diagnosis using the pulse involves determining its quality and the relative strength of each of the internal organs taken at six positions along the radial artery of both wrists. This procedure reflects diagnostic practice in China (see pages 104–105). However, the positioning of the practitioner's hands differs; rather than using one hand to feel each wrist in turn, as is normal in China, the Japanese practitioner usually uses both hands to palpate each wrist simultaneously, and the thumb plays an important role.

To have the pulse taken, the patient lies on the treatment couch, or floor mat, resting their wrists naturally on the abdomen. Standing or kneeling at the patient's side, the practitioner adopts a wide stance and strengthens their lower abdomen. This is consistent with the Japanese focus on the *tanden* (*dan tian* in Chinese), a source of power and concentration (see pages 124–125).

Rather than using strength in the fingers, the Japanese practitioner creates it first in the abdomen and then in the thumbs, which are used for support behind the patient's wrists. The practitioner's left hand takes the patient's right wrist and the right hand the patient's left wrist. The thumbs are placed in a natural position around the wrist. Master acupuncturists in Japan have long taught that the secret of palpation is to perceive the pulse through the thumbs. This shift of focus allows the fingers to be placed lightly and to develop great sensitivity with no strain. If the patient is weak, the abdomen may be needled or palpated first in

This woodblock illustration of a pregnant woman is from an Edo-period text about abdominal palpation, Fukusho Kiran Yoku. *The skilled application of pressure is said to have therapeutic effects.*

order to strengthen the wrist pulses and make them easier to take. Other hand positions can also be used, depending on the preference of the practitioner. In one common technique, the palms are used around the wrist for support in place of the thumbs. Pulse diagnosis clarifies the relative balance of each channel (meridian) and organ and the patterns of *kyo* and *jitsu*.

Alongside pulse-taking, the abdomen is palpated (see box, right) using significant points, including those along the acupuncture channels. Certain major points are selected on the basis of symptoms or diagnostic signs already elucidated and pressure is applied using the finger or thumb. The points most often used are on the lower arms and legs, the abdomen and either side of the spine. If the point is sensitive to pressure, this indicates a *jitsu* condition of the meridian and corresponding internal organ. If little sensation is felt this indicates a *kyo* condition. For example, pain upon pressure to the large intestine point between the index fingers and thumbs indicates sluggish digestion, while pain upon palpation of the inner-ankle meeting point of the liver, kidney and spleen meridians suggests menstrual problems.

Another sensation-based diagnosis is the *akabane* test whereby a lighted incense stick is passed repeatedly over the starting and end points of the meridians in the fingers and toes. The sooner that warmth is felt the more likely that there is a *jitsu* condition in the corresponding organ.

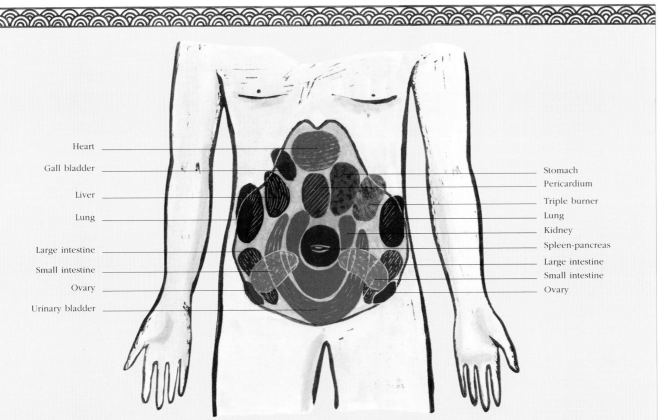

Heart
Gall bladder
Liver
Lung
Large intestine
Small intestine
Ovary
Urinary bladder

Stomach
Pericardium
Triple burner
Lung
Kidney
Spleen-pancreas
Large intestine
Small intestine
Ovary

Japanese ampuku *is based on the premise that different abdominal areas correspond to particular internal organs. As with acupoint theory, it is believed that the application of pressure will have a therapeutic effect on the balance of energy.*

ABDOMINAL DIAGNOSIS (AMPUKU)

Abdominal diagnosis originated at the beginning of the seventeenth century, probably developing out of the rivalry between different schools of acupuncture and herbalism. It was particularly favoured by the monk Mubunsai, who controversially advocated diagnosis and treatment using the abdomen alone. His Mubun School became prominent during that century and the approach was favoured by the Imperial court during the Edo period (1603–1868). By the eighteenth century abdominal diagnosis had become so firmly established in Japan that one master acupuncturist, Yoshimasu Todo, said in 1752, "The abdomen is the source of life and therefore the myriad diseases have their root there. The abdomen must always be examined in order to diagnose disease." This has now become a part of the nation's folklore and Japanese people today often express the belief that disease begins in the intestines and the abdomen.

The patient lies on a treatment couch or floor mat with the legs extended, hands by the sides and abdomen exposed. The practitioner kneels or stands on the left side of the patient, places strength in the abdomen (as with pulse-taking) and then starts by placing a warmed hand below the patient's sternum. The hand is kept there for five or six breaths while the practitioner synchronizes his or her breathing with that of the patient and the patient relaxes. The practitioner then applies gentle pressure to different diagnostic areas of the abdomen corresponding to each internal organ (see illustration, above). Pain upon pressure indicates a *jitsu* ("excess") condition while a feeling of comfort on pressure indicates *kyo* ("deficiency"). The point that is four finger-widths below the navel may also be used to determine life expectancy (rather like the "life pulse" in Tibetan medicine, see pages 66–67). If this feels completely hollow and empty then death may be imminent. A patient's abdomen is also felt for any lumps or intestinal blockage. By the twentieth century, different styles of abdominal diagnosis were developed, giving rise to separate and distinct schools of treatment.

CHAPTER 16

HEALING IN JAPANESE MEDICINE

The Japanese word for health, *kenko*, is made up of two Chinese characters – *ken* means "human" or "upright", while *ko* expresses the manner of being relaxed and at ease. Thus health embodies uprightness and correct living according to the laws of nature as well as the development and maintenance of inner peace and calm. In Japan there has always been, and there remains today, an underlying belief that disease is due to living out of harmony with the natural laws of life. A study published in 1980 by the American social anthropologist Margaret Lock reveals that, when asked their view of the cause of their disease, some patients said it was due to "not keeping the rules of life correctly" ("*Kisoku tadashii seikatsu o shinakata*").

The focus in Japanese healing is on bringing one's life back into balance and in harmony with the laws of nature. This starts with the home environment, which should enable you to cultivate a sense of tranquillity and an appreciation of beauty (see page 141), and goes on to cover every aspect of lifestyle and daily habits, including diet, breathing and exercise, daily activities and relationships within the community. Much of this can be achieved through the use of preventive and therapeutic techniques in the home. These include careful diet and exercise, herbal medicine, self-massage and moxibustion techniques, magnet therapy and so on (see pages 144–159). There is also an emphasis on cleanliness and purity, and so bathing, both at home and in outdoor spa baths (*onsen*), is also used for health promotion and healing.

A HEALTHY LIFESTYLE

The Japanese believe that health can be promoted, and illness prevented, by means of a moderate lifestyle and self-help health techniques. The underlying concept for this is the ideal of living according to the Middle Way (*Chu yo*) – that is, of avoiding extremes and of balancing *in* and *yo* in every aspect of daily life.

The first consideration is the home environment. It is thought that the home should be built from, or contain, as many natural materials as possible and should display individual items of great artistic merit and beauty to provide inspiration. Traditional dwellings in Japan have always been made primarily of wood and paper and have been designed with the principles of *in* and *yo* in mind. The *shoji* screens or *fusuma* sliding doors used to divide rooms and the *tatami*-grass mats for flooring are all natural and are thought to help promote a sense of domestic peace. The sides of the house are easily opened to allow in light and air and present the inhabitants with exterior views, which are reflected inside the home in floral arrangements (*ikebana*) or miniature trees (*bonsai*).

Such dwellings have for centuries enabled agrarian Japanese communities to live in close contact with nature and to follow the rhythm of the seasons. By developing an appreciation of nature and cultivating a sense of inner tranquillity at home, it is thought that the foundations of health and healing can be built. It is therefore still common practice for city-dwellers to take periodic breaks in rural retreats

This Japanese pavilion epitomizes tranquillity and the beauty of natural materials and surroundings – all considered beneficial to health. Such environments serve to invoke harmonious feelings.

so as to refresh body, mind and spirit. This may take the form of a Zen weekend retreat for businessmen or a trip to a mountain *onsen* (see pages 154–155).

Moderation and harmony are also ideally reflected in lifestyle. Clothing should be modest and, as far as possible, made from natural ingredients. Many Japanese favour cotton, linen, jute and silk over manmade fibres. It is thought that these fabrics allow the skin to breathe, helping to balance fluid metabolism and temperature regulation. Natural materials are also favoured for dental hygiene and skin and hair care.

The mind and emotions should be kept in balance. Japanese children are shown how to keep their emotions within their control, because expressions of extreme emotion, such as anger, are thought to be not only socially undesirable but also injurious to the body. Respect for ancestors and the cultivation of a sense of gratitude are also thought to be an important aspect of overall health and harmony with the universe. Specific days are set aside in the annual calendar to honour ancestors and to express gratitude to deities (see also pages 156–157) and to the people who help you, such as your teachers.

Daily contact with nature and self-improvement through artistic skills such as calligraphy, the tea ceremony, archery, music, poetry, dance and flower arranging are all thought to enable people to refine both personality and spirituality, leading to greater mental and spiritual health.

FOOD AS MEDICINE

In Japan food is seen as essential to health-maintenance and healing. Japanese cuisine relies on fresh, local, seasonal produce selected in balanced combinations. An ideal meal contains a variety of colours and at least one item from each of the main sources – sea, land and mountain.

Japanese researchers have long been interested in identifying foods for health. One great pioneer of the 1870s, Dr Sagen Ishizukato, spent years studying optimum nutrition

levels and developing cures. In particular he identified the importance of the balance of potassium and sodium in the body and the maintenance of an acid/alkaline balance. He realized that many diseases were linked to excess body acid and concluded that food was the best medicine.

Ishizukato's concept of "foods for health and happiness" became well known (termed *shokuyo* – *shoku* means nourishment and *yo* is the way to nourish oneself perfectly). After his death, his ideas were further developed by one of his disciples, George Ohsawa, who had cured his own prolonged ill-health by using Ishizukato's dietary methods.

Ohsawa, born in 1893, linked Ishizukato's work on acid and alkaline to the oriental medical concepts of *in* and *yo*, and in the 1950s he coined the term macrobiotics (from the Greek *macro*, meaning "big", and *bio*, meaning "life"). The word is used to describe a way of life and of eating that is in harmony with the universal life principles outlined in oriental medicine and philosophy. Ohsawa's work has been hugely influential and has been spread around the world, especially in the West, notably by his followers Herman Aihara and Michio and Eveline Kushi.

In macrobiotics all foods are classified according to their *in* and *yo* properties and eaten according to certain rules and principles. The ideal macrobiotic diet recommends that 50 per cent of consumption is wholegrains and cereals supported by 20–30 per cent vegetables, 10–15 per cent beans and seaweed, and the remainder comprising locally grown fruit, nuts, and seeds and occasional white fish or seafood. However, animal produce should never exceed 15 per cent of the meal.

Grains include brown rice, whole wheat, buckwheat, rye, barley and millet. Vegetables include sea vegetables (seaweeds) such as *konbu*, *hijiki*, *wakame*, *nori* and dulse,

MISO AND MISO SOUP

Miso soup is believed to offer numerous health benefits. To make this dish, select vegetables of different colours and sources (sea, land, mountain). A good combination is *wakame* seaweed, carrot or *daikon* (Japanese radish) and small or finely chopped mushrooms. Sauté the vegetables in sesame oil and simmer, then slowly add 20 fl. oz. (600ml) of boiled water, cover and simmer for fifteen minutes. Dissolve a tablespoonful of *miso* paste in a ladle full of this broth, then stir into the soup. Simmer gently for five minutes and serve with *tofu* and spring onion.

HEALTHY FOODSTUFFS

Food and drink are vital parts of healthy living in Japan. Popular foods include various types of rice; seaweed (such as long, dark *konbu*; small, curly *hijiki*; bright green *wakame*; or dried sheets of *nori*); *miso* (*hacho*, *mugi* and *kome* are three common types); *tofu* (made from soy bean curd); and vegetables. Common drinks are green leaf tea (*o cha*); brown-rice tea (*genmai cha*); and roast-twig tea (*ban cha*).

Clockwise, from top left: Hijiki *seaweed,* wakame *seaweed, half-dried plums* (umeboshi, *which aid digestion), green tea* (o cha), *brown rice tea* (genmai cha), ama koji miso *(top),* oku shinano miso *(bottom) and* tofu.

which are used in smaller amounts than locally grown land vegetables. Beans include soy beans, which when fermented with barley or rice produces the thick *miso* paste used in many dishes. *Miso* is said to alkalinize the blood, aid digestion, help expel intestinal worms and parasites, and regulate metabolism. It is also thought to build vitality, relieve arthritic pain and promote youthful skin (for this reason soy beans are sometimes called "beauty beans"). Seasonings such as salt are limited and only used in unrefined forms. Dairy produce, refined sugar, chemical preservatives and hot spices are excluded from the diet.

Beverages are made from local herbs and include teas such as *ban cha* (roasted twig tea) and *mu* tea made from mixtures of tonifying herbs, including ginger root, peony root, Japanese parsley, mandarin orange peel, Japanese ginseng, liquorice and cinnamon.

Foods may be classified as *in* and *yo* according to their constituents, where and how they are grown, the part of the food used, the way in which it is cooked, and so on. The acid or alkaline-forming nature of the food – that is, its effect on the body after being ingested – also needs to be considered. For example, a lemon may be acid in nature but after ingestion it actually has an alkalinizing effect on the body. Tables of acid and alkaline foods can be found in all macrobiotic cookbooks. The Japanese also have a clear understanding of foods that should not be eaten together (*kuiwase*) – it is said that eating watermelon with fried food (*tempura*) or bamboo shoots with brown sugar will cause stomach ache; eating eels with dried plums (*umeboshi*) is believed to cause food poisoning.

It is recommended that all foods are eaten in a calm environment, chewed very well and consumed at least three hours before sleep to allow for proper digestion. There is a sense of the sacred in food and eating. In Zen establishments, the preparation of food is akin to an act of worship and is an essential part of spiritual discipline. A Zen abbess once commented, "The entire universe is represented in my plate; seeing it I understand the nature of my existence."

ACUPUNCTURE AND ADJUNCT THERAPIES

Acupuncture was brought to Japan from China, but while its theoretical roots are the same (see pages 92–93), its practice is very different. In Japan, distinct instruments and subtle techniques have been developed over several centuries; in addition, there is a wide variety of methods used within Japan. This has come about partly due to the Japanese fondness for refining ideas in innovative ways and partly because of the place of acupuncture therapy within Japanese medicine as a whole.

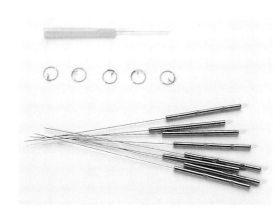

An assortment of Japanese acupuncture equipment: a guide rod or tube (top) to assist with the painless insertion of a needle, ring needles (centre) and stainless steel needles of varying thicknesses (bottom).

focus on symptomatic treatment (the selection of particular acu-points for specific ailments) and often utilize mechanical devices, infra-red lamps and even lasers to stimulate acupoints. One such technique is that of *ryodoraku*, which uses a small device to pulse mild electrical currents through the needles. There are also more eso-teric styles of acupuncture, created by those who are adepts in spiritu-al practices and meditation such as *zazen* (see pages 156–157). These practitioners often use extremely subtle needle techniques where the skin is barely touched.

Unlike China, where acupuncture developed alongside herbal medicine for a millennium and was eventually adopted into the state medical system, Japanese acupuncture developed separately from herbal medicine and has remained in private practice. For centuries acupuncture and massage were the almost exclusive preserve of blind practitioners. An association between these two forms of therapy remains today: in Japan's acupuncture colleges both disciplines are taught together to non-medical practitioners, whereas herbal medicine (*kanpo*) is taught to doctors as a clinical specialization (see pages 152–153).

The basic training required to gain a licence in acupuncture lasts for three years. Graduates then apprentice themselves to a "master" for many more years in order to develop clinical skills according to a particular style of acupuncture. There are many different styles practised in modern Japan, ranging from the "scientific" to the esoteric. So-called "scientific" methods, based on Western medicine,

In addition, there are various approaches based firmly on the Chinese classics of acupuncture. Prominent among them is Meridian Therapy, inspired by the work of Sorei Yanagiya in the 1930s and developed by Okabe Sodo and Inoue Kiri. In this therapy, diagnosis and treatment of meridian imbalance, based on pulse diagnosis and palpation, is seen as more primary than symptomatic treatment.

Because the Japanese pay privately for acupuncture there is an emphasis on service quality and patient comfort. Many subtle, painless techniques have been developed for those who do not favour strong needle stimulation. The needles are generally finer than those used in China, and a guide tube enables painless insertion. Made from stainless steel, silver or gold, needles are normally between 0.16mm and 0.2mm thick (Japanese needle sizes 1–3) and 25 and 40mm in length, excluding the handles. Short needles are often preferred and the guide tube, which is slightly longer, is used to tap the needle in swiftly and comfortably. In Chinese acupuncture, when the needle is inserted the focus is on obtaining a strong needle sensation (*de qi*) which is felt by both the patient and the practitioner. In Japan, the practitioner tries instead to sense the arrival of *ki* – known as *ki itaru* – in their own supporting or needling fingers and hands. The patient may feel nothing at all. The practitioner's supporting hand also plays a prominent role in preparing the acupuncture points to be needled by applying slight pressure and rotations with the fingertips. The actual needle techniques themselves are quite gentle and the depth of needling is often much more superficial than in China.

During treatment, acupuncture needles may be inserted and left for twenty minutes or so, or they may be inserted and immediately withdrawn in synchrony with the patient's breathing. This is a favourite tonification technique for use when the meridian is very "empty" or deficient. If the patient is very sensitive or weak then "contact" needling may be used where the needle is simply touched against the skin rather than inserted.

Intradermal needles are popular for prolonging and enhancing the effects of treatment. These are small needles attached to a plaster which are inserted vertically or horizontally into the skin where they remain between treatments. They can often be seen on the necks and backs of Japanese people at the public baths (see pages 154–155). Also used on acupoints are small magnets, with their north and south poles close together, encased in a waterproof shell and stuck onto the body with a plaster. The poles set up a magnetic charge, which appears to stimulate the acupoint. These magnets sell in their millions over the counter and appear to be particularly effective for pain relief.

Very sharp, three-edged needles were traditionally used for blood-letting: for chest infections, for example, a few drops of blood would be extracted from the end point of the lung meridian on the corner of the nail bed of the thumb. This technique is rarely used today.

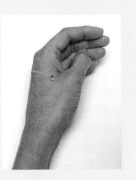

In direct moxibustion the "wool" is lightly compacted to the size and shape of a rice grain and placed on the appropriate acupoint (here, Large Intestine 4). The lit end of an incense stick is then applied to ignite the herb.

MOXIBUSTION TECHNIQUES

Moxibustion is widely used in Japan as an adjunct to acupuncture. However, whereas the Chinese favour indirect (off-the-skin) moxibustion (see pages 116–117), in Japan the most popular techniques involve direct (on-the-skin) moxibustion. A refined moxa "wool" is gently rolled between the index finger and thumb and made into tiny rice-grain-sized pieces. These are then placed on the skin and lit with an incense stick, either being allowed to burn right down to the skin or extinguished between the fingertips just before reaching the skin's surface.

Although this sounds painful it is actually a very comfortable and warming treatment. The moxa is very fine and the technique is carefully controlled. The tiny moxa pieces are repeatedly placed on the acupuncture point until the patient feels generalized warmth.

Indirect moxa techniques are also used. Little metal "hats" are used on top of acupuncture needles to hold lit moxa "wool" and pass heat into the body by warming the needle. Moxa cones can also be placed on slices of ginger on the patient's back, in order to "warm" the kidneys, or on the abdomen to boost vitality.

Moxibustion is an industry in Japan. Packaged moxa is sold ready to use on relevant acupoints selected according to a self-help guide included in the packet. People use moxa in this form for pain-relief and to ease common ailments.

MASSAGE AND MANIPULATION THERAPY

Three main types of massage and manipulation therapy have developed side by side in Japan and are practised widely today. They are *anma*, *shiatsu* and "Western massage". The three have many similarities, yet their overall approach and underlying theory are quite different. *Anma* is used mainly for relaxation and comfort; *shiatsu*, which is firmly based on meridian theory, is used for diagnosis and treatment of a wide range of disorders; "Western massage" is based on a knowledge of anatomy and physiology and is used mainly for the relief of muscle tension and pain.

Anma is the oldest of the traditions and is believed to have pre-dated the arrival of Chinese medicine in Japan. In the nineteenth century its techniques were part of a doctor's formal training, but as Western ideas gained in prominence, it was dropped and became associated almost exclusively with blind practitioners whose sense of touch was believed to be acute. Gradually the medical aspects disappeared and *anma* survived as a recreational therapy. A revival of interest in the early twentieth century has meant that it is now widely taught and practised once more.

"Western massage" was introduced in the early 1900s. The aim of it is to stimulate the sympathetic nervous system and circulation to release muscle tension. All the movements are made from the extremities towards the heart and they include vigorous kneading, grasping and rolling techniques. Never a part of the Japanese mainstream, some practitioners have incorporated certain of its techniques into their forms of *shiatsu*.

The term *shiatsu* was first coined to get round government licensing procedures for *anma* practitioners, but over time it became a general term for a number of different massage and manipulation techniques. Whereas *anma* and "Western massage" stimulate blood circulation directly and aim to release stiffness, *shiatsu* also aims to correct structural alignment and muscular tension by means of a series of gentle stretches and manipulations, as well as a rebalancing of the meridians through acupressure. The techniques used mainly involve pressure from the fingertips, thumbs, elbows, knees and feet directly onto the skin or through clothing.

An early 20th-century "practitioner" massages a patient's arm. Different forms of manual therapy offered today include shiatsu, seitai *(structural realignment),* honetsugi *(structural adjustment) and* katsu *(emergency survival techniques).*

Neck and shoulder tension can be relieved with self-massage. Place the fingers of one hand over the large muscle (trapezius) covering the shoulder blade.

Support the elbow with the opposite hand and, using a "squeeze-and-release" movement, work along the muscle from the neck to the shoulder.

SELF-MASSAGE TECHNIQUES

In Japan there is an extensive tradition of self-massage, used to relieve pain and stiffness of the joints and muscles and for the general promotion of good health. Self-massage is easy to practise as it requires no special materials, equipment or clothing – just a pair of hands. It is based on knowledge of both the acupuncture meridian system (see pages 144–145) and the muscular system of Western anatomy. It utilizes both acupressure (see page 117) and moves and stretches derived from the *shiatsu* and *do-in* traditions (see pages 148–149 and 158–159).

To perform self-massage it is best to wear loose, comfortable clothing. Make sure your position is comfortable and always support the part of the body applying pressure (see top right). Always use a gentle touch first to locate the spot and then gradually but firmly apply pressure, hold it for a few seconds and then release. This principle is known as "touch-press-release". Work from the top to the bottom of the body, or body part, and from the inside to the outside. Keep your body relaxed throughout and breathe evenly and deeply.

Use the fingertips to massage the outside edges of the cervical vertebrae (neck bones) from top to bottom. Use a "press-and-release" technique to aid circulation and reduce tension.

ZEN SHIATSU AND IMAGERY EXERCISES

The status of *shiatsu* as a recognized therapy is largely due to the work of three great twentieth-century practitioners – Tokujiro Namikoshi, Katsusuke Serizawa and Shizuto Masunaga. Tokujiro Namikoshi originally trained in *anma* massage (see page 146), then, after further study of Western anatomy and massage, he worked hard to gain official recognition for *shiatsu*, eventually achieving it in 1964.

Namikoshi explained *shiatsu* in Western medical terms and removed all reference to *ki* energy and the meridians from his work. His technique emphasizes pressure on neuro-muscular points aimed at releasing pain and tension and facilitating healing. The focus is on the physical body and specific symptoms. Its appeal has been extended both by his son, Toru, and by Wataru Ohashi in the United States.

Katsusuke Serizawa based his *shiatsu* work more on traditional oriental medicine, albeit with a modern medical approach. After researching the explanations for the meridians and their effects, he favoured a theory of nerve reflexes and became particularly interested in the therapeutic use of individual acupoints, which he tested electrically to verify their location and observe their precise effects on the body. He called these points *tsubo* and investigated ways of stimulating them and their associated reflexes. His *tsubo* therapy, as it came to be known, incorporates finger pressure, massage, acupuncture, moxibustion and electrical stimulation of the points. In the United States this has been developed into acupressure *shiatsu*, in which pressure on specific acupoints is used to relieve particular ailments.

MASUNAGA'S IMAGERY EXERCISES FOR THE TWELVE MAIN MERIDIANS

Start and end the exercise sequence with a few minutes of imagery breathing in which you visualize the flow of *ki*. Move smoothly from one position to the next.

1. Exercise A: Lung and Large Intestine meridians.
Link the thumbs as shown here and, exhaling, bend forwards. Relax in this position and focus on the sensation along the two meridians. Return slowly to the upright.

2. Exercise B: Stomach and Spleen meridians.
Sit in the seiza position (see page 159) and slowly lean backwards. With back and shoulders resting on the floor, and without forcing, allow your knees to dip and raise your hands above your head with fingers interlinked and palms facing down. Relax and practise imagery breathing – focusing on the two meridians – before returning slowly to the upright position.

3. Exercise C: Heart and Sm Intestine meridians.
Sit with the knees bent and together. Place the fingers a the toes and, with the elbows to the side, bend forwards to the floor. Do not force too far; instead, simply hold the positi the point at which it is comfor and begin imagery breathing, ing on the two meridians. Unc the body slowly to the upright seiza position.

148

Shizuto Masunaga was the first to develop a comprehensive theory for the application and effects of *shiatsu* based on traditional oriental medicine. He termed it "Zen *shiatsu*" because he wished to elucidate the profound wisdom underlying *shiatsu* rather than focusing on it as merely mechanical. Masunaga felt *shiatsu* was a supreme method for not only healing the body and preventing disease, but also for developing personal and spiritual awareness.

He advocated two-handed, continuous, steady pressure rather than vigorous massaging movements. Instead of using muscular force the practitioner is taught to "lean" into the body using one hand as a support and the other to apply relaxed, gentle, perpendicular pressure. This relaxes the sympathetic nervous system and allows the parasympathetic system to calm the body. In addition, rather than applying pressure to just one part of the meridian or specific points only, Masunaga recommended applying this relaxed pressure along the whole length of the meridian in order to balance *ki* flow.

Masunaga identified extended pathways for the major meridians and developed a series of stretches to be used to diagnose meridian imbalance. Applying pressure to the limbs reveals which meridians (and organs) are *kyo* or *jitsu* in their function. *Kyo* meridians feel flabby and weak even when they are completely stretched, whereas *jitsu* meridians feel tight, hard and elastic. Masunaga also developed abdominal (*hara*) and back diagnosis and treatment techniques (see page 139). His final work was devoted to developing a series of daily exercises (see below). Like Zen *shiatsu*, these were meant to integrate body, mind and spirit by combining stretches with breathing and mental imagery of *ki* flowing within the meridian lines. His six basic exercises balance the six pairs of meridians. They start with imagery breathing, in which the body is visualized as a balloon with the *hara* as the centre that fills with *ki* upon inhalation and deflates with exhalation. Through practice, the meridians themselves can be sensed and, in Masunaga's words, "the joy of being alive is experienced".

4. Exercise D: Kidney and Urinary Bladder meridians.
Stretch the legs out in front and slowly bend forwards, extending the hands out with the palms facing outwards and the thumbs pointed downwards. Keep the knees flat and, as always, do not force, strain or bounce. Practise imagery breathing and focus on the kidney and bladder meridians before slowly returning to the upright position.

5. Exercise E: Pericardium and Triple Burner meridians.
Sit cross-legged or adopt the half or full lotus position. Cross the arms over and, with the same arm uppermost as the leg, grasp the knees. Slowly bend forwards, pulling down with the arms. Ideally the forehead should touch the floor but simply move as far as is comfortable. Breathe and focus on the meridians for a moment, as before, then release the stretch.

6. Exercise F: Liver and Gall Bladder meridians.
Sit on the floor with the legs spread wide open. Raise the arms and interlock the fingers with the palms facing upwards. Keeping the torso facing forwards, bend down slowly to one side. Hold the stretch for a moment or two, practising the imagery breathing and focusing on the sensation in the two relevant meridians. Repeat this exercise for the opposite side of the body before returning to the upright position and releasing the stretch.

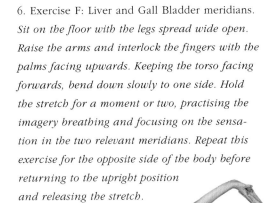

WORKING WITH LIFE ENERGY

Japan has a long tradition of *ki* healing – using life energy to heal oneself and others. This tradition is seen in acupuncture, *shiatsu* and self-massage and is also found in both martial arts and exercise therapies and in specific healing techniques that have a spiritual or religious basis (see box, right).

All traditional Japanese martial arts, such as judo, karate, *kendo* and *aikido*, are based on the generation and control of *ki*. This emphasis is designed, firstly, to facilitate one's own health, strength and mental functions, and only secondly to enhance one's fighting ability. Many martial arts also utilize specific healing and first aid techniques through the practice of acupressure, massage and manipulation (see pages 148–149).

Great masters teach that the power and speed behind all the moves comes from *ki* and from the breath generated in the *hara* or abdominal centre rather than from muscular strength alone. *Aikido* contains specific exercises for developing the ability to use *ki*. An example is the practice of the "unbendable arm", whereby you first try to resist an opponent's pressure on your outstretched arm using muscular control alone, and then try to resist using only breathing and the visualization of *ki* flowing through and out of the arm. Surprisingly, when done properly, the latter is stronger. The *ki*, once mastered, can be directed to different parts of the body to facilitate healing or can be directed at others either for healing or to overcome an attacker. An example of this is the martial art of *toate*, also known as "distance hitting", whereby the practitioner draws up *ki* in their own

Kendo *is, literally, "the way of the sword" and first developed as a training technique for samurai. By harnessing* ki *the swordsman increased his effectiveness.*

body and then "throws" it at a distant opponent, winding them or even knocking them to the floor.

More recently developed martial arts and exercise therapies also stress the role of *ki* in order to strengthen the physical, mental and spiritual health of the practitioner. *Shintaido*, developed in the latter part of the twentieth century by Master Hiroyuki Aoki, evolved out of Aoki's long study of traditional martial arts. He became very interested in movement as a form of communication and expression as well as a method of energizing and healing the body. He sought to move away from the stiff, more formal moves of martial arts, such as karate, to gentler, freer movements that would allow the experience and celebration of the life force and even the attainment of spiritual communion.

Shintaido exercises are carried out either in silence or with strong vocal vocalization and may involve stillness or free movement, such as running barefoot with the arms outstretched so as to experience a sense of freedom. The basic *kata* (exercise sequence), called *tenshingoso*, involves moving symbolically in five stages, from nothingness through birth and awakening, exploring and expressing life potential, giving and taking, fruition, and then back to nothingness; it is described as an "embodiment of the hidden cosmic breath". The exercises are practised individually or in pairs and regular participants describe feeling energized, invigorated, and discovering a new sense of freedom with their bodies and within themselves.

Noguchi taiso, a system of movement developed by Michizo Noguchi in the 1980s, involves letting go of conscious movement and allowing nature to take over in order to experience one's full potential. Noguchi, a former physical education and gymnastic instructor, was disappointed with movement theories based on the understanding of anatomy derived from the dissection of corpses. After his retirement he sought to evolve his own theory of movement based on living nature. Rather than focusing on building muscle, correcting posture and so on, he sought to return to more natural movement, working with gravity rather than against it, just as a waterfall cascades down a mountain.

In his exercises, muscular effort is used only briefly and lightly to initiate a movement, after which the emphasis is on relaxing the body and surrendering it to gravity and the earth. He argues that in this way energy is returned to the body, empowering the movement naturally. Through this method Noguchi believed that the movement of energy could be experienced in the body and the person would become both more relaxed and stronger.

The system of "laying on of hands" and healing with *ki* energy was first documented in Japan in the mid-1800s. Various approaches have been developed more recently for using the hands to share "divine light" or "divine energy" for the purpose of healing and renewal. Three of the most famous are *reiki*, *johrei* and *mahikari*. *Reiki* (see box) uses symbols, hand positions and mental intention to connect the person to "universal life-force energy". This is thought to awaken healing ability in both the self and others. *Johrei*, which literally means "purification of the spirit", is a technique whereby, with a prayer that the receiver be happy, the giver holds a hand in front of, and then at the back of, the receiver and channels love and healing energy. It is believed that this initiates a process of purification and detoxification that prepares the person for spiritual progress. *Mahikari* is the transfer of divine light, (*ma* is "truth" or "reality" and *hikari* is "light"), again by means of the hands, to facilitate healing and spiritual upliftment.

To feel ki, *place the palms close together without touching. Keeping the arms relaxed, slowly move the palms apart and almost together several times. You will feel a "pull" – this is* ki *energy*.

REIKI: THE UNIVERSAL POWER OF KI

Reiki (*rei* means "universal"; *ki* is life energy) is believed to have its origins in ancient Tibetan healing techniques, which were rediscovered in the nineteenth century by Dr Mikao Usui, a theologian, who was researching the healing powers of both Jesus and the Buddha. The technique was eventually revealed to him in a vision and he passed it on to a pupil, Chujiro Hayashi, who formalized it. There are now thousands of practitioners worldwide.

Reiki is taught at three levels. At the first level, the master attunes the person to *reiki* healing energy and teaches the basic hand positions that are used for self-healing. At the second level, symbols used for healing others and for distant healing are taught. At the third level, the ability to teach others is passed on. During a *reiki* session the practitioner holds their hands on, or just away from, the recipient's body, in twelve basic positions: four on the head, four on the front and four on the back. There is little scientific evidence for the efficacy of *reiki* but countless testimonials confirm its beneficial effects on stress and on conditions such as asthma and psoriasis.

HERBAL MEDICINE

Herbal medicine has been practised in Japan since it arrived from China via Korea during the fifth century CE. While Japan's relations with China flourished, herbalism enjoyed a prominent role in Japanese medicine, but with the beginnings of trade with the West during the mid-sixteenth century, all things Chinese suffered a loss of prestige in Japan and herbal medicine declined. It was not until the nineteenth century that it was reinstated as a part of mainstream medicine.

In the second half of the twentieth century there was a revival of interest in herbal medicine, as a result of which *kanpo* training was formalized, an officially approved licensing system was introduced and certain herbal formulas were permitted within Japan's health insurance system. Today, pharmacists can advise on over-the-counter remedies and products, of which there is an extensive range. Health insurance covers the use of herbs prescribed in extract form; if raw herbs are required a licensed practitioner must be consulted and the herbs must be privately paid for.

The term *kanpo* means "the way of Han", and refers to the Han dynasty-period Chinese text the *Shang han lun*, known as the *Shokanron* in Japan. Translations and interpretations of this text form the basis of *kanpo* theory and practice, but there are also important differences between the two countries' systems of herbal medicine. In general *kanpo* formulas use fewer and smaller quantities of herbs than traditional Chinese ones, and refined granules are

A 19th-century Japanese illustration showing women collecting herbs for medicinal purposes.

often preferred to raw herbs (see box, opposite). *Kanpo* places great emphasis on abdominal diagnosis, which has been developed into a fine art in Japan (see pages 138–139).

The *kanpo* diagnosis (*sho*) uses the Eight Principles (see pages 100–101), which determine whether the patient's constitution and symptoms are *kyo* or *jitsu* (see pages 134–135); whether the condition and stage of illness is *in* (usually chronic and serious) or *yo* (usually acute and easier to treat); whether the disease is *hyo* (external and superficial) or *ri* (internal and affecting organ function); and whether the symptoms are mainly *netsu* (hot – as in fevers, temperature and reddened skin) or *kan* (cold – as in chills, shivering and pallor). Chronic *in* diseases are classified according to the concept of *ki-ketsu-sui* (vital energy, blood and body fluids). The relative strength and normality of function of each is diagnosed and the herbs selected accordingly. *Ki-zai* herbs help restore and balance abnormal *ki*, while *risui-zai* herbs treat abnormalities in body fluids. Acute *yo* diseases are classified according to their stage. *Taiyo* diseases affect the skin, tonsils and central nervous system; *yomei* diseases affect the lungs and digestive organs; *shoyo* diseases affect the circulatory system and bone marrow.

Determining the *sho* is crucial in deciding which combination of herbs to use in treatment. The practitioner aims to identify the body system, organ or organs that are most affected and then to support and strengthen them through herbal treatment. In this way, the *kanpo* practitioner,

instead of attempting to identify a particular disease, focuses on the patient's constitution, the nature and severity of symptoms and their effect on the body, the part(s) of the body affected and stage of disease. This holistic picture is then used to determine the most appropriate herbal remedy. Thus, in *kanpo*, a "cure" is brought about by restoring balance to weak areas of the body rather than only by attacking the invading pathogen, or germ, as is often the case in Western medicine. Moreover, treatment is individually tailored and patients with the same "disease label" may receive completely different herbal formulas rather than an identical treatment, as is common in the West. Furthermore it is recognized that not everyone will react in the same way to particular herbs and so the effects of dosage and the formulation used are observed and then altered as necessary.

Kanpo formulas can have anything from two to thirty separate ingredients; between five and ten, however, is the most common. The ingredients may be of plant, mineral or animal origin, although all-plant ingredients are the most common and may include the roots, bark, leaves, flowers and fruit. Everyday items, such as cinammon, liquorice and ginger, have their place, as do rarer, less well-known ingredients, such as certain fungi and even cicada. Constituents are chosen for their effects both singly and in combination with one another in order to enhance efficacy and lessen side effects.

There are various ways of taking *kanpo*. Because herbal tea can taste unpleasant and be laborious to make, the Japanese prefer the more refined and processed forms of herbal medicine – these are also ideal for Western markets. *Kanpo* can be used for any health problem, as it has almost no side effects if prescribed and taken properly. A large number of research trials in recent years have demonstrated its effectiveness for asthma, eczema, menstrual problems and digestive problems and other disorders. It can also be taken together with Western medicine but such combinations must be carefully monitored by experienced practitioners because of possible interactions.

HYDROTHERAPY

Water plays a central role in everyday Japanese health and healing. Daily bathing is believed to cleanse spiritual impurity and ward off disease. In the Japanese style of bathing, the body is washed before entering the bath, using water – drawn either from the bath itself or from a small tap next to the tub – which is poured over the body from a jug or small bucket. Coarse towels are used to lather up soap and the skin is rubbed vigorously all over. This removes dead cells and leaves the rest soft and smooth; it is also a

People relaxing in a natural hot spring or onsen. *Bathing, either singly or in groups, has been popular for centuries in Japan and is associated with both physical and spiritual regeneration.*

self-massage that invigorates circulation in the extremities. Once the soaping and skin-rubbing is complete, water is poured over the body until all traces of soap have been removed. The person then climbs into the tub to enjoy a relaxing, hot soak. Since the water remains clean, it is usual for families to take turns in the same bath. Occasionally, on special days or according to the seasons, herbal ingredients may be added to the bath for medicinal and aromatic effects (see box, right).

Bathing can also be a social occasion. Traditionally each village or town had its own *sento* (communal bathhouse) where bathing took place at the end of every day. Nowadays, most family homes are equipped with their own

baths and many *sento* have closed, but the remaining ones are still popular. These public baths are generally segregated and nudity in the company of others of the same sex is seen as quite natural.

It is also a common pastime in Japan to bathe in rural and mountain spring baths, for both relaxation and health. There are more than 1,000 natural spring baths (*onsen*) in Japan. They are classified as hot spring baths or cold spring baths or according to their mineral content, which may be sulphurous, alkaline, carbonated with iron, and so on. The bathing procedure is as described above, where all impurities are first washed away and then people enjoy soaking together. When both sexes mix at the spa baths swimsuits are generally worn. The *onsen* are believed to be therapeutic because of the medicinal properties of the water and the beauty of the surroundings.

Water is also an essential part of the purification rites associated with the Shinto religion (see page 131). At the entrance to every shrine is an ablution basin from which a ladle is used to draw a small amount of water for washing the hands and rinsing the mouth before entering the sacred space. Water is also used for purification in certain spiritual rituals and ascetic practices such as *taki-gyo*, or "waterfall practice", where the waterfall itself is held to be sacred. The adept washes, dons a white garment and then stands under the powerful cascade of mountain water while chanting sacred texts. The force of the water has a hugely invigorating and cleansing effect on both mind and body – it is said to activate the subtle energetic centres, but is not for the faint-hearted.

In preparation for the traditional tea ceremony (*chanoyu*), water is sprinkled over the entrance to the teahouse for purification. The guest performs ritual cleansing from a basin of water before entering, and during the ceremony itself water is treated with enormous respect and care. There are also special "water tea" ceremonies in which the tea is made with water sourced from places renowned for their sacred or healing properties.

Finely chopped ginger tied in muslin bags for a warming winter bath. The ginger has a stimulant effect and increases circulation.

SEASONAL HERBAL BATHS

Special baths can be enjoyed at different times of the year for specific purposes. During December, on the day of *toji* (the winter solstice and the shortest day of the year, usually around the twenty-first or twenty-second of the month), citron baths are popular. It is said that eating pumpkin and taking a bath containing fragrant slices of lemon on this day will provide protection against colds all winter. On 5 May there is a festival day for young boys known as *kodomo no hi* on which people bathe in *shobu-yu*, that is a bath in which leaves of the festival's flower, the *shobu* (sweet flag), are floated. This bath is aromatic and medicinal – it aids digestion and clears phlegm; it is also symbolic, for the word *shobu* also means "fighting spirit". (There is a festival for girls – *kodomo no matsuri* – on 3 March which is dedicated to a Shinto goddess.) Other seasonal baths include those with mandarin orange peel (aromatic and a digestive aid) in late autumn and ginger baths (warming) in winter. The peel or freshly chopped ginger is tied up in a muslin bag and strung over the edge of the bath to infuse in the warm water.

ZEN AND SPIRITUAL HEALING

Rinzai Zen Buddhist monks in contemplation in the garden of Ryoanji Temple, Kyoto, executed in the 16th century in the karesansui *or "waterless stream" style.*

Buddhism and Shintoism exist side by side in Japan and most people will visit both religions' places of worship during the year for specific events and draw on spiritual aspects of both religions to influence their daily life and health. For example, ceremonies for new-born babies are traditionally carried out at Shinto shrines, while cremation ceremonies take place at Buddhist temples. Certain rituals may also be performed in private houses for people who are sick, and talismans (see box, right), prayer books and images of deities may be obtained for use in ritual prayers for healing at home.

Zen Buddhism in particular has had a huge influence on many aspects of daily life and culture in Japan. The influence of Zen is apparent in Japanese gardens, architecture, interior design, the tea ceremony, flower arrangements, poetry, calligraphy, archery, martial arts, medical practices such as Zen *shiatsu* and specialized kinds of acupuncture.

The goal of Zen is to achieve enlightenment – *satori* – through meditation, wisdom, stillness (*samadhi*) and the experience of pure consciousness. These qualities and practices are thought to be crucial to spiritual health, which has a direct influence on mental, physical and emotional health.

For this reason, many people enjoy visiting Zen gardens to gaze at the rocks and sand or stone patterns on the ground, which are designed to soothe the mind and calm the spirit, or to take in the beauty of a carefully designed floral arrangement, which may contain all the elements of balance and harmony necessary to elevate the senses. Activities such as archery, the tea ceremony or *noh* dance drama are also designed to focus and calm the mind. To a Western eye, some of these activities may appear aimlessly slow, but within the context of Zen they create inner stillness and heightened awareness. All are welcome to join in a meditative *sesshin*, or "sitting session", a common feature at Zen, or other, temples. Many businesses even send their executives each year, in what is regarded as a character-building tradition.

Zen practice first involves the student adopting a *zazen* posture. Usually, a small, round, hard cushion is placed on a larger one – the small one raises the hips, while the lower one protects the knees. Generally, the full-lotus or half-lotus posture is used, but the important thing is to sit in a stable, straight-backed position that can be held for twenty minutes or more. The hands are usually placed in the lap with the left fingers in the right palm. The eyes are kept slightly open, although some people prefer to shut them in order to focus within. Breathing should be natural but as still as possible, to the point where it becomes almost imperceptible and energy is drawn from the *tanden* point in the abdomen. Focus is achieved by counting and following the breath. Once the student has developed some control over their thoughts, a *koan* may be introduced. These are words or phrases that are worked with in meditation and experienced in many ways until they produce some sort of realization or awareness of stillness or pure consciousness. It may be that the sounds of the words are repeated, taken syllable by syllable, combined with certain breathing techniques or allowed to produce thought impulses, known as *nen*. Ultimately the *koans* are intended to lead to an experience of your "original self".

A taster of Zen can be obtained by trying "one-minute *zazen*". Sit in a comfortable position and fix your eyes on a point in your line of vision (a spot on a wall, detail in a picture or a petal). Stare at it and do not allow your eyes to move. While doing this slow your breathing down until it has virtually stopped. While you concentrate, try to stop any thoughts from entering your mind. You may find this hard at first, but after a while you will notice that by holding the breath you are able to gain more control over your thoughts and that, although your eyes are fixed on a point or object, you will no longer even see it. Instead perception is turned within and your mind is stilled and becomes calm.

Sacred talismans contain prayers to help protect against disease, promote a healthy pregnancy, facilitate success in exams or to ensure general good fortune.

SACRED TALISMANS: OMAMORI

Amulets or sacred talismans are used to invoke deities who are thought to protect against illness and facilitate cures. The devout worshipper will bathe, put on clean clothes and recite morning prayers before setting off to the shrine which favours the chosen deity. After passing through the *torii* gates, which symbolically purify the visitor, the hands and mouth will be rinsed at the water basin and the shoes discarded.

Once in front of the deity, the visitor will bow, drop a coin or money envelope into the offering box, clap the hands twice to attract the attention of the deity, and then bow once more, perhaps offering a prayer in-between. After this, a sacred talisman may be bought. These are covered in beautiful brocade silk of different colours and designs; inside they contain tiny wooden tablets and/or pieces of rice paper on which prayers and sacred words have been written.

The talisman can be carried with the person or placed on the altar at home. They bring a useful source of revenue to the shrines and offer real comfort to the purchasers, who feel protected and reminded of the deity's divine power.

DO-IN EXERCISE FOR HEALTH

Do-in and *an-kyo* both have their origins in the health exercises that were practised in Confucian times (around 500BCE) in ancient China. The latter are thought to have absorbed influences, including elements of yoga, from India. Exercises which were said to circulate the "life essences" of the kidneys throughout the subtle channels of the body were used to promote longevity. They are thought to have been based on a knowledge of the acupuncture meridians and subtle energy, as well as close observation of nature. In China these activities developed into *qi gong*, still used widely today (see pages 124–125), while in Japan they evolved into *do-in* and *an-kyo*.

Do literally means "to guide or lead" and *in* is "to pull or stretch". In the context of *do-in* exercises, the terms refer to the use of movements and stretches to enable energy to circulate in the channels of the body. This practice is mentioned in the oldest Japanese medical text, the *Ishinpo* (see page 129), and is said to be useful for promoting, or restoring, a good flow of *ki* and for helping to dispel "bad" *ki* and disease from the body.

An means "to conduct the flow" – in this context the flow of *ki* through the body via massage. *Kyo* refers to "correcting or making straight" – referring in *an-kyo* to the joints, bones and structural alignment of the body through manipulation techniques. *An-kyo* involves one person acting on another; it generated the *anma* and *shiatsu* techniques (see pages 146–149). *Do-in* is performed on oneself, requires no special equipment and so can be performed by anyone, anytime and almost anywhere.

Do-in exercises can be incorporated into one's daily routine for the purpose of both physical and, ultimately, spiritual development. They include breathing techniques, stretches and a series of movements to balance the

functioning of the meridians, organs, glands and body systems, and meditative exercises to calm the mind and lift the spirit. It is believed that in ancient times these exercises were combined with the drinking of elixirs which were said to enhance longevity, although little is known about these.

Many of the exercises start and end with a basic sitting posture designed to calm the mind and focus the attention

THE SITTING POSITIONS

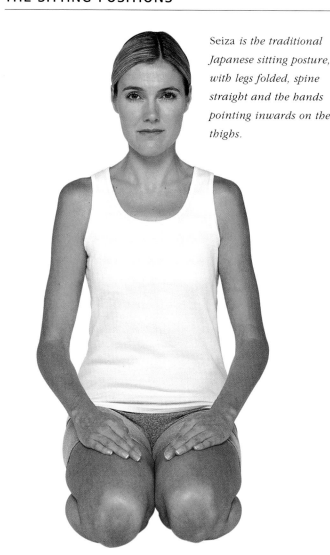

Seiza is the traditional Japanese sitting posture, with legs folded, spine straight and the hands pointing inwards on the thighs.

(see below). The posture must be stable, with the spine erect, and the breathing even and rhythmical. Attention is focused on the *tanden* point in the lower abdomen, which connects with the second, or navel, *chakra* to link with the energy of the earth. This has a "grounding" effect while carrying out the exercises.

Koto-dama can be used to accompany the exercise. This is the science of the vibrational effects of the sounds that constitute words, according to which every syllable has an effect on different parts of the body and on the mind. Each of the fifty sounds of the Japanese alphabet are thought to represent different vibrational forces and these

have been used since ancient times, in different chants and mantras, for physical, mental and spiritual development.

Particular sounds or words may activate healing in parts of the body, or longer chants may be used to enhance general well being. In Shintoism there is also a tradition of using ten-syllable "divine chants" to summon a protective deity, one of the most famous being "A-MA-TE-RA-SU-O-O-MI-KA-MI", which invokes the goddess Amaterasu. The single sound of "SU" has long been used to create feelings of peace and harmony: repeating it vocally or mentally in a sitting position for several minutes with each exhalation creates feelings of calmness and peace.

Spread the heels and sit within them for increased comfort. This relieves the ankles. The big toes should rest on top of one another.

If seiza *is uncomfortable, you can sit in a chair or in the half-lotus position with the heels drawn into the body.*

GLOSSARY

acupressure the application of fingertip pressure on acupuncture points.

acupuncture the insertion of needles at various precise points on the body (known as acupoints) to regulate the flow and distribution of vital energy.

adibalapravritta genetic disease, one of seven main disease categories in Ayurveda (India).

agni the individual's "digestive fire"; also the fire element (India).

abamkara individualized identity (India).

ai rong jiu moxibustion (China).

akabane incense stick diagnostic test (Japan).

akasha the space or ether element (India).

ampuku abdominal diagnosis (Japan).

anma the oldest of Japan's massage traditions, perhaps 1,000 years old.

asadbya disease that can neither be cured nor eased, for it is untreatable (India).

asanas postures used in yoga (India).

Ayurveda system of medicine taking its name from the words *veda* ("knowledge" or "science") and *ayus* ("life" or "longevity") in Sanskrit (India).

ba gua eight trigrams representing the balanced energies of nature (China).

bodhisattva a figure embodying compassion who stands on the verge of enlightenment but delays it to assist others.

bo-shin observation (Japan).

bu a method of tonifying *qi* (China).

bun-shin diagnostic technique of listening and smelling (Japan).

chakras energy centres associated with the flow of the body's subtle energy (India).

chen classification of herbs as "middle" or "ministerial" (China).

chi "rear" pulse position (China).

chu the water element (Tibet).

Chu yo an ideal of living in a balanced manner, the Middle Way (Japan).

"Congenital" *qi* a form of *qi* inherited from one's parents (China).

Cinnabar Fields three major energy fields, including the upper, middle and lower *dan tian* (China).

cun a unit used in proportional measurement for finding the location of acupoints. Also the front pulse-taking position on the wrist (China).

daivabalapravritta divine disease, one of the seven main disease categories in Ayurveda (India).

dan tasteless, in reference to herbs (China).

dan tian the three major energy centres in the body (China).

Daoism a belief system in which the universe is considered to exist as a unified whole, symbolized by a circle, which is made up of two great opposing yet mutually interdependent creative forces known as *yin* and *yang* (China).

dao yin various Chinese healing techniques that include self-massage, massage and breathing exercises.

dhatus seven tissues of the physical body (India).

dinacharya beneficial daily health routine (India).

do-in a system of exercise for physical and spiritual development (Japan).

doshabalapravritta constitutional or metabolic disease, one of the seven main disease categories in Ayurveda (India).

doshas the three humours that make up the physical body, being *vata*, *pitta* and *kapha*; also used to describe three constitutional types (India).

feng the environmental factor of wind (China).

feng shui the art of creating a harmonious flow of *qi* in the home or working environment in order to promote health and healing.

Five Phase theory also known as Five Elements theory, a concept explaining the cycle of mutually productive, supportive and potentially destructive relationships between all natural phenomena. The phases are wood, fire, earth, metal and water (China).

Four Medical Tantras the core of Tibetan medical knowledge, also known as the *rGyud-bzhi*.

fu organs the "hollow organs" are the stomach, small and large intestines, gall bladder and urinary bladder, responsible for extracting, receiving and transforming nutrients and excreting waste matter and considered *yang* in nature. The sixth *fu* "organ" is the triple burner (China).

gan sweet taste (China).

gunas three interdependent universal constitutents: *sattva* (purity), *rajas* (activity) and *tamas* (solidity) (India).

ban cold in nature (China).

hara the abdomen and centre of vital energy (Japan).

he harmonizing (China).

ho a tonification technique (Japan).

Huang di Nei jing (*The Yellow Emperor's Inner Canon*) important Chinese medical text, see *Nei jing*.

Huang ting jing (*The Canon of the Yellow Court*) a major Daoist text (China).

in the Japanese word for *yin*.

indriyas the eleven sense and motor organs recognized in Ayurveda (India).

ja-ki evil or pathogenic energy that causes disease (Japan).

jala the water element (India).

janmabalapravritta congenital disease, one of the seven main disease categories in Ayurveda (India).

japa the recitation of mantras (India).

jin means "dews" and refers to thin, clear body fluids such as sweat and tears, which moisten the skin and nourish the muscles (China).

jing "constitutional essence", which is combined with the extracts from the *fu* organs and stored in the kidneys. It is inherited from one's ancestors over many generations (China).

jin ye body fluids. See *jin* and *ye* (China).

jitsu an excess of *ki* (Japan).

jun category of herbs in China, meaning upper or "ruler" herbs.

kalabalapravritta seasonal disease, one of the seven main disease categories in Ayurveda (India).

kanpo Japanese herbal medicine – "the way of Han".

kapha phlegm, one of the three *doshas* or humours in Indian medicine.

karma the law of cause and effect through which the roots of an illness may lie in actions performed in a past life, the fruits of which are resulting in the present time.

kenko the Japanese word for health, made up of two Chinese characters; *ken* means "human" or "upright", while *ko* expresses the manner of being relaxed and at ease.

ki literally "vital force" and equivalent to *qi* (Japan).

kostha bowel function (India).

ku bitter taste (China).

kuiwase a Japanese concept of foods which should not be eaten together.

kum nye a Tibetan form of massage and subtle energy exercises.

kyo a *ki* deficiency (Japan).

liang cool in nature (China).

likhita japa the practice of writing mantras (India).

linga a smooth, phallic or egg-shaped stone, either naturally occurring or carved, used in Indian worship and representing male energy.

liu yin six pathogenic factors in disease (China).

mahagadas the eight "great" diseases described in Ayurveda (India).

mahat intellect (India).

mala prayer beads (India).

malas waste products (India).

mandala a circular diagram used as a meditation aid (Tibet, India).

mantra syllables, words or sentences in Sanskrit that have a particular sound vibration conducive to meditation and spiritual development.

materia medica comprehensive text listing medicinal ingredients and their properties.

me the fire element (Tibet).

meridian channels of vital energy (*qi*, *ki*) located within the skin tissue and connecting with each of the inner organs (China, Japan).

ming men a gateway of moving energy in the kidney area, and where *yin* and *yang* originate (China).

mon-shin questioning diagnosis (Japan).

mudra symbolic hand positions used in meditation (India).

nadis the subtle nerve channels of the astral body, said to number more than 72,000, through which *prana* flows (India).

nam-mkha the space element (Tibet).

Nan jing (*The Classic of Difficult Issues*) a second-century CE Chinese medical text that explains passages from the *Nei jing*.

nasya nasal cleaning, one of the five *panchakarma* purification techniques in Ayurveda (India).

Nei jing an important work that still forms the basis of Traditional Chinese Medicine as it is practised today.

nyes-pa see Three Humours.

onsen spa bath (Japan).

panchakarma five purification techniques used in Ayurveda for cleansing and detoxifying the body and for rectifying any imbalances of the *doshas*. It has three parts, a preparatory *purva karma*, a main *pradhana karma* and an after-care period called *paschatah karma* (India).

panchamahabhutas the five primordial elements (India).

paschatah karma the after-care element of *panchakarma* treatment (India).

ping xing neutral herbs (China).

pitta choler or bile, one of the three *doshas* in Indian medicine.

pradhana karma the main treatment element of *panchakarma* (India).

prajnaparadha a term in Ayurveda meaning "a crime against wisdom", which refers to the mental attitudes that prevent us from taking good care of ourselves (India).

prakriti individual constitution (India)

prana vital energy of life-force. Also one of the types of *vata* (India).

prithvi the element of earth (India).

puja prayer and worship rituals performed at home, in temples and in ceremonies on religious festival days (India).

purva karma two preparatory techniques used in *panchakarma* (India).

qi pronounced "chee" and sometimes written as *ch'i*, the all-pervasive vital energy of the universe and the body. There are many types of *qi* in the body. See also *wei qi, ying qi, yuan qi* and *zong qi* (China).

qie zhen touch diagnosis (China).

qi gong form of physical exercise meaning "directing" or "mastering" *qi* (China).

qing purifying (China).

qi qing seven emotional factors (China).

rajas activity, one of the three *gunas* (India).

raktamokshana blood purification, one of the five *panchakarma* techniques in Ayurveda (India).

re hot in nature (China).

reiki Japanese healing energy technique whose name derives from the words *rei* (universal) and *ki* (vital force).

rGyud-bzhi the key texts of Tibetan medicine, known in English as the *Four Medical Tantras*.

rinchen ribu the seven different types of Precious Pill, made from minerals and gems (Tibet).

rishi ancient Indian seer.

ritucharya living according to the seasons (India).

rlung the air element (Tibet).

sa the earth element (Tibet).

sadachara the non-suppression of natural urges (India).

sadhya disease that may be cured (India).

sanghatabalapravritta traumatic disease, one of the seven main disease categories in Ayurveda (India).

san jiao (triple burner) organ that balances the function of the upper, middle and lower parts of the body, regulates circulation, temperature and sexual function (China).

se astringent taste; also means rough (China).

seiza traditional Japanese sitting posture.

setsu-shin touch diagnosis (Japan).

sha to disperse *ki* (Japan).

shakti the invigorating and healing power of a divine being (India).

Shang han lun (*Treatise on Cold Damage Disorders*) medical text on the symptoms and herbal treatment of febrile diseases (China).

shen the "spirit" of a person. Refers to consciousness, mental faculties and spiritual awareness. Also refers to the kidneys (China).

Shen nong ben cao jing (*Shen Nong's Materia Medica Canon*) the earliest surviving complete text of herbal remedies, compiled *c.*500CE (China).

shi an excess or replete condition; also means dampness (China).

shiatsu literally "finger pressure", this form of therapeutic massage has been developed in Japan for over 100 years.

shin the spirit or vivacity of a patient (Japan).

shokuyu concept of "foods for health and happiness" – *shoku* means "nourishment' and *yo* is the way to nourish oneself perfectly (Japan).

shu points a series of acupoints along the urinary bladder meridians on either side of the spine; also means heat (China).

si qi four types of *qi* used in the classification of herbs, see *re, wen, liant* and *han* (China).

si zhen the four diagnostic procedures in Traditional Chinese Medicine.

snehana oil therapy using vegetable oils, *ghee* or herbal remedies (India).

suan sour taste (China).

sukta Sanskrit verse.

svedana sweating therapy (India).

swabhavbalapravritta natural disease, one of the seven main disease categories in Ayurveda (India).

t'ai ch'i an exercise therapy originally based on animal movements (China).

tamas solidity or

GLOSSARY

stagnation, one of the three *gunas* (India).

tanden the energetic centre of the *hara*, see *dan tian* (Japan).

Three Humours wind or air (*nyes-pa*), bile (*mKhris-pa*) and phlegm (*bad-gan*) (Tibet).

Three Treasures the triad of *qi* (vital energy), *jing* (essence) and *shen* (spirit) (China).

trimurti the holy trinity of the Hindu pantheon: Brahma, Vishnu and Shiva (India).

triple burner see *san jiao* (China).

tu vomiting (China).

vamana therapeutic vomiting, one of the five *panchakarma* purification techniques in Ayurveda (India).

vasti enemas, one of the five *panchakarma* purification techniques in Ayurveda (India).

vata wind, one of the three *doshas* or humours in Indian medicine.

vayu the element of air (India).

virechana purgatives, one of the five *panchakarma* purification techniques in Ayurveda (India).

wang zhen observational diagnosis (China).

wei qi "defensive *qi*" which protects the body from external pathogens (China).

wen zhen listening, smelling and questioning diagnosis (China).

wu qin xi the "five animal play" exercise sequence (China).

wu shu the martial arts tradition (China).

wu xing see Five Phases (China).

xian salty taste (China).

xie a method for dispersing *qi* (China).

xin pungent taste (China).

xu a *qi*-deficient condition (China).

xue a body fluid generally translated as "blood", but it has a wider meaning than that. Its relationship with *qi* is interdependent: *qi* plays a role in *xue*'s formation and circulation, while *xue* affects the amount and flow of bodily *qi*. (China).

yang a universal energy force whose characteristics are active, expanding, hot, bright, hard and masculine (China).

yang sheng the "cultivation of life" (China).

yantra symbolic diagrams used in meditation (India).

yapya disease that cannot be cured, only eased (India).

ye means "juices" and refers to body fluids which maintain joints and brain function (China).

Yi jing (I Ching) (the *Classic of Changes*) an ancient Chinese book of divination and wisdom.

yin a universal energy force whose characteristics are passive, contracting, cold, dark, soft and feminine (China).

ying qi "nutritive *qi*", which is obtained from digested food and nourishes the body. (China).

yo the Japanese word for *yang*.

yoga from the Sanskrit word for "union", an ancient health system incorporating physical exercises (*asanas*) and meditation techniques for spiritual development (India).

Yoga Sutras Patanjali's eight-part framework for yoga practice. It consists of *yamas* (moral codes), *niyamas* (daily observances), *asanas* (exercise postures), *pranayama* (breathing exercises), *pratyahara* (withdrawal of the senses), *dharana* (concentration), *dhyana* (meditation) and *samadhi* (superconsciousness and spiritual union) (India).

yoni a rounded shape that represents the vulva and female energy (India).

yuan qi "congenital *qi*", also known as "source *qi*", inherited from parents and related to vitality, lifespan and reproductive capacity (China).

***yu* points** a series of acupuncture points along the urinary bladder meridian on either side of the spine (Japan).

***zang–fu* organs** the twelve main organs of the body in Traditional Chinese Medicine, classified according to their functions rather than their structure, see *zang organs*, *fu organs* (China).

***zang* organs** the "solid organs" of lungs, spleen, heart, kidneys and liver. They create and store vital essences and fluids and are *yin* in nature. The sixth *zang* "organ" is the pericardium which relates to the physical functions of the heart (China)

zhen jiu acupuncture (China).

zong qi "gathering *qi*", also known as "essential *qi*", made up of *qi* from air and food (China).

zuo shi classification of herbs as "lower" or "assistant" (China).

163

FURTHER READING

INDIA

Chishti, G.M. *The Traditional Healer: A Guide to the Principles and Practice of Unani Herbal Medicine*, Thorsons: Northampton, 1988.

Conrad, Lawrence, I. et al. *The Western Medical Tradition 800 BC to AD 1800*, Cambridge University Press: Cambridge, 1995.

Dash, Vaidya Bhagwan, and Ramaswamy, Suhasini. *The Science of Traditional Indian Medicine*, Lustre Press: New Delhi, 1998.

Dharmalingam, Vaidya, V., Radhika, Vaidya, M., and Balasubramanian, A.V. *Maram Chikitsa in Traditional Medicine*, Lok Swaasthya Parampara Samvardhan Samithi: Chennai, India, 1991.

Frawley, David. *Ayurvedic Healing: A Comprehensive Guide*, Passage Press: Salt Lake City, 1989.

Godagama, Dr. Shantha. *The Handbook of Ayurveda*, Kyle Cathie: London, 1997.

Hiriyanna, M. *Essentials of Indian Philosophy*, Diamond Books: London, 1996.

Ibn Qayyim Al-Jawziyya (trans. by Penelope Johnstone). *Medicine of the Prophet*, Islamic Texts Society: Cambridge, 1998.

Jeffery, Patricia., Jeffery, Roger, and Lyon, Andrew. *Labour Pains and Labour Power: Women and Childbearing in India*, Zed Books: London and New Jersey, 1989.

Lad, Dr Vasant. *Secrets of the Pulse: The Ancient Art of Ayurvedic Pulse Diagnosis*, The Ayurvedic Press: New Mexico, 1996.

Lad, Usha, and Dr. Vasant. *Ayurvedic Cooking for Self Healing*, The Ayurvedic Press: New Mexico, 1994.

Larson, Gerald James. *Classical Samkhya*, Motilal Banarsidass: New Delhi, 1998.

Leslie, Charles (editor). *Asian Medical Systems: A Comparative Study*, University of California Press: Berkeley, 1976.

Liebeskind, Claudia. *Unani Medicine of the Subcontinent*, in *Oriental Medicine*, edited by Van Alphen, Jan, and Aris, Anthony, Serindia Publications: London, 1995.

Morningstar, Sally. *Ayurveda: Traditional Indian Healing for Harmony and Health*, Lorenz: London, 1999.

Morrison, Judith. *The Book of Ayurveda*, Gaia Books: London, 1995.

Nagarathna, Dr., Monroe, Robin, and Nagendra, Dr. *Yoga for Common Ailments*, Gaia Books: London, 1994.

Patel, Ramesh. *The Mandeer Ayurvedic Cookbook*, Curzon: London, 1997.

Raichur, Pratima, with Cohn, Marian. *Absolute Beauty*, Bantam: London, 1998.

Ray, Priyadaranjan, and Gupta, Hirendra Nath. *Caraka Samhita (A Scientific Synopsis)*, National Insitute of Sciences of India: New Delhi, 1965.

Ray, P., Gupta, H., and Roy, M. *Susruta Samhita (A Scientific Synopsis)*, Indian National Science Academy: New Delhi, 1980.

Santa Maria, Jack. *Anna Yoga, The Yoga of Food*, Rider: London, 1978.

Shankar, Darshan, and Manohar, Ram. *Ayurvedic Medicine Today – Ayurveda at the Crossroads*, in *Oriental Medicine*, edited by Van Alphen, Jan, and Aris, Anthony, Serindia Publications: London, 1995.

Sharma, Harry, and Clark, Christopher. *Contemporary Ayurveda: Medicine and research in Maharishi Ayurveda*, Churchill Livingstone: Pennsylvania, 1998.

Sharma, Prof. Priya Vrata (editor and translator). *Caraka Samhita*, Vols 1-3, Chaukhambha Orientalia: Varanasi, India, 1981-5.

Singhal, Dr. G. D., and Guru, Dr. L.V. *Ancient Indian Surgery*, Chaukhamba Vidyabhawan: Varanasi, India, 1973.

Sivananda Yoga Centre. *The Book of Yoga*, Ebury Press: London, 1983.

Svoboda, Robert. *Ayurveda: Health, Life and Longevity*, Arkana: London, 1992.

Svoboda, Robert. *Theory and Practice of Ayurvedic Medicine*, in *Oriental Medicine*, edited by Van Alphen, Jan, and Aris, Anthony, Serindia Publications: London, 1995.

Van Alphen, Jan, and Aris, Anthony. *Oriental Medicine*, Serindia Publications: London, 1995.

Vishnudevanada, Swami. *The Complete Illustrated Book of Yoga*, New York, 1972.

Waterstone, Richard. *India*, Macmillan/Duncan Baird Publishers: London, 1995.

Wujastyk, Dominik. *Indian Medicine* in Bynum, W.F., and Porter, Roy. *Companion Encyclopaedia of the History of Medicine*, Vol. 1, Routledge: London, 1993.

Wujastyk, Dominik. *Medicine in India*, in *Oriental Medicine*, edited by Van Alphen, Jan, and Aris, Anthony, Serindia Publications: London, 1995.

Wujastyk, Dominik. *The Roots of Ayurveda*, Penguin Books: India and London, 1998.

Wujastyk, Dominik. *Miscarriages of Justice: Demonic Vengeance in Classical Indian Medicine*, in Hinnells, John, and Porter, Roy. *Religion, Health and Suffering*, Kegan Paul: London and New York, 1999.

Zimmerman, Francis. *The Jungle and The Aroma of Meats: An Ecological Theme in Hindu Medicine*, University of California Press: Berkeley, 1987.

Zvelebil, Kamil V. *The Siddha Quest for Immortality*, Mandrake: Oxford, 1996.

Zysk, K.G. *Religious Healing in the Veda*, American Philosophical Society: Philadelphia, 1985.

TIBET

Baker, Ian A. *The Tibetan Art of Healing*, Thames and Hudson: London, 1997.

Clifford, Terry. *Tibetan Buddhist Medicine & Psychiatry: The Diamond Healing*, Aquarian Press: Northamptonshire, 1984.

Donden, Dr. Yeshi. *Health Through Balance*, Snow Lion: N.Y., 1986.

Dummer, Tom. *Tibetan Medicine & other Holistic Health Care Systems*, Routledge: U.K., 1988.

Finckh, Dr. Elisabeth. *Foundations of Tibetan Medicine*, Vols I & II, Watkins: U.K., 1978 and 1988.

Finckh, Dr. Elisabeth. *Studies in Tibetan Medicine*, Snow Lion: N.Y., 1988.

Hoffman, Helmut. *The Religions of Tibet*, George, Allen & Unwin: London, 1956.

Meyer, Fernand. "Theory and Practice of Tibetan Medicine" in Aris, Anthony (general editor) *Oriental Medicine*, Serindia Publications: London, 1995.

Parfionovitch, Y., Dorje, G., and Meyer, F. (editors). *Tibetan Medical Paintings*, Serindia Publications: London, 1993.

Rapgay, Dr. Lobsang. *The Art of Tibetan Urinalysis*, (self-published in India), 1986.

Snellgrove, David. *Indo-Tibetan Buddhism*, Serindia Publications: London, 1987.

Sogyal, Rinpoche. *The Tibetan Book of Living and Dying*, Random House: London, 1992.

Tarthang, Tulku. *Kum Nye Parts I & II*, Dharma Publishing: California, 1978.

Tsarong, T.J. *Handbook of Traditional Tibetan Drugs*, Tibetan Medical Publications: Kalimpong, India, 1988.

Tsarong, T.J. (editor). *Fundamentals of Tibetan Medicine*, Tibetan Medical Centre: Dharamsala, India, 1981.

Van Alphen, Jan, and Aris, Anthony, (editors). *Oriental Medicine: An Illustrated Guide to the Asian Arts of Healing*, Serindia Publications: London, 1995.

Ven Rechung, Rinpoche. *Tibetan Medicine*, The Wellcome Trust: London, 1973, and University of California Press: California 1976.

CHINA

Craze, Richard, and Tang, Stephen. *Chinese Herbal Medicine*, Piatkus: London, 1995.

Craze, Richard, with T'ieh Fou, Jen. *Traditional Chinese Medicine*, Hodder Headline: London, 1998.

Flaws, Bob. *Imperial Secrets of Health and Longevity*, Blue Poppy Press: Colorado, 1994.

Gach, Michael Reed, with Marco, Caroline. *Acu-Yoga: Self-Help Techniques to Relieve Tension*, Japan Publications: Tokyo and New York, 1981.

Gach, Michael Reed. *How to Cure Common Ailments the Natural Way*, Piatkus: London, 1990.

Guorui, Jiao. *Qigong Essentials For Health Promotion*, China Reconstructs Press: Beijing, 1985.

Harper, Jennifer. *Body Wisdom: Chinese and Natural Medicine for Self-Healing*, Thorsons: London, 1997.

Hill, Sandra, and Firebrace, Peter. *A Guide to Acupuncture*, Constable: London, 1998.

Hill, Sandra. *Reclaiming the Wisdom of the Body*, Constable: London, 1997.

Hsu, Elizabeth. *The Transmission of Chinese Medicine*, Cambridge Studies in Medical Anthropology Number 7, Cambridge University Press: Cambridge, 1999.

Hsu, Hong-yen (trans.). *Shang Han Lun*, Oriental Healing Arts Institute: California, 1981.

Kaptchuk, Ted. *The Web That Has No Weaver: Understanding Chinese Medicine* (2nd edition), Contemporary, NTC Publishing: Lincoln Wood, Illinois, 2000.

Kingston, Karen. *Creating Sacred Space with Feng Shui*, Piatkus: London, 1996.

Lam, Kam Chuen. *Step-by-Step Tai Chi*, Gaia Books: London, 1994.

Lam, Kam Chuen. *The Way of Energy*, Gaia Books: London, 1991.

Lao Tsu. *Tao Te Ching*, trans. by Gia-gu Feng and Jane English, Vintage Books: New York, 1972.

Larre, Claude, Schatz, Jean, and Rochat de la Valle, Elizabeth. *Survey of Traditional Chinese Medicine*, trans. by Stang, S. Elizabeth, Traditional Acupuncture Foundation: Maryland, 1986.

Lee, Hor Ming, and Whincup, Gregory. *Chinese Massage Therapy*, Shambala: Colorado, 1983.

Liu, Da. *Taoist Health Exercise Book*, Quick Fox: New York, 1974.

Lu, Gwei-djen, and Needham, Joseph. *Celestial Lancets: A History and Rationale of Acupuncture and Moxa*, Cambridge University Press: Cambridge, 1980.

Manaka, Yoshio, and Urquart, Ian. *The Layman's Guide to Acupuncture*, John Weatherill: New York, 1972.

Mercati, Maria. *Step-by-Step Tui-Na*, Gaia Books: London, 1997.

Mitchell, Emma (general editor). *Your Body's Energy*, Duncan Baird Publishers: London, 1998.

Taylor, Louise, and Bryant, Betty. *Acupressure Yoga and You*, Japan Publications: Tokyo and New York, 1984.

Teeguarden, Iona Marsaa. *Acupressure Way of Health: Jin Shin Do*, Japan Publications: Tokyo and New York, 1978.

Too, Lillian. *The Complete Illustrated Guide to Feng Shui*, Element: Dorset, 1996.

Tse, Michael. *Qigong for Health and Vitality*, Piatkus: London, 1995.

Veith, Ilza (trans.). *The Yellow Emperor's Classic of Internal Medicine*, University of California Press: California, 1949.

Yeoh, Eileen. *Longevity: The Tao of Eating and Healing*, Times Books International: Singapore, 1989.

Young, Jacqueline. *Acupressure for Health*, Thorsons: London and New York, 1994.

Young, Jacqueline. *Vital Energy: Oriental Exercises for Health and Wellbeing*, Hodder: Kent, 1988.

JAPAN

Accolla, Dylana, with Yates, Peter. *Back to Balance: A Self-Help Encyclopaedia of Eastern Holistic Remedies*, Boxtree: London, 1996.

Aihara, Herman. *Acid and Alkaline*, Ohsawa Macrobiotic Foundation: C.A., 1982.

Benedict, Ruth. *The Chrysanthemum & the Sword: Patterns of Japanese Culture*, Mariner Books: 1989.

Birch, Stephen and Ida, Junko. *Japanese Acupuncture*, Churchill Livingstone: London, 1998.

Dawes, Nigel. *The Shiatsu Workbook*, Piatkus: London, 1991.

Denmai, Shudo, trans. by Stephen Brown. *Introduction to Meridian Therapy*, Eastland Press: Seattle, 1990.

Doi, Takeo. *The Anatomy of Dependence*, Kodansha International: Tokyo, 1973.

Fukuhara, Hiroko and Takahata, Yasuko. *Natural Remedies from the Japanese Kitchen*, Weatherhill: New York and Tokyo, 1998.

Hashimoto, Keizo, and Yoshiakai, Kawakami. *Sotai: Balance and Health Through Natural Movement*, Japan Publications: Tokyo and New York, 1983.

Kosoto, Hiroshi. *Kanpo: The History of chinese-Japanese Medical Traditions*, 1999.

Kushi, Michio. *The Book of Do-In: Exercises for Physical & Spiritual Development*, Japan Publications: Tokyo and New York, 1979.

Kushi, Michio. *The Book of Macrobiotics: The Universal Way of Health and Happiness*, Japan Publications: Tokyo and New York, 1977.

Liechti, Elaine. *The Complete Illustrated Guide to Shiatsu*, Element: Dorset, 1998.

Lock, Margaret. *East Asian Medicine in Urban Japan*, University of California Press: Berkeley, C.A., 1980.

Masunaga, Shizuto. *Meridian Exercises: The Oriental Way to Health and Vitality*, Japan Publications: Tokyo and New York, 1987.

Masunaga, Shizuto, and Ohashi, Wataru. *Zen Shiatsu: How to Harmonise Yin & Yang for Better Health*, Japan Publications: Tokyo and New York, 1977.

Matsumoto, Keiko, and Birch, Stephen. *Hara Diagnosis: Reflections on the Sea*, Paradigm Publications: Brookline, Mass., 1988. (See Chapters 12 & 13 for Shiatsu and Anma.)

Motoyama, Hiroshi. *Karma & Reincarnation*, Piatkus: London, 2000.

Motoyama, Hiroshi. *Theories of the Chakras*, Theosophical Publishing House: Illinois, 1981.

Muramoto, Naboru. *Healing Ourselves*, Avon Books: New York, 1973.

Namikoshi, Tokujiro. *Shiatsu: Japanese Finger-Pressure Therapy*, Japan Publications: Tokyo and New York, 1972.

Namikoshi, Toru. *The Complete Book of Shiatsu Therapy*, Japan Publications: Tokyo and New York, 1981.

Norbeck, E., and Lock, Margaret (editors). *Health, Illness & Medical Care in Japan; Cultural & Social Dimensions*, University of Hawaii Press: Honolulu, 1987.

Ohashi, Wataru. *Do-It-Yourself Shiatsu: How to Perform the Ancient Art of 'Acupuncture Without Needles'*, Dutton: N.Y., 1976.

Ohnuki-Tierney, E. *Illness and Culture in Contemporary Japan*, Cambridge University Press: Cambridge, 1984.

Rister, Robert. *Japanese Herbal Medicine*, Avery: 2000.

Sekida, Katsuki. *Zen Training: Methods and Philosophy*, Weatherhill: New York and Tokyo, 1983.

Serizawa, Katsusuke. *Effective Tsubo Therapy*, Japan Publications: Tokyo and New York, 1984.

Sonoda, K. *Health & Illness in Changing Japanese Society*, University of Tokyo Press: Tokyo, 1988.

Standlee, M.W. *The Great Pulse: Japanese Midwifery & Obstetrics Through the Ages*, Charles Tuttle & Co.: Tokyo, 1959.

Tohei, Koichi. *Book of Ki: Co-ordinating Mind and Body in Daily Life*, Japan Publications: Tokyo and New York, 1979.

Tsumura, Akira. *Furo: The Japanese Trendy Bath Life*, Japan Publications: Tokyo and New York, 1992.

Van Alphen, Jan, and Aris, Anthony. *Oriental Medicine: Illustrated Guide to Asian Arts of Healing*, Serindia Publications: London, 1995. (Part III contains excellent chapters on *kanpo* and Japanese medicine).

Young, Jacqueline. *Self Massage*, Thorsons: London, 1992.

USEFUL ADDRESSES

There is a wide variety of services available, ranging from professional bodies with highly qualified members to individuals or groups with less training. It is important that potential users seek to establish the nature of the organization or the qualifications of the person being consulted. Always attempt to seek a referral or recommendation from a health professional. If not, approach the discipline's professional association and try to ensure that practitioners are registered and that a code of professional conduct exists. The bodies listed below are merely a selection of the many available and are presented here to enable any further enquiries to begin; they are not endorsed in any way by the author or publisher.

UNITED KINGDOM

Acumedic Centre
(for Oriental health supplies)
101 Camden High Street
London NW1 7JN
Tel: 020 7388 5783/6704
Website: www.acumedic.com

The Ayurvedic Company of Great
  Britain
81 Wimpole Street
London W1M 7DB
Tel: 020 7224 6070

Ayurvedic Living Ltd.
(Seminars and Information)
P.O. Box 188
Exeter
Devon EX4 5AB

Ayurvedic Medical Association U.K.
59 Dulverton Road
Selsdon
South Croydon CR2 8PJ

The Ayurvedic Trading Company
East West Centre
10c The High Street
Glastonbury BA6 9DU
Tel: 01458 833382

British Acupuncture Council
63 Jeddo Road
London W12 9HQ
Tel: 020 8735 0400
Website: www.acupuncture.org.uk

British Complementary Medicine
  Association (BCMA)
Kensington House
33 Imperial Square
Cheltenham GL50 1QZ
Tel: 0845 345 5977
Website: www.bcma.co.uk

British Massage Therapy Council
Greenbank House
65a Adelphi Street
Preston
Lancashire PR1 7BH
Tel: 01772 881063
E-mail: info@bmtc.co.uk
Website: www.bmtc.co.uk

British Medical Acupuncture Society
  (BMAS)
12 Marburg House
Higher Whitley
Warrington
Cheshire WA4 4QW
Tel: 01925 730727
Fax: 01925 730492
E-mail:
  Admin@medical-acupuncture.org.uk
Website:
  www.medical-acupuncture.co.uk

The British Wheel of Yoga
25 Jermyn Street
Sleaford
Lincolnshire NG34 7RU
Tel: 01529 306859
Fax: 01529 303233
E-mail: office@bwy.org.uk
Website: www.bwy.org.uk

Chinese Heritage Ltd
Qigong Healing
15 Dawson Place
London W2 4TH
Tel: 020 7229 7187

Community Health Foundation
188, Old Street
London EC1

Feng Shui Network International,
P.O. Box 2133
London W1A 1RL
Fax: 01423 770940
Email: Feng1@ad.com
Website: www.fengshuinet.com

Institute for Complementary Medicine
P.O. Box 194
London SE16 7QZ
Tel: 020 7237 5165

The Register of Chinese Herbal
  Medicine
Office G4, Garden Studios
11–15 Betterton Street
London WC2H 9BP
Tel: 020 7470 8740
Website: www.rchm.co.uk

The Reiki Association
Cornbrook Bridge House
Clee Hill
Ludlow
Shropshire SY8 3QQ
Tel: 01584 891197
Website: ww.reikiassociation.org.uk

The Research Council for
  Complementary Medicine (RCCM)
60 Great Ormond Street
London WC1N 3JF
E-mail: info@rccm.org.uk
Website: www.rccm.org.uk

The Shiatsu Society, U.K.
Eastlands Court
St. Peter's Road
Rugby
Warwickshire CV21 3QP
Tel: 01788 555051
Fax: 01788 555052
E-mail: admin@shiatsu.org
Website: www.shiatsu.org

School of Tai Chi Chuan
Centre for Healing
5 Tavistock Place
London WC1H 9SN
Tel: 020 8444 6445

Sivanda Yoga Vedanata Centre
51 Felsham Road
London SW15 1AZ
Tel: 020 8780 0160

Tai Chi Union of Great Britain
69 Kilpatrick Gardens
Clarkston
Glasgow G76 7RF
Tel: 0141 638 2946
Fax: 0141 621 1220
E-mail: secretary@taichiunion.com
Website: www.taichiunion.com

Tibet Foundation
1 St James's Market
London SW1Y 4SB
Tel: 020 7930 6001
E-mail: enquiries@tibet-foundation.org
Website: www.tibet-foundation.org

Tse Qigong Centre,
P.O. Box 59
Altringham
Cheshire WA15 8FS
Tel: 0161 929 4485

UK Reiki Federation
P.O. Box 261
Wembley HAO 4FP
E-mail: enquiries@reikifed.co.uk
Website: www.reikifed.co.uk

Yoga for Health Foundation
Ickwell Bury
Biggleswade
Bedfordshire SG18 9EF
Tel: 01767 627271

Yoga Therapy Centre
Royal Homoeopathic Hospital
60 Great Ormond Street
London WC1N 3HR
Tel: 020 7419 7195
Website: www.yogatherapy.org.uk

UNITED STATES

Acupuncture and Oriental Medicine
   Alliance
14637 Starr Road SE
Olalla, Washington 98359
Tel: (253) 851 6896

American Association of Acupuncture
   and Oriental Medicine
National Acupuncture Headquarters
1424 16th Street NW, Suite 501
Washington DC 20036

American Institute of Vedic Studies
P.O. Box 8357
Santa Fe, New Mexico 87504
Tel: (505) 983 9385
Fax: (505) 982 5807
Website: www.vedanet.com

American Oriental Bodywork Therapy
   Association (AOBTA)
1010 Hoddonfield-Berlin Road,
   Suite 408
Voorhees, New Jersey 08043
Tel: (856) 782 1616
E-mail: AOBTA@prodigy.net

The Ayurvedic Institute
P.O. Box 23445
11311 Menaul Boulevard NE, Suite 28
Albuquerque, New Mexico 87112
Tel: (505) 291 9698

College of Maharishi Vedic Medicine
Maharishi University of Management
Fairfield
Iowa 52557
Tel: (641) 472 1110
E-mail: administration@mum.edu

East-West Foundation
PO Box 40012
Washington DC

George Ohsawa Macrobiotic Foundation
PO Box 3998
Chico, California 95927
Tel: (530) 533 7702

International Association of Reiki
   Professionals
P.O. Box 481
Winchester, Massachusetts 01890
Tel: (781) 729 3530
E-mail: info@iarp.org
Website: www.iarp.org

The International Center for Reiki
   Training
21421 Hilltop Street, Suite 28
Southfield, Michigan 48034
Toll Free: (800) 332 8112
E-Mail: center@reiki.org
Website: www.reiki.org

National Accreditation Commission for
   Schools and Colleges of Acupuncture
   and Oriental Medicine (NASCAOM)
1010 Wayne Avenue, Suite 1270
Silver Springs, MD 20910
Tel: (301) 608 9680
E-mail: acom1@compuserve.com

National Certification Commission for
   Acupuncture and Oriental Medicine
11 Canal Center Plaza, Suite 300
Alexandria, Virginia 22314
Tel: (703) 548 9084
Fax: (703) 548 9079
Website: www.nccaom.org

National Council of Acupuncture
   Schools and Colleges
P.O. Box 954
Columbia, MD 21044.

Qigong Resource Associates
1755 Homet Road
Pasadena, California 91106

Qigong Academy
5553 Pearl
Cleveland, Ohio 44129
Tel: (440) 842 8042
Website: www.qigongacademy.com

Traditional Acupuncture Institute
America City Building, Suite 100
Columbia, MD 210044
Tel: (301) 596 6006
Website: www.tai.edu

AUSTRALIA

Acupuncture Association of Victoria
126 Union Road
Surrey Hills
Victoria 3127

Acupuncture Ethics and Standards
 Organisation
P.O. Box 84
Merrylands
New South Wales 2160

Australian Acupuncture and Chinese
 Medical Association
P.O. Box 5142
West End
Queensland 4101
Tel: (61) 7 3846 5866
E-mail: aacma@acupuncture.org.au
Website: www.acupuncture.org.au

Australian College of Ayurvedic
 Medicine
19 Bowey Avenue
Enfield
South Australia 5085
Tel: (61) 8 8349 7303
Website: www.ayurvedahc.com

Maharishi Ayurveda Health Centres
P.O. Box 81
Bundoora
Victoria 3083
Tel: (61) 3 9467 4633

Qigong Association of Australia
458 White Horse Road
Surrey Hills
Victoria 3127
Tel: (61) 3 836 6961

Shiatsu Therapy Association
of Australia
332 Carlisle Street
Balaclava
Victoria 3183

CANADA

Canadian Acupuncture foundation
7321 Victoria Park Avenue, Suite 302
Markham
Ontario L3R278

CHINA

The World Academic Society of Medical
 Qigong
No11 Heping Jie Nei Kou
Beijing 100029

INDIA

Faculty of Ayurveda
Institute of Medical Sciences
Benaras Hindu University
Varanasi 221005

ITALY

European Shiatsu Federation
Piazza S. Agostino 24
20123 Milano

JAPAN

Iokai Centre
1-8-9 Higashiuena
Daito-ku
Tokyo

Japan Institute of Traditional Medicine
Chushoto Building
3–4–10 Nihonbashi
Chio-ku
Tokyo 103

Motoyama Institute for Life Physics
Inokashira
4-11-7 Mitaka-shi
Tokyo 181

NEW ZEALAND

New Zealand Register of Acupuncturists
P.O. Box 9950
Wellington 1

New Zealand School of Acupuncturists
Tel: (4) 801 6400

THE AUTHOR

Jacqueline Young can be contacted at:

Health systems
P.O. Box 2211
Barnet
Herts EN5 4QW
United Kingdom
Website: www.jacquelineyoung.com

INDEX

Page references in **bold** type are to glossary entries; those in *italics* indicate picture captions and feature boxes on pages where the indexed entry does not appear in the main text.

ACKNOWLEDGMENTS AND PICTURE CREDITS

AUTHOR'S ACKNOWLEDGMENTS

I would like to thank all my Japanese, Tibetan, Chinese and Indian teachers, patients and students, to whom I owe a deep debt of gratitude. In particular I wish to acknowledge: Dr Hiroshi Motoyama, Mr Todo Ishii (Yuki Tohdoh), the late Dr Yoshio Manaka and the late Shizuto Masunaga and his successors; Ven. Dr Trogawa Rinpoche, Ven. K.C. Ayang Rinpoche, Dr Choedak, Dr Tamdin, Dr Dorje and Dr Dolma; Professor Chen, Dr Gao, and Professor Jiao Guorui; Dr K. Ramalingam, Dr S. Venkataraman, Mrs P. Nagpal, Mr K. Mahadevia and family and Mr Ramesh Patel; and in the West, Dr Elisabeth Finck, Dolores Hand and Professor Henri van Praag. Also Sri Sathya Sai Baba, Swami Sivananda, Swami Sivanada-Hridyananda, and Swami Sivananda Radha who have been my guides.

Warm and heartfelt thanks too to my four consultants, Marianne Winder, Dr Dominik Wujastyk, Dr Elisabeth Hsu, and Gretchen de Soriano. The contact and discussions I have had with all of you have been the most enjoyable and stimulating part of writing this book and I am deeply grateful for your contributions. Special thanks go to Phuntsog Wangyal and Karma Hardy at the Tibet Foundation, London; to Dr Tamdin for taking part in the photoshoot; and to Professor Ma Kanwen for his expert calligraphy for the cover. Also to the photographer, Matthew Ward, his assistant, Michel Labat, and the models Cate Williams, Gabriella Cemengova and Michael Young; it was a joy working with you. At Duncan Baird Publishers I would like to thank everyone who worked on the book.

Finally I would like to thank Kiyomi Kuratani and Yukihiro Takeshima to whom I owe so much for my time in Japan; my dear friend and colleague, Stephen Brown, without whom the amazing Qi gong tuition from Professor Guorui in China and Japan would never have happened and whose translations of Japanese texts have vastly enriched the oriental medical literature; and special friends and loving family who have been there during the two years it took to write this book: Selina and Theo Shah, Nic and Kirsten Rowley, Annie Sinnott, Chris Archer, my wonderful mother and step-father, Joanne and Don Angel, the best grandparents and supporters ever, my brothers Mark and Ken who kept up the email encouragement and my darling son, Shanphan Norbu who put up with it all and gave me a fantastic celebration once it was all finished.

PUBLISHER'S ACKNOWLEDGMENTS

The publisher would like to thank George Askounis for supplying *kanpo* herbs, and Stephanie Jacob.

PICTURE CREDITS

The publisher would like to thank the following people, museums and photographic libraries for permission to reproduce their material. Every care has been taken to trace copyright holders. However, if we have omitted anyone we apologise and will, if informed, make corrections in any future edition. The publishers would also like to thank Pictures of Health.

Pages 8–9 P. Rauter/TRIP; 11 Musee Guimet, Paris/Michael Holford, London; 12 Bridgeman Art Library/Victoria & Albert Museum; 13 Bridgeman; 14 The Wellcome Institute; 15 The Wellcome Institute; 17 Bridgeman/Freud Museum, London; 18 Stone/Joel Simon; 21 British Library/AKG, London; 22 Ian Cumming/Axiom; 25 The Wellcome Institute; 26 Peter Barker/Panos Pictures; 29 British Library(Add.27255f.340b); 30 Stone/Hilaire Kavanagh; 31 Stone/Anthony Cassidy; 34 Alison Wright/Panos Pictures; 36 Zen Icknow/Corbis; 38 Resource Foto/TRIP; 39 D. Sansoni/Panos Pictures; 44 Chris Caldicott/Axiom; 45 H. Rogers/TRIP; 46–47 Tiziana and Gianni Baldizzone/Corbis; 49 Tiziana and Gianni Baldizzone/Corbis; 50 Christophe Langridge/Tibet Images; 51 Werner Forman Archive; 53 British Museum(OA1906.12–26.09); 56 Mimi Lipton, London; 58 Serindia Publications, London; 59 Panos Pictures; 61 Serindia Publications, London; 62 Victoria & Albert Museum/Michael Holford; 63 Tibet Images; 67 Serindia Publications, London; 68 Serindia Publications, London; 69 Serindia Publications, London; 70–71 Serindia Publications, London; 72 Galen Rowell/Corbis; 73 British Museum(OA1983.3–20.5); 75 Norma Joseph/Royal Geographical Society; 78 Diane Barker/Tibet Images; 81 Serindia Publications, London; 83 Jirina Simajchlora/Tibet Images; 87 Musee Guimet/Michael Holford; 88 Wolfgang Kaehler/Corbis; 91 Ancient Art & Architecture; 92 Images Colour Library; 93 British Museum/Michael Holford; 99 The Wellcome Institute; 101 Ted Streshinsky/Corbis; 103 Science and Society Picture Library; 109 Dean Conger/Corbis; 112 Stone/Karen Su; 114 Stockmarket; 118 The Wellcome Institute; 122 Stockmarket; 123 Paul Schermeister/Corbis; 126–127 Images Colour Library; 129 Needham Research Institute/Cambridge; 131 Michael Yamashita/Corbis; 133 Science & Society Picture Library; 137 Science & Society Picture Library; 141 Luke White/Axiom; 146 Hulton/Corbis; 150 Michael Yamashita/Corbis; 152 Archive Iconografico, SA/Corbis; 154 Michael Yamashita/Corbis; 156 Stone/Paul Chesley.